ROMAN SILVER COINS

Vol. III.

PERTINAX TO BALBINUS AND PUPIENUS
A.D. 193-238

ROMAN
SILVER COINS

BY

H. A. SEABY

REVISED BY

DAVID R. SEAR

VOL. III.

PERTINAX TO
BALBINUS AND PUPIENUS

Arranged according to *Cohen*

2nd edition

Seaby

London

First edition, 1969

Second (revised) edition, 1982

Published and distributed by

B. A. SEABY LTD.

Audley House, 11 Margaret Street, London W1N 8AT

also distributed by

M. R. Roberts,

Wynyard Coin Centre, 7 Hunter Arcade, Sydney, N.S.W. 2000, Australia

Numismatic Fine Arts, Inc.,

P.O.B. 3788, 342 North Rodeo Drive,

Beverly Hills, California 90210, U.S.A.

Trade Winds Inc.

P.O. Box 401, Clementon, N.J. 08021, U.S.A.

Printed in England by ROBERT STOCKWELL LTD., London SE1 1YP

PREFACE AND INTRODUCTION TO VOL. III.

As in the case of the earlier volumes, there is very little original research in this work; and as explained before, the purpose is to give collectors and dealers a quick and ready help in identifying their coins and a guide to present day values. The arrangement is not technically sound as it is alphabetical. The scientific works to which we refer are arranged chronologically and under mints, which makes quick reference difficult.

I have continued to use Cohen's *Médailles Imperiales* as the basis, as it is still used by most dealers and auction sale cataloguers as a reference. His numbers will be found in black on the left hand side commencing each item. Cohen's system was to list the coins alphabetically according to their reverse legends; where there are a number of pieces with the same legend he started with the old gods and goddesses and then followed with the allegorical personifications (see *Roman Coins and Their Values*, pp. 16-26), the emperor, etc., animals and finally inanimate objects. Where I have varieties not in Cohen I have added them by putting a, b, c, etc. to his numbers.

In many cases when there is definitely an error in Cohen I have put it right, sometimes with, but often without any indication. In other cases where it is not certain whether Cohen's coin exists, I have left it in without a price. In some cases a known coin, which may be the piece that Cohen intended, is given an a number.

There are other numbers also without prices. This indicates that either I am not certain if the piece exists, that a genuine piece is known or that it is a hybrid.

Hybrids. These are coins that do not fit into the normal series and are for the most part contemporary forgeries, many of which are plated. A few genuine hybrids may have come from the mint, where the moneyer or one of his workmen had used the wrong combination of dies.

Obverses. I have put the obverse legends and types at the beginning of each reign with letters A, B, C, etc. for the legend. For the earlier reigns I have given the head or bust description, a, b, c, etc., but for the later reigns where there is less variety I have put—1. for laureate, d. for draped, etc. In the catalogue I have given Aa, Bc, Ald, etc. as the case may be; this has been done to save space and a lot of repetition.

Value. The value given in the right hand column is that which I would have placed on a VF (*very fine*) specimen. By this I mean the price a dealer might reasonably charge, but not the price a dealer would pay for such a piece.

I cannot stress too strongly that the value of any coin depends very largely on its state of preservation and Roman coins are no exception. A poor denarius, unless a great rarity, is of little value; on the other hand a coin in superb state of preservation would be worth considerably more than the stated price.

Additional coins. I have to thank many collectors for supplying details of new coins in their collections, especially Mr. G. R. Arnold.

My thanks are also due to Monsieur F. Willems of Belgium for lending me two of Monsieur Tinchant's mss. catalogues in which he had listed all the Roman coins he had seen or knew of.

I am also particularly indebted to Mr. Curtis L. Clay of Oxford for reading the proofs and giving me details of new coins from his plaster casts of material in European museums.

Illustrations. As will be seen we have used photographs of real coins to illustrate this volume instead of line blocks. All the denarii are from the collection of Mr. G. R. (Bob) Arnold of Burford (Tom Forrest of the radio series "The Archers"). The other pieces illustrated (cistophori and quinarii) are British Museum coins. We are greatly indebted to both these sources for allowing their coins to be photographed.

I have to thank Mr. Frank Purvey for his excellent photographs, which were taken with his own specially constructed camera.

In conclusion. My appreciation is due to Mr. David Sear for looking through the mss. and giving me so much help with the pricing of the coins.

May, 1969   H. A. SEABY.

INTRODUCTION TO SECOND (REVISED) EDITION

Thirteen years have elapsed since the original publication of this volume, so a thorough revision has been long overdue. The intervening years witnessed a dramatic surge in coin values, up to the mid-70s, followed by a much quieter period during which prices stabilised at their new levels. Only pieces of exceptional quality have continued to appreciate significantly. Nevertheless, a comparison between the valuations in this edition and those in the 1969 catalogue provides solid evidence of the growing popularity of Roman silver coins amongst collectors. Additional interest in the hobby has arisen as a result of metal-detecting which has become so popular over the past few years. A significant proportion of the Roman silver coins uncovered by metal-detector users in Great Britain are from the period encompassed by this volume, A.D. 193-238, so this revision has been eagerly awaited by large numbers of the hobby's newest recruits.

Frank Purvey has provided some additional photographic illustrations to augment those which he supplied for the original edition, and my thanks are due to everyone who sent me information on new varieties, all of which have been incorporated in the text.

February, 1982

DAVID R. SEAR.
Hawstead, Suffolk

ABBREVIATIONS.

Æ	= copper	laur.	= laureate
Æ	= silver	O. or ὄυ.	= obverse
Ν	= gold	p.	= page
cuir.	= cuirassed	pl.	= plate
diad.	= diademed	quad.	= quadriga
dr.	= draped	r.	= right
ex.	= exergue	rad.	= radiate
hd.	= head	Ɽ. or *rev.*	= reverse
(Hy.)	= hybrid or probable hybrid	stg.	= standing
l.	= left		

⌒ indicates that the letters below the sign are ligate.

Books of reference

The numbers given here in black on the left of each description are the same as those in H. Cohen, *Description Historique des Monnaies frappées sous L'Empire Romain, communément appelées Médailles Impériales*, 2nd edition, 1880.

B.M.C. = British Museum Catalogue, in this case *Coins of the Roman Empire in the British Museum*, Vols. V-VI.

R.I.C. = Mattingly and Sydenham, *The Roman Imperial Coinage*, Vols. IV-V.

C.R.B. = *The Coinage of Roman Britain*, by Gilbert Askew. A history and catalogue of the coins struck in the Roman province of Britannia and of coins that refer to campaigns fought in Britain.

Most of the coins designated as in the Lawrence collection are now in the British Museum. Coins marked Oldroyd came from the L. A. Lawrence collection via the Oldroyd Bequest.

PERTINAX

193 A.D.

Publius Helvius Pertinax, son of a charcoal-burner, was born in 126 A.D. *at Alba Pompeia in Liguria. He was a studious youth and became a teacher of grammar but soon adopted the military profession. He distinguished himself in Parthia, Britain and Noricum, and M. Aurelius made him a senator; he then received the command of the first legion and lastly the consulate was conferred upon him. At the death of Commodus he was Prefect of Rome and consul for the second time. He reluctantly accepted the vacant throne when offered it by the Senate. He immediately instituted many reforms for the public good, but these made him unpopular, especially with the Praetorians. On* 28th *March a band of military debauchees rushed the palace and Pertinax was slain after a reign of only* 87 *days.*

Obverse legend and type:

IMP . CAES . P . HELV . PERTIN . AVG . laureate head right

As all obverses are the same except for nos. **6** and **56b,** descriptions are of the reverses

All the regular denarii are attributed to the Rome mint, except **33a**

2   17

2 **Denarius.** AEQVIT . AVG . TR . P . COS . II, Aequitas stg. l., holding scales and cornucopiae. *B.M.C.* 15-17; *R.I.C.* 1 (a) £500
5a AEQVITAS AVG . TR . P . COS., as last. *B.M.C.* p. l, 6 (*fine modern forgery*) ..
6 DIVVS PERT . PIVS PATER, his bare hd. r. ℞. CONSECRATIO, eagle stg. half-right on globe, hd. l. *B.M.C.,* Wars of the Succession 37; *R.I.C.* Septimius Severus 24A 1000
6a Similar, but eagle stands on cippus instead of globe. *B.M.C.* pl. 6, 6 .. 1000
14 DIS CVSTODIBVS (*under the guardianship of the gods*), Fortuna stg. l., holding rudder on globe and cornucopiae. *B.M.C.* 1; *R.I.C.* 2 1000
17 IANO CONSERVAT., Janus stg. front, holding sceptre, l. hand on hip. *B.M.C.* 2; *R.I.C.* 3 850

20   28

20 LAETITIA TEMPOR . COS . II, Laetitia stg. l., holding wreath and sceptre. *B.M.C.* 8-9; *R.I.C.* 4 (a) 500
20a Similar, but sceptre on globe. *B.M.C.* 8 note (*regular issue?*); *R.I.C.* 4A
28 LIBERATIS CIVIBVS, Liberalitas stg. l., holding abacus (accounting board) and cornucopiae. *B.M.C.* p. 2, *; *R.I.C.* 5 1150
28a — Libertas stg. l., holding pileus (?) and vindicta (rod looking like a long sceptre). *B.M.C.* 3; *R.I.C.* 6 1150

30 Denarius. MENTI LAVDANDAE (*to praiseworthy judgment or counsel*), Bona-
Mens stg. l., holding wreath and sceptre. *B.M.C.* 4; *R.I.C.* 7 ..   .. £1350

33 OPI DIVIN . TR . P . COS . II, Ops seated l., holding two corn-ears, l. hand
on seat of throne. *B.M.C.* 19-20; *R.I.C.* 8 (a)   550

33a As last, but very odd style. *B.M.C.* p. 616 (*Oldroyd; possibly of Alexandria ?*)

33b As 33, curious style. *B.M.C.* 21 (*ancient forgery ?*)   ..   ..   ..

37 OPI DIVINAE TR . P . COS . II, as last. *B.M.C.* 21 note (*probably does not
exist*); *R.I.C.* 9..   ..   ..

33   43

40 PROVID . DEOR . COS . II, Providentia stg. l., raising both hands towards
a large star. *B.M.C.* 10 note; *R.I.C.* 10 (A)   650
There is a Becker forgery of this reverse, but with draped bust.

43 — Providentia stg. l., raising r. hand towards a smaller star. *B.M.C.* 13;
R.I.C. 11 (a)   550

47 PROVDENTIA DEORVM COS . II, woman stg., two stars in field. *B.M.C.* p. 3,
* note; *R.I.C.* 10 note (*very doubtful*)   ..   ..

54 SAECVLO FRVGIFERO (*to the age of fertility or plenty*), caduceus with six
corn-ears attached to it in the form of wings. *B.M.C.* 5; *R.I.C.* 12..   .. 1150

56 VOT . DECEN . TR . P . COS . II, Pertinax, veiled, stg. l., sacrificing out of a
patera over altar. *B.M.C.* 24; *R.I.C.* 13 (a)   550

56a As last (*base ?*). *B.M.C.* 25   ..   ..

56b As last, but with *obv.* legend IMP . CAES . P . HELV . PERTINAX AVG . (*British
Museum*)   650

DIDIUS JULIANUS
193 A.D.

Marcus Didius Severus Julianus was the son of Petronius Didius Severus and Clara Aemilia. He had had a successful career, having amongst other things succeeded Pertinax as consul and in government in Africa. At the time of the murder of Pertinax he was in Rome, and when the praetorians put the empire up for auction he was the highest bidder, offering 25,000 sestertii per man. The death of Pertinax and the circumstances of the elevation of Didius aroused much indignation amongst the populace. They assembled in the Circus and cried out for some provincial governor to come to their assistance—their favourite was Pescennius Niger in Syria. Two other provincial governors, Clodius Albinus in Britain and Septimius Severus in Upper Pannonia also determined to answer their appeal. Severus quickly advanced on Rome. Didius made several attempts to negotiate with his rival, into sharing the Empire, which failed. The praetorians deserted him, the Senate deposed him and he was beheaded on the 2nd June, after a reign of only 66 days, at the age of sixty.

Obverse legend and type:
IMP . CAES . M . DID . IVLIAN . AVG., his head laureate right

All are attributed to the Rome mint

2 **Denarius.** CONCORD . MILIT., Concordia stg. l., holding legionary eagle and vexillum. *B.M.C.* 2-3; *R.I.C.* 1 (*Cohen omits* DID *on obv. in error*) .. £800

10 P . M . TR . P . COS, Fortuna stg. l., holding rudder on globe and cornucopiae. *B.M.C.* 6; *R.I.C.* 2 .. ..⟍ 800

There is a Becker forgery of this reverse, but with draped bust.

| 2 | 10 | 15 |

10a Similar, but without globe. *B.M.C.* 6 note; *R.I.C.* 2 note .. ..

10b IMP . CAES . M . DID . SEVER . IVLIAN . AVG., laur. bust dr. and cuir r. R . — Jupiter seated l. *B.M.C.* p. li, 16 (*cast*)

10c — — R . P . M . TR . P . COS . II . TIBERIS, Tiber reclining l. *B.M.C.* p. li, 17 (*cast; rev. of Hadrian*) .. ..

10d Normal obv. R . PONT . MAX . TR . POT . COS . II, Pax stg. l. *B.M.C.* p. li, 18 (*cast; rev. of Hadrian*) .. ..

15 RECTOR ORBIS (*master of the world*), Didius stg. l., holding globe and perhaps roll. *B.M.C.* 7-8; *R.I.C.* 3 800

19a SECVRITAS P . R., Securitas stg. l., holding wreath and sceptre (Hy.; *type of Otho*). *B.M.C.* p. 12 (*certainly false—perhaps ancient*); *R.I.C.* 4 .. ..

19b As 10b, but *rev.* legend, S . P . Q . R . OPTIMO PRINCIPI. *B.M.C.* p. lii, 19 (*cast*) .. ..

The British Museum has an ancient plated forgery of a denarius (slightly gilded) with obv. of Didius and obv. of Manlia Scantilla. B.M.C. p. 12; R.I.C. p. 16 .. ..

MANLIA SCANTILLA

Manlia Scantilla was the wife of Didius Julianus, by whom she had the beautiful Didia
Clara; she being herself the most deformed of women.

2 Denarius. MANL . SCANTILLA AVG, her bust dr. r. R. IVNO REGINA, Juno
stg. l., holding patera and sceptre, at her feet l., peacock. *B.M.C.* Didius
11; *R.I.C.* Didius 7 ..   .. £1500
There are two Becker forgeries of this type, one has a stop after IVNO
5a Similar, but MANLIA. *B.M.C.* 12 (*looks like an ancient forgery*) ..   ..
7 As last. R. PIETAS PVBLICA, Pietas, veiled, stg. with hands raised before
altar. *B.M.C.* p. 13 (*certainly a forgery, perhaps ancient*); *R.I.C.* 8   ..

DIDIA CLARA

Daughter of the last two, she is described as the most beautiful young woman of her age.
On her father's accession named Augusta by the Senate.

1 Denarius. DIDIA CLARA AVG., her dr. bust r. R. FORTVNAE FELICI,
Fortuna stg. l., holding rudder and cornucopiae (Hy.; *rev. of J. Domna*).
B.M.C. p. 14 (*certainly a forgery, perhaps ancient or perhaps obv. has been*
tooled from Julia Domna); *R.I.C.* Didius 9 ..   ..

3 — R. HILAR. TEMPOR, Hilaritas stg. l., holding long palm and cornucopiae. *B.M.C.* Didius 14-16; *R.I.C.* 10 ..   .. £1500
There is a Becker forgery of this type.

PESCENNIUS NIGER

193-194 A.D.

Caius Pescennius Niger came from a middle class family and had an honourable career in the army. Under Commodus he was made a consul in 190 and in the next year appointed to command of the legions in Syria. On the murder of Pertinax and the purchase of the empire by Didius the troops of Niger proclaimed him emperor. Severus, however, having secured Rome, turned his attention to his rival in the East, and thrice defeated the forces of Niger. The latter, after the fall of Antioch, fled but was eventually overtaken, captured and put to death together with his whole family.

Obverse legends.

A. IMP . CAES . C . PESC . NIGER
B.   ,,   ,,   ,,   ,,   ,,   AVG.
C.   ,,   ,,   ,,   ,,   ,,   IVST.
D.   ,,   ,,   ,,   ,,   ,,   IVST . AVG.
E.   ,,   ,,   ,,   ,,   ,,   IVST . AVG . COS . II
F.   ,,   ,,   ,,   ,,   ,,   IVS . AVG . COS . II
G.   ,,   ,,   ,,   ,,   ,,   IVS . AVG . COS
H. IMP . C . PESC . NIGER IVS . AVG . COS . II

The IVST. or IVS. is for IVSTVS, a title Niger assumed on becoming emperor.

Obverse type:

His laureate head right, unless otherwise stated.

All his coins were struck in the East, mostly at Antioch.

British Museum numbers are under the Wars of Succession

1 Denarius. H. ℞. AETERNITAS AVG., crescent and seven stars. *B.M.C.* p. 71, †; *R.I.C.* 1..   ..   ..   £800

1a D, but IVSTVS. ℞. — As last (*false*). Numismatische Zeitschrift, 1871, pl. 2, 1 ..   ..

2 D, but AV. ℞. APOLLINI SANCTO, Apollo, naked, stg. l. by column, on which he rests r. arm; he holds branch, l. hand on hip. *B.M.C.* 297 note; *R.I.C.* 2 (a)   700

3 B ?, but PESCE (*Cohen* PESI *is incorrect*). ℞. — As last. *B.M.C.* 297; *R.I.C.* 2 (b)   700

3a E. — As last. *B.M.C.* p. 71, §; *R.I.C.* 2 (c)   700

4 F. ℞. BONAE SPEI, Spes advancing l., holding flower and raising skirt. *B.M.C.* p. 71, ‖; *R.I.C.* 3(d)   650

5 G ?, ℞. — As last, but Spes wears polos (modius) on hd. *B.M.C.* p.82,(a); *R.I.C.* 3 (e)   650

6 D, but PESCE. ℞. — As last. *B.M.C.* 298 note; *R.I.C.* 3 (b)   650

7 D, but IVS . AV. ℞. — As last. *B.M.C.* 298 note; *R.I.C.* 3 (a)..   ..   650

7a D ? but IVT . AV. ℞. — As last. *B.M.C.* p. 616 (*in B.M.*)   650

8 D, but PESCEN. and AV. ℞. — As **4**, *B.M.C.* 298; *R.I.C.* 3 (c) and (f)..   650

8a F. ℞. — As **4**, but Spes stg. *R.I.C.* 3 (d) note   650

It is not quite certain on which of these Spes wears polos.

9 Denarius. D, but IVT . AV. ℞. BONI EVENTVS, Bonus Eventus or Fides
stg. r., holding two corn-ears and plate of fruit. *B.M.C.* 299 note; *R.I.C.*4   £650

10 E. ℞. — Similar, but Bonus Eventus or Fides stg. front, hd. l. *B.M.C.*
p. 72, * note; *R.I.C.* 5 (c)   650

10a F. ℞. — As last. *B.M.C.* p. 72, *; *R.I.C.* 5 (a) note   650

10b IMP . ACES . C . PESCE . NIGER IVSTI . AV. ℞. — As last. *B.M.C.* 299;
R.I.C. 5 (d)   650

10c D, but PES. and IVS . A. ℞. — As last. *B.M.C.* 299 note; *R.I.C.* 5 (a);
(*Mazzini cat.*)..   650

10d D. ℞. — As last. *B.M.C.* 299 note; *R.I.C.* 5 (d); *R.I.C.* 5 (b)   ..   650

10e D, but PESCE . or PESCO . and IVSTI . AG. or AV. ℞. — As last. *B.M.C.* 299
note; *R.I.C.* 5 (e)   650

10f C. ℞. — As last. *B.M.C.* 299 note; *R.I.C.* 5 (f)   650

11 F (*Cohen omits* CAES. *in error*). ℞. — Fides or Bonus Eventus stg. l.,
holding wreath and two corn-ears. *B.M.C.* p. 72, †; *R.I.C.* 6   650

11a D, but NIG . IVSTI. ℞. CELERI FRVGIFE, Ceres stg. l., holding torch in
each hand. *B.M.C.* p. 616 (*in B.M.*)   650

12 E and/or F. ℞. CERER . FRVG . (*the fruit bearing Ceres*), Ceres, stg. l.,
holding two corn-ears and sceptre. *B.M.C.* 291; *R.I.C.* 7 (a) and (b);
(*Mazzini cat.—obv.* F)   650

13 IMP . CAES . PESCE . NIGER ISTI. AVG. ℞. CERERI FRVGIF, as **12**. *B.M.C.* p. 75,
*; *R.I.C.* 8   650

13a D. ℞. CER . . . FRVGIFE. ℞. — As last. *B.M.C.* p. 75, † note; *R.I.C.* 9   650

13b IMP . CAES . C . PESCE . NIGER IVS. . . . ℞. CERERI FRVGIFER, Fides stg. l.,
holding plate of fruit and corn-ears. *B.M.C.* p. 75, ‡; *R.I.C.* 11 (a)   ..   650

13c D, but PESCEN. and IVSTI . AV. ℞. — As last. *B.M.C.* p. 75, ‡ note;
R.I.C. 11 and 7 note   650

13d C. ℞. CERERI FRVGIFERE, as **14b**. *B.M.C.* p. 75, † note; *R.I.C.* 10 note   650

13e D, but PESE. and IV.A. ℞. CERERI FRVGIFERI, as last. *B.M.C.* p. 75, †;
R.I.C. 10   650

14 IMP. . . . GER ISTI . AVG. ℞. CERERI FRVFER, as last. *B.M.C.* p. 75 * note;
R.I.C. 7 note   650

14a C, but PES. ℞. — As last. *B.M.C.* p. 75, * note; *R.I.C.* 7 note   ..   650

14b D, but PESCEN . and AV. ℞. — As before, but Ceres holds torch in each hand.
B.M.C. p. 75, † note; *R.I.C.* 10A   650

14c D, but PESCE . and IVSTI. AV. ℞. — As last. *B.M.C.* p. 75, † note   ..   650

15a E. Laur. and dr. bust r.   ℞. CONCORD. MILIT., Concordia stg. l. between
two standards. (*British Museum*)   850

15b IMP . CAES . C . PESC . NIG . . . AVG. ℞. FELICIA TEMPORA, two cornuacopiae
crossed. *B.M.C.* p. 76, *; *R.I.C.* 13 (a)   750

15c D, but AV. ℞. — As last. *B.M.C.* p. 76, * note; *R.I.C.* 13 (b)   ..   750

16 F. ℞. FELICITAS TEMPOR., vase-shaped basket of fruit, a bunch of grapes
hanging over each side. *B.M.C.* 293, note; *R.I.C.* 16   800

16a F. ℞. FELICITAS TEMPORVM, as last. *B.M.C.* 293; *R.I.C.* 17   800

16b F. ℞. — As last, but with three corn-ears stg. up in centre, and no
grapes. *B.M.C.* 294   800

17 B. ℞. FELICIT . TEMPOR., corn-ear between two cornuacopiae crossed.
B.M.C. p. 76, †; *R.I.C.* 14 (a)   750

18 D, but PESCE . and IVSTI . AV. ℞. — As last. *B.M.C.* p. 76, † note;
R.I.C. 14 (b)   750

18a G? ℞. — As **15b**. *B.M.C.* 292; *R.I.C.* 15 (*obv. incorrect*)   750

19 ? Ŗ. FIDEI EXER., three standards, a shield inscribed VIC . AVGG. is attached
to the central one. *B.M.C.* p. 76, ‡ note; *R.I.C.* 18 (*doubtful*) . . . .

20 D, his laur. bust. dr. and cuir., r. Ŗ. FIDEI EXERCTVI, three standards
with vexilla, the centre one inscribed VIC . AVG. *B.M.C.* p. 76, ‡; *R.I.C.* 19 £900

21 D, but AV. Ŗ. FORTVNAE RE., Fortuna or Concordia seated l., holding
patera and wreath. *B.M.C.* p. 77, †; *R.I.C.* 20 700

22 C, but IVS. Ŗ. FORTVNAE RED., Fortuna or Pax, seated l., holding branch
and cornucopiae (*C.* has " wreath "). *B.M.C.* p. 77, *; *R.I.C.* 21 . .

23 D, but PESCE . and IVSTI . A. Ŗ. — Fortuna seated l., holding rudder and
cornucopiae. *B.M.C.* 301 note; *R.I.C.* 23 650

23a C, but IVSI ? Ŗ. — As last. *B.M.C.* 301 650

24 D, but IVST . A. Ŗ. FORTVNAE REDV., Fortuna stg. l., holding rudder and
cornucopiae. *B.M.C.* p. 76, ‖; *R.I.C.* 25 650

24a F. Ŗ. — Fortuna or Felicitas stg. l., holding caduceus and cornucopiae.
B.M.C. p. 72, ‖; *R.I.C.* 27 700

25 D, but IVSTI . AV. Ŗ. FORTVNAE REDVC., Fortuna or Aequitas stg. l.,
holding scales and cornucopiae. *B.M.C.* p. 76, ¶; *R.I.C.* 30 . . 750

26 F. Ŗ. FORTVNAE REDVCI, Fortuna or Pax seated l., holding branch and
wreath. *B.M.C.* p. 73, *; *R.I.C.* 24 700

26a F. Ŗ. — Fortuna or Pax stg. l., holding branch and cornucopiae.
B.M.C. p. 73, † note; *R.I.C.* 29; (*not in B.M. as stated*) . . . . . .

27 F or E? Ŗ. — As **24a.** *B.M.C.* 300? 700

27a A. Ŗ. — As last. *B.M.C.* 300 note; *R.I.C.* 28a; (*not in B.M. as stated*)

27b IMP . CAES . C . PESC . NIGER IVS . . . . Ŗ. — As last. *B.M.C.* 300 note;
R.I.C. 28 (b) 700

27c F. Ŗ. — As **22.** *B.M.C.* p. 73, †; *R.I.C.* 22 700

27d F. Ŗ. — Fortuna, wearing polos, stg. front, hd. l., holding two corn-ears
and cornucopiae. *B.M.C.* 295 700

27e C, but IVSTI. Ŗ. — As last. (*Numismatic Fine Arts auction, Dec.* 1980,
lot 543) 700

27f F. Ŗ. — Fortuna or Providentia, wearing polos, seated l., holding rod
and cornucopiae, globe at feet. (*Frank Sternberg auction, Nov.* 1981, *lot*
671) 700

28 D, but A. Ŗ. — As **24,** but Fortuna sometimes wears polos. *B.M.C.*
p. 76, ‖ note; *R.I.C.* 26 (b) 650

28a D, but AV. Ŗ. — As last. *B.M.C.* p. 76, ‖ note; *R.I.C.* 26 (c) . . 650

28b D. Ŗ. — As **24** or **28.** *B.M.C.* p. 76, ‖ note. *R.I.C.* 26 (d) 650
There is a Becker forgery with obv. D, but PESCE *and* ISTI.

28c B. Ŗ. — As last. *B.M.C.* p. 76, ‖ note. *R.I.C.* 26 (a) 650

28d B. Laur. bust r., with slight drapery. Ŗ. — As last. (*Tinchant cat.*) . . 700

28e F. Ŗ. — As last. *B.M.C.* p. 72, ‡; *R.I.C.* 26 (e) 650

29 IMP . CAES . C . PESCE . NI . IT . AV. Ŗ. FR FR FRVG or/and FRFRF AVG, Ceres
stg. l., holding two corn-ears and sceptre. *B.M.C.* p. 75, * note; *R.I.C.*
7 note 650

29a B, slight drapery. Ŗ. HILARITAS AVG . S . C., globe, on which four stars,
held by two capricorns. *B.M.C.* p. 77, ‡; *R.I.C.* 30A 750

30 D ? but PESCE and ISTI. Ŗ. IMVISTO IMPER, trophy. *B.M.C.* p. 77, § note;
R.I.C. 32 700

30a B ? Ŗ. INVIC . IMP., trophy with arms below. *B.M.C.* p. 77, §; *R.I.C.* 30 700

N.B.—*In the following it is not always clear whether there are arms or not
below the trophy.*

31 D ? Ŗ. INVICT . IMPERAT., trophy. *B.M.C.* p. 77, § note; *R.I.C.* 33 . . 700

32 D, but AV. Ŗ. INVICTO IMP., trophy with arms below. *B.M.C.* p. 77, §
note; *R.I.C.* 31 (a) 700

32a B. Ŗ. — As last. *B.M.C.* p. 77, § note; *R.I.C.* 31(c) 700

32b B, but PESCE. R. — As last. *B.M.C.* p. 77, § note; *R.I.C.* 31 (b) .. £700
32c B, slight drapery. R. — As last. (*Tinchant cat.*) 750
33 **Denarius.** D, but AV. R. INVICTO IMPERAT., trophy with arms below. *B.M.C.* p. 77, § note; *R.I.C.* 34a 700
33a D, but IVSTI . AV . R. — As last. *B.M.C.* p. 77, § note and p. 616 (*in B.M.*); *R.I.C.* 34 (b) 700
33b D, but IVSTI . A. R. — Trophy. *B.M.C.* p. 77, § note; *R.I.C.* 35 .. 700
34 F. R. INVICTO IMP . TA., trophy with arms below. *B.M.C.* 296 note; *R.I.C.* 36 700
35 E. R. INVICTO IMP . TROPAE, as last. *B.M.C.* 296 note; *R.I.C.* 37 (a) (*Perhaps a misreading of next*) .. ..
35a F. R. — As last. *B.M.C.* 296; *R.I.C.* 37 (b) 700
35b F. R. INVICTO IMP . TROPACA, as last. (*Ryan coll.*) 700
36 E, but IVSTVS. R. INVICTO IMP . TROPAEA, as last. *B.M.C.* 296 note; *R.I.C.* 38 (a) 700
36a E. R. — As last. (*Tinchant cat.*) 700
36b F. R. — As last. *B.M.C.* 296 note; *R.I.C.* 38 (b) 700
37 E. R. INVICTO IMP . TROPHAEA, as last. *B.M.C.* 296 note (*in B.M., exceptionally good style, probably false*); *R.I.C.* 39 .. .. ..
38 D, but PESCEN. R. INVICTO MPERAI or IMPER, as last. *B.M.C.* p. 77, § note; *R.I.C.* 40 700
40 D, but PES . and IVS . AV. R. IOVI CONSER., Jupiter seated l., holding Victory on globe and sceptre; at his feet, eagle. *B.M.C.* 302; *R.I.C.* 41 750
41 D. R. IOVI PRAE . ORBIS (*Jupiter; Governor of the World*), Jupiter, naked to the waist, seated l., holding Victory and sceptre surmounted by eagle. *B.M.C.* 303 note, *R.I.C.* 43 (a) (*has eagle for Victory in error*) 700
41a D, but PESCEN. R. — As last, but without eagle on sceptre. *B.M.C.* 303; *R.I.C.* 43 (b) 700

33   41b

41b IMP . CAES . C . PESCEN . NIG . IVST . AVG . R. — As last. (*G. R. Arnold coll.*) 700
41c H. R. — As **41**. *B.M.C.* p. 73, ‡; *R.I.C.* 43 (c) 700
41d F. R. — As last *B.M.C.* p. 616 (*in B.M.; also in Tinchant cat.*) 700
42 D, but PESCEN . and AV. R. IVSTI . AVG., two capricorns, back to back, bearing globe on which seven stars; against their hind-quarters, small shield. *B.M.C.* 304 note; *R.I.C.* 44 (a) (*possibly a mistake for next*) ..
42a D, but PESCEN . and IVSTI . AV. R. — As last. *B.M.C.* 304; *R.I.C.* 44 (b) 850
43 D, but AV. R. IVSTITIA AVG., Justitia stg. front, hd. l., holding scales and cornucopiae. *B.M.C.* 305-6; *R.I.C.* 45 (a) 650
43a D. R. — As last. *B.M.C.* 305 note; *R.I.C.* 45 (c) 650
43b D, but PESCE. R. — As last. *B.M.C.* 305 note; *R.I.C.* 45 (b) 650
44 D, but no C. after CAES. R. — Justitia stg. l., holding scales and sceptre. *B.M.C.* 305 note; *R.I.C.* 49 650
44a D, bust dr. and cuir. seen from the front. R. — As last (*Tinchant cat.*) 700
45 D ? R. — Justitia or Providentia stg., holding globe and sceptre. *B.M.C.* 305 note; *R.I.C.* 50 650
45a D, but AV. R. IVSTITIA AVGV., as **43**. *B.M.C.* 305 note; *R.I.C.* 46 .. 650
47 D, but without C. after CAES. R. IVSTITIA AVGVSTI, as last. *B.M.C.* 305 note; *R.I.C.* 47 (b), (*possibly a misdescription of* **47b**—*confirmation required*) .. ..

47a As last, but AV. R. — As last. *B.M.C.* 305 note; *R.I.C.* 47 (a) (*possibly a misdescription of* **47c**—*confirmation required*) .. ..

47b D. R. — As last. *B.M.C.* 305 note; *R.I.C.* 47 (d); (*Mazzini cat.*) .. £650

47c D, but AV. R. — As last. *B.M.C.* 305 note; *R.I.C.* 47 (c) .. 650

47d D, bust dr. and cuir. seen from behind. R. — As last (*Tinchant cat.*) 700

47e D. R. — Genius(?) stg. l., holding scales and branch(?) (*Tinchant cat.*)

47f D. R. MARTI AVG., Mars advancing r., holding spear and trophy. *B.M.C.* 307; *R.I.C.* 51 700

48 D, but AV. R. MARTI AVGVSTO, as last. *B.M.C.* 307 note; *R.I.C.* 52 .. 700

49 D. R. MARTI INVICTO, as last. *B.M.C.* 307 note; *R.I.C.* 53 .. ..

50 D. R. MARTI VICTOR, Mars stg. front, hd. l., holding spear and leaning on shield. *B.M.C.* p. 79, * note; *R.I.C.* 54 650

50a B? R. — As last. *B.M.C.* p. 79, *; *R.I.C.* 54A 650

51 D, but PESCEN . and AV. R. MARTI VICTORI, Mars stg. l., holding Victory and spear, shield at feet. *B.M.C.* 308 note; *R.I.C.* 55 650

51a IMP . C . PESC . [NI]GER [IV]S (*B.M.C. version*) or IMP . C . PESCE . [NI]GER AVG? (*R.I.C. version*). R. — As last. *B.M.C.* 308; *R.I.C.* 56; (*both quoted from very poor specimen in the B.M.*) 650

52 B. R. — Mars walking, holding parazonium and trophy. *B.M.C.* p. 79, † note; *R.I.C.* 57 650

52a B? R. — Mars advancing l., holding spear and trophy. *B.M.C.* p. 79, †; *R.I.C.* 58 650

52b D, but PESCEN. and IVSTI . AV. R. — (but VCTORI for VICTORI), as last. (*Mazzini cat.*) 650

52c D, but PESCEN . and AV. R. — Mars stg. l., holding trophy and spear. *B.M.C.* p. 79, ‡; *R.I.C.* 58A 650

53 G. R. MINER . VICT., Minerva stg. l., holding Victory and spear, shield at feet. *B.M.C.* p. 73, §; *R.I.C.* 59 650

53a C, but PESCE. R. MINER . VICTRIC (or VICTRIS), as last. *B.M.C.* 309; *R.I.C.* 60 650

53b D, but PESCEN . and A. R. — Similar, but no shield. *B.M.C.* 309 note; *R.I.C.* 61A 650

53c D, but PESCEN . and AV. R. — Minerva stg. l., holding owl and spear. *B.M.C.* p. 616 (*in B.M.*) 700

42a 54a

54 IMP . CAES . C . PESC . NIGER ... R. MINER . VICTRIS, Minerva stg. l., holding shield in raised r. hand and spear with rounded end in l. *B.M.C.* 309 note; *R.I.C.* 61 700

54a D, but AV. R. — As last. (*Tinchant cat. and G. R. Arnold coll.*) .. 700

N.B.—*Moneta sometimes wears polos (modius) on nos.* 55-57.

55 H. R. MONET . AVG., Moneta stg. l., holding scales and cornucopiae. *B.M.C.* p. 73, ‖; *R.I.C.* 62 650

55a B. R. — As last. *B.M.C.* 310 note; *R.I.C.* 62 note 650

55b H. R. MONETA AVG., as last. *B.M.C.* p. 73, ‖ note; *R.I.C.* 63 (a).. 650

55c F. R. — As last. *B.M.C.* p. 73, ‖ note; *R.I.C.* 63 (a) note .. 650

55d B, but PESE. R. — As last. *B.M.C.* 310 note; *R.I.C.* 63 (b) .. 650

55e Denarius. H. ℞. MONETE AVG., Moneta stg. l., holding scales and cornucopiae. *B.M.C.* p. 73, ‖ note; *R.I.C.* 65 (a) £650

55f B, but PESCE. ℞. — As last. *B.M.C.* 310 note; *R.I.C.* 65 (b) 650

55g B, but PISE. ℞. — As last. *B.M.C.* 310 note; *R.I.C.* 65 (c) 650

55h F, but AV. ℞. — As last (*Tinchant cat.*) 650

56 D, but PESCEN. ℞. MONETAE AVG., as last. *B.M.C.* 310 note; *R.I.C.* 64 (b) 650

56a D, but PESCEN. and AV. ℞. — As last. *B.M.C.* 310 note and p. 617 (*in B.M.*) 650

56b D, by PESCEN . NIG. ℞. — As last. *B.M.C.* 310; *R.I.C.* 64 (a).. .. 650

56c B. but PESCEN. ℞. — As last. (*Frank Sternberg auction, Nov.* 1981, *lot* 673) 650

56d H. ℞. — As last. *B.M.C.* p. 73, ‖ note; *R.I.C.* 64 (c) 650

56e F. ℞. — As last. *B.M.C.* p. 73, ‖ note 650

56f B. ℞. MONETE AVG., Moneta stg. l., holding scales and raising skirt. *B.M.C.* 310 note and p. 617 (*in B.M.*); *R.I.C.* 66 (b) 650

56g B, but without CAES. ℞. — As last. *B.M.C.* 310 note; *R.I.C.* 66 (a) .. 650

56h B, but PESCE. ℞. — As last (*Tinchant cat.*) 650

57 D, but PESCEN. and A. ℞. MONETA COS, as **55,** *B.M.C.* p. 82, (b) (*somewhat doubtful*); *R.I.C.* 67 .. ..

58 IMP . CAES . PESCE . NIGER IVST. ℞. PIETATI AVG., Niger stg. l., sacrificing out of patera over lighted and garlanded altar. *B.M.C.* 311 note; *R.I.C.* 68 750

58a A? but PESCEN. ℞. — As last. *B.M.C.* 311 750

60 D, but PESCEN. ℞. ROMAE AETERNAE, Roma seated l., holding Victory and spear, shield at feet. *B.M.C.* p. 80, * note; *R.I.C.* 70 (b) 650

60a D? but AV. ℞. — As last. *B.M.C.* p. 80, * note; *R.I.C.* 70 (c) .. 650

61 F, but without C. ℞. — As last. *B.M.C.* p. 74, *; *R.I.C.* 70 (a) ..

61a F. ℞. — As last. *B.M.C.* p. 74, * note and pl. 13, 7 (*probably false*) ..

62 D, but PESCEN. ℞. ROMAE AETERN., as last. *B.M.C.* p. 80, *; *R.I.C.* 69 650

62a As last. ℞. ROMAE ATERAE, as last. *B.M.C.* p. 80, * note; *R.I.C.* 70 (b) note 650

62b D, but PESCEN . and IVSTI . A. ℞. ROMAE AETERNAE, Roma seated l., holding sceptre and Victory. *B.M.C.* p. 80, * note; *R.I.C.* 70 (d) note (? *true variant of rev.*).. 650

64b

63 A, but PESCE. ℞. SAECVLI FELICITAS, seven stars above crescent. *B.M.C.* 312; *R.I.C.* 73 (a) (*Cohen has normal* A *legend in error*) 750

63a D, but AV. ℞. — As last (*Mazzini cat.*) 750

64 D, but PESCEN . and IVSTI . A. ℞. — As last. *B.M.C.* 312 note; *R.I.C.* 73 (b) 750

64a D, but PESCEN. ℞. — As last. *B.M.C.* 312 note; *R.I.C.* 73 (c) .. 750
There is a Becker forgery with obv. D, *but* PESCEN *and* IVSTI.

64b D, but PESCE . and ISTI . A. ℞. SAECVLI FLICITAS, as before. *B.M.C.* 312 note; *R.I.C.* 74

64c F. ℞. As **63** (*Dr. Busso Peus*) 750

65 D, but AV. ℞. SALVTI AVG., Salus, Moneta or Aequitas stg. l., holding scales and cornucopiae. *B.M.C.* 313 note; *R.I.C.* 78 650

65a D? touch of drapery on l. shoulder. ℞. — As last, but goddess stg. front, hd. l. *B.M.C.* 313 (*it could be that* **65** *and* **65a** *are similar*) .. . 650

66   D, but AV. R. SALVTI AVG., Salus stg. r. before altar, feeding snake held in her arms. *B.M.C.* p. 80, ‡; *R.I.C.* 75 (a) £650

66a   D. R. — As last. *B.M.C.* p. 80, ‡ note; *R.I.C.* 75 (b) (*Mazzini cat.*) ..   650

66b   D. but without c. R. SALVTI AVGV., as last. (*Leu auction, May* 1981, *lot* 488)   650

67   D, but without c. R. SALVTI AVGVS., type as before. *B.M.C.* p. 80, ‡ note; *R.I.C.* 76   650

68   D. R. SALVTI AVGVSTI, as last. *B.M.C.* p. 80, ‡ note; *R.I.C.* 77   650

68a   D, but without c. R. — As last. (*Lucerne sale,* 24/4/69, *lot* 270)   ..   650

69   D. R. SPEI FIRM . . ., Spes walking l., star on her forehead, holding flower and raising skirt. *B.M.C.* p. 80, §; *R.I.C.* 79   800

70   F (*Cohen,* CAE.). R. VICTO . IMP . TROPAEA, trophy with arms below. *B.M.C.* p. 74, †; *R.I.C.* 80   750

71   D, but PESCEN. R. VICTORIA AVG., Victory flying l., holding wreath and palm (*plated*). *B.M.C.* 314 note; *R.I.C.* 82 (b)   ..   ..   ..

71a   D, but IVS . AV. ? R. — As last. *B.M.C.* 314 note; *R.I.C.* 82 (a) (*not in B.M., possibly a wrong description of* **75h**) ..   ..   ..

72   D, but without c. after CAES. R. VICTORIAE, Victory stg. l., inscribing AVG. on shield set on column. *B.M.C.* 316 note; *R.I.C.* 83 (a)   800

72a   D. R. — As last. *B.M.C.* 316 note; *R.I.C.* 83 (b)   800

73   D, but possibly with a longer form of PESC. Laur. dr. and cuir. bust r. R. VICTORIAE AVG., as last. *B.M.C.* 316 note; *R.I.C.* 84 (*omitting the* AVG. *in rev. legend*)   850

73a   D, but without c. after CAES. R. — As last, but shield is set on trophy. *B.M.C.* 316 (*omitting the* AVG. *on shield, but see pl.* 14, 6); *R.I.C.* 85 (*omitting the* AVG. *in rev. legend*)   850

74   D, but IVS. R. VICTORIAE AVG., Victory stg. r., holding wreath and palm. *B.M.C.* 314 note; *R.I.C.* 86   750

75   D, but without c. R. — As last, but Victory stg. l. (in some of the following it may be stg. front, hd. l.). *B.M.C.* 314 note (*gives wrong obv.*); *R.I.C.* 87 (a)   650

75a   D. R. — As last (*Tinchant cat.*)   650

75aa   D. Laur., dr. and cuir. bust r. R. — As last (*Tinchant cat.*)   700

75b   D, but PES. and IVS . AV. R. — As last. *B.M.C.* 314 note; *R.I.C.* 87 (b)   650

75bb   D, but PES. R. — As last. *B.M.C.* 314 note; *R.I.C.* 87 (c)   650

75c   D, but AV. R. — As last. *B.M.C.* 314 note; *R.I.C.* 87 (d)   650

75d   D. R. — As last, but Victory advancing l. *B.M.C.* 314 note; *R.I.C.* 88 (a)   650

75e   D, but PES. and IVS . AV. R. — As last. *B.M.C.* 314 note and p. 617 (*in B.M.*); *R.I.C.* 88 (b)   650

75f   D, but IVS . AV. R. — As last. *B.M.C.* 314 note; *R.I.C.* 88 (c)   650

75g   D, but NGER IVS . M. R. — As last. *B.M.C.* 314 note; *R.I.C.* 88 (d) ..   650

75h   D. R. — Victory stg. l., holding wreath, l. hand on hip or raising dress. *B.M.C.* 315 (*Tinchant cat.*)   650

75i   D, but AV. R. — As last (*Tinchant cat.*)   650

75j   D. R. — As last, but holds cornucopiae. *B.M.C.* p. 81, *; *R.I.C.* 89 ..   700

75k   D, but IVS. R. — As last (*Tinchant cat.*)   700

76   F, but without AVG. R. VICTOR . IVST . AVG., Victory walking l., holding wreath and palm. *B.M.C.* p. 74, ‡ (*gives* IVSTI *on rev.*); *R.I.C.* 81 (e)   650

76a   F. R. — As last. *B.M.C.* p. 74, ‡ note; *R.I.C.* 81 (f)   650

77   G, but PESCE. and without AVG. R. — As last. *B.M.C.* p. 82, (c) (*doubtful*); *R.I.C.* 81 (d) ..   ..

78 Denarius. D, but PESCÉ. and AV. R. VICTOR. IVST. AVG., Victory walking
l., holding wreath and palm. *B.M.C.* 314 note; *R.I.C.* 81 (b) £650
78a C, but IVS. R. — As last. *B.M.C.* 314 note; *R.I.C.* 81 (a) 650
78b D, but PESCE. R. VICTOR . IVSTI . AVG., as last. *B.M.C.* 314; *R.I.C.* 81 (c)
(*has* IVST *on rev. in error*)   650
78c G, but PESCE. and without AVG. R. VICTOR.IVSTI AV.,as last (*Mazzini cat.*) 650
79 . . . CAI . . . ESC . NIGER IVS . COS. R. VIRTVS AVG. retrograde, Minerva
stg. l., holding spear and leaning on shield. *B.M.C.* p. 82, (d) (*doubtful*);
R.I.C. 91   ..   ..
79a D, but IVS. R. VIRTVS AVG., Mars advancing r., holding spear and shield.
B.M.C. p. 81, †; *R.I.C.* 90 650
79b D, but IVSTI M (or AVG mon.). R. — As last (*Ryan coll.*) 650
79c D? R. — As last, but Mars stg. l. *B.M.C.* 317 note; *R.I.C.* 94 (b)
(*where rev. legend gives* VIRTVTI AVG.)   ..   ..   ..
80 D, but without C. R. VIRTVTI AVG., Virtus or Mars stg. r. (or front, hd. r.),
holding spear and leaning on shield. *B.M.C.* 317 note; *R.I.C.* 92 (a) .. 650
80a D. R. — As last. *B.M.C.* 317 650
80b D, but IVT ? R. — As last. *B.M.C.* 317 note; *R.I.C.* 92 (b) 650
80c D ? but AV. R. — As last, but Mars possibly advancing r. *B.M.C.* p. 81,
† note; *R.I.C.* 93   650
80d D. R. — As before, but Mars advancing r. (*Tinchant cat.*) 650
81 D, but without C. R. — As last, but Mars stg. l. *B.M.C.* 317 note;
R.I.C. 94 (a) 650
81a D, but AV. R. — As last (*Tinchant cat.*) 650
81b B. R. VOTIS PVBLICIS, emperor, veiled and togate, stg. l., sacrificing
out of patera over altar. (*British Museum*) 800

CLODIUS ALBINUS

195-197 A.D.

Decimus Clodius Septimius Albinus was born at Hadrumentum in Africa. He entered the army at an early age and served with great distinction until, at the death of Pertinax, he was governor of Britain. Severus, in order to keep the West quiet whilst he consolidated his position and dealt with Didius and Niger, offered Albinus the rank of Caesar, which he accepted. However, as soon as Italy and the East were under his control, Severus determined to be absolute master of the Empire. Accordingly, in 195 Severus persuaded the Senate to declare Albinus a public enemy and prepared to attack him. Albinus, having been saluted as Augustus by his legions, made preparations for the forthcoming struggle and had some initial successes. A great battle was fought on 19th Feb., 197, near Lugdunum (Lyons) and ultimately the victory went to Severus. Albinus committed suicide.

Obverse legends.

As Caesar, struck at Rome

A. D . CLODIVS ALBINVS CAES. 193 A.D.

B. D . CLOD . SEPT . ALBIN . CAES. 193-195 A.D.

C. D . CL . SEPT . ALBIN . CAES. 193-195 A.D.

As Augustus, struck at Lugdunum, late 195 or early 196-197 A.D.

D. IMP . CAE . D . CLO . SEP . ALB . AVG.

E. IMP . CAES . D . CLO . ALBIN . AVG.

F. IMP . CAES . D . CLO . SEP . ALB . AVG.

G. IMP . CAES . D . CLOD . SEP . ALB . AVG.

Obverse types.

a. Bare head right.
b. Laureate head right.
c. Laureate head right, light drapery on far shoulder.
d. Laureate head right, draped and cuirassed.

References.

The *B.M.C.* numbers are under "The Wars of the Succession."

R.I.C. on page 44 has an error, *obv.* (a) and (b) should be reversed.

Mints.

B.M.C. numbers before 104 and *R.I.C.* 1-12A are attributed to Rome, others to Lugdunum.

1	**Denarius.** Fb. ℞. AEQVITAS AVG . COS II, Aequitas stg. l. (or front, hd. l.), holding scales and cornucopiae. *B.M.C.* 280; *R.I.C.* 13 (a)	£200
1a	Gd. ℞. — As last. *B.M.C.* 279; *R.I.C.* 13 (b)	200
1b	Gc. ℞. — As last. *B.M.C.* p. 616 (*in B.M.*)	200
1c	F. Laur. r., cuir. bust almost half-length. ℞. — As last. *B.M.C.* p. 616 (*in B.M.*)	350
5	Is almost certainly a very incomplete description of the next, though with one possible variation—APOLLINI for APOLINI. *B.M.C.* p. 70, bottom (a); *R.I.C.* p. 46, * (*Belgrade*)	
5a	Db. ℞. APOLINI AVG . COS . II., Apollo, in female dress, stg. half l., holding patera and lyre (*Mazzini cat.*)	300
6	Db. ℞. CLEMENTIA AVG . COS . II, Clementia stg. front, hd. l., holding patera and sceptre. *B.M.C.* 269-70; *R.I.C.* 14	225

N.B.—*R.I.C. nos.* 2-10 (*C.* 9, 15, 30, 48, 65) *have the obv. legends reversed, his (a) should be (b) and vice versa.*

9   15

9   **Denarius.** Ba. ℞. COS . II, Aesculapius stg. l., holding snake-wreathed rod on ground, or holding round object that he offers to snake which coils upwards around rod. *B.M.C.* 88-9; *R.I.C.* 2   ..   ..   £200

13   Eb. ℞. FEL . AVG . COS . II, Felicitas stg. l., holding caduceus and sceptre. *B.M.C.* p. 63, †; *R.I.C.* 15   250

14   Db. ℞. FELICITAS AVG . COS . II, Felicitas stg. l., holding branch and cornucopiae. *B.M.C.* p. 65, *; *R.I.C.* 16 (*Cohen quotes B.M. probably in error for next*) ..   ..

14a Fb. ℞. — As last, but described as holding caduceus and cornucopiae, also stg. front, hd. l. *B.M.C.* 281; *R.I.C.* 16   250

15   Ba. ℞. FELICITAS COS . II, as **13.** *B.M.C.* 91-2; *R.I.C.* 4   ..   150

19   Ba. ℞. FEL . P . R. in ex., P . M . TR . P . COS . III around, Felicitas seated l., holding caduceus and cornucopiae (Hy.; *rev. of Hadrian*). *B.M.C.* p. 38 (*probably an ancient forgery*); *R.I.C.* 12A (*wrong in saying ' not in B.M.'*)

20   Db. ℞. FIDES AVG . COS . II, Fides stg. r., holding corn-ears and basket or plate of fruit. *B.M.C.* p. 65, †; *R.I.C.* 17 (*Cohen quotes B.M., probably in error for next*)   ..   ..

20a Fb. ℞. — As last. *B.M.C.* 282 (*described as ' head l.,' but see pl.* 12, 14); *R.I.C.* 17   250

20b Fb. ℞. — Clasped hands, holding legionary eagle. *B.M.C.* 283; *R.I.C.* 18   225

21   Db. ℞. FIDES LEGION . COS . II, legionary eagle on perch l., hd. r., between two standards, each surmounted by a hand. *B.M.C.* 271; *R.I.C.* 19 ..   225

22   Db. ℞. — As **20b.** *B.M.C.* p. 65, ‡; *R.I.C.* 20 (a)   ..   ..

22a Db. ℞. As last, but LEG. *B.M.C.* p. 65, ‡ note; *R.I.C.* 20 note   ..   225

23   F. Laur. bust dr. r. ℞. As **22** or **22a.** *B.M.C.* p. 65, ‡ note; *R.I.C.* 20 (c)

24   30

24   Fb. ℞. FIDES LEGION . COS . II, as **22.** *B.M.C.* 284; *R.I.C.* 20 (b)   ..   200
    N.B.—*The normal perch for the eagle on the last five is a thunderbolt.*

25   Fb. ℞. — As last, but eagle not on thunderbolt. *R.I.C.* 20 note   ..   200

26   *Obv.?* ℞. FORTITVDO AVG . INVICTA, Hercules stg., leaning on club and holding globe or apple. *B.M.C.* p. 70, bottom (b); *R.I.C.* 21 ..   ..

27   D . CL . SEPT . ALBINO CAE., a. ℞. FORT . RE., Fortuna seated l., holding rudder and cornucopiae, wheel under seat. *B.M.C.* 94 note; *R.I.C.* 5 note (*very doubtful*) ..   ..

30   Ca. ℞. FORT . REDVCI . COS . II., as last, but rudder on globe. *B.M.C.* 94; *R.I.C.* 5 (c)   150

30a Ca. ℞. — As last, but without wheel. *B.M.C.* 94 note; *R.I.C.* 5 note (*Réka Devnia hoard*)   150

36   48

36 D, but ends ALBINV, b. R. FORTVNA AVG . COS . II, Fortuna stg. l., holding
a rudder and cornucopiae. *B.M.C.* p. 70, (b) (*irregular; ancient forgery ?*);
R.I.C. 22   ..   ..   £300

37 Db. R. — As last. *B.M.C.* p. 71; *R.I.C.* 21 note (*if this is the obv.
Cohen means, it makes sense, if the coin exists*)   ..

40 Eb. R. GEN . LVG . COS . II, the Genius of Lugdunum, towered, stg. front,
hd. l., holding sceptre and cornucopiae, eagle at feet. *B.M.C.* p. 63, ‡;
R.I.C. 23 (c)   275

40a Fb. R. — As last. *B.M.C.* 285; *R.I.C.* 23 (b)   250

40b Fc. R. — As last. *B.M.C.* 286   250

40c Fd. R. — As last. *B.M.C.* 285 note; *R.I.C.* 23 (d)   275

41 Dd. R. — As last. *B.M.C.* 285 note (*possibly an error for last*)   ..

43 IMP . C . D . CLO . SEP . ALBIN . AVG., b. R. IOVIS VICTORIAE COS . II, Jupiter
stg. r., holding Victory and sceptre. *B.M.C.* 272 note; *R.I.C.* 26 note
(*both suggest Cohen's description is inaccurate, and may be the same coin as
next*)   ..   ..

43a Db. R. — Jupiter stg. l., holding Victory and spear, eagle at feet.
B.M.C. 272; *R.I.C.* 26   300

44 *Obv.* as **43**. R. IOVI VICTORI, Jupiter seated l., holding Victory and
thunderbolt. *B.M.C.* p. 65, §; *R.I.C.* 27 (*both think that Cohen's description
is imperfect, and that the variety may not exist at all*)   ..   ..

45 *Obv.* as **43**. R. MARS PATER COS . II, Mars advancing r., holding spear
and trophy. *B.M.C.* 273 note; *R.I.C.* 29 note (*both suggest Cohen's
description is inaccurate and may be the same coin as next*)   ..   ..

45a Db. R. — As last. *B.M.C.* 273; *R.I.C.* 29   300

46 IMP . CAES . D . CL . ALBIN . AVG., b. R. MAR . VLT . COS . II, Mars stg. r.,
holding spear and leaning on shield. *B.M.C.* p. 70 (d); *R.I.C.* 28 (*believed
to be incorrectly reported*)

48 Ba. R. MINER . PACIF . COS . II, Minerva stg. front, hd. l., holding branch
of olive and shield on ground, spear rests against l. arm. *B.M.C.* 98-102;
R.I.C. 7   120

48a Ca. R. — As last. *B.M.C.* 95-7   130

48b Ba. R. — Minerva stg. r., holding branch. *Seaby's Bull. Mar.* 1950,
B356   175

51 Eb. R. MIN . PAC . COS . II, as **48**. *B.M.C.* 265A; *R.I.C.* 30   ..   200

52 F, but without ALB. R. MONET . AVG . COS . II, Moneta stg., holding scales
and cornucopiae. *B.M.C.* p. 70, (e); *R.I.C.* 31 (*doubtful*)   ..   ..

53 Fb. R. PAX AVG . COS . II, Pax stg. l., holding branch and cornucopiae.
B.M.C. 287-8; *R.I.C.* 32 (a)   200

53a Db. R. — As last. *B.M.C.* p. 66, *; *R.I.C.* 32 (a) (*Lawrence coll.*) ..   225

54 Fa. R. — As last. *B.M.C.* 287 note (*very doubtful*); *R.I.C.* 32 (b)   ..

55 Denarius. Ca. ℞. PROVID . AVG . COS., Providentia stg. front, hd. l.
(or half-left), holding wand, over large or small globe, and sceptre.
B.M.C. 41-2; *R.I.C.* 1 (c) £140

56 A, but ALBIN., a. ℞. — As last. *B.M.C.* 38 note; *R.I.C.* 1 (b) .. 150

58 Aa. ℞. — As last. *B.M.C.* 38-40; *R.I.C.* 1 (a) 140

58a A, but AES . for CAES., a. ℞. — As last. *B.M.C.* 38 note; *R.I.C.* 1 (a)
note (*R.D. hoard*)

60 Db. ℞. PROV . AVG . COS . II, as last. *B.M.C.* 274 note; *R.I.C.* 33 .. 225

60a Db. ℞. PROVIDEN . AVG . COS . II, as last. *B.M.C.* 274 note; *R.I.C.* 34 225

60b Db. ℞. PROVIDENT . AVG . COS . II, as last. *B.M.C.* 274 note; *R.I.C.* 35 225

60c Db. ℞. PROVIDENTIA AVG . COS . II, as last, but the II of COS . II l. and r.
of Providentia. *B.M.C.* 274; *R.I.C.* 36 note 225

60d Fb. ℞. — As last, but legend normal. *B.M.C.* p. 69, *; *R.I.C.* 36 (a) 225

60e Gb. ℞. — As last. *B.M.C.* p. 67, †; *R.I.C.* 36 (b) 225

61   76

61 Ca. ℞. ROMAE AETERNAE, Roma seated l. on round shield, holding
palladium and sceptre. *B.M.C.* 43-4; *R.I.C.* 11 (a) 140

61a Ba. ℞. — As last. *B.M.C.* 45; *R.I.C.* 11 (b) 150

62 Db. ℞. SAEC . FEL . COS . II, Felicitas stg. front, hd. l., holding caduceus
and branch. *B.M.C.* 275 note; *R.I.C.* 37 225

63 Ca? ℞. — As last. *B.M.C.* p. 70; *R.I.C.* 37 note (*very doubtful*) ..

64 Db. ℞. SAECVLI FEL . COS . II, as last. *B.M.C.* 275-6; *R.I.C.* 38 .. 225

65 Ca. ℞. SAEC . FRVGIF . COS . II, Saeculum Frugiferum, rad., bare to waist,
stg. l., holding caduceus and fork. *B.M.C.* p. 37, *; *R.I.C.* 8 .. 200

66 Db? ℞. — As last. *B.M.C.* p. 37, * note; *R.I.C.* 8 note (*very doubtful*)

67 B, but CLO . SEP ., a. ℞. SAECVLO FRVGIFERO, Sol stg., holding caduceus
(or type as last). *B.M.C.* p. 26; *R.I.C.* 12 250

72a Fb. ℞. SAL . AVG . COS . II ?, Salus stg. l., holding sceptre and feeding
out of patera a snake coiled round altar. *B.M.C.* p. 69, † note; *R.I.C.* 39
note .. ..

73 Fb. ℞. SALVTI AVG . COS . II, as last. *B.M.C.* p. 69, †; *R.I.C.* 39.. .. 225

74 Ca? ℞. As last. *B.M.C.* p. 70; *R.I.C.* 39 note (*very doubtful*) ..

75 Fb. ℞. — Salus seated l., feeding snake coiled round altar. *B.M.C.*
p. 69, ‡; *R.I.C.* 40 225

76 Eb. ℞. SPE . AVG . COS . II, Spes advancing l., holding up flower and
raising skirt. *B.M.C.* 266; *R.I.C.* 41 225

76a Ed. ℞. — As last. *B.M.C.* 267 225

76b Eb. ℞. SPES . AVG . COS . II, as last. *B.M.C.* 266 note and p. 616 (*in B.M.*);
R.I.C. 42 (a) 225

77 E. Laur. bust dr. r. ℞. As **76** and/or as last. *B.M.C.* 267 note; *R.I.C.*
42 (b) ..

78   IMP . CAES . CL . SEPT . ALBIN . AVG ., b. R. S . P . Q . R . P . P . OB C . S in laurel wreath. *B.M.C.* p. 70, (c) (*modern forgery*); *R.I.C.* p. 50, *   ..

79B

79	Db. R. VICT . AVG . COS . II, Victory advancing r., holding wreath and palm or trophy. *B.M.C.* 277; *R.I.C.* 43 (a)	£225
79a	Dc. R. — As last. *B.M.C.* 278 (see pl. 12, 10); *R.I.C.* 43 (b).. ..	225
79b	Fb. R. — As last. *B.M.C.* 289; *R.I.C.* 43 (c)	225
80	Ca ? R. — As last. *B.M.C.* p. 71; *R.I.C.* 43 (a) note (*very doubtful*) ..	
81	E. Laur. bust dr. r. R. — As last. *B.M.C.* p. 64, * note; *R.I.C.* 43 (d)	250
81a	Eb. R. — As last. *B.M.C.* p. 64, *; *R.I.C.* 43 (e) (*Lawrence coll.*) ..	225
81b	Db. R. — Similar type, but standard for trophy. *B.M.C.* 277 note; *R.I.C.* 44	250
82	Fb. R. — Victory stg. r., foot on globe, inscribing shield balanced on knee. *B.M.C.* p. 69, §; *R.I.C.* 45	250
82a	Fb ? R. — Victory stg. l. on globe, holding wreath and palm. *B.M.C.* p. 69, ‖; *R.I.C.* 46	250
82b	Fc. R. — As last. (*Mazzini cat.*)	250
83	Eb. R. — Victory seated l. on cuirass, holding palm and balancing shield on knee. *B.M.C.* 268; *R.I.C.* 47	250
83a	Db. R. VIRTVTI AVG . COS . II, Virtus stg. l., holding parazonium and spear. *B.M.C.* p. 67, *; *R.I.C.* 48 (b) (*Lawrence coll.*)	250
83b	Fa. R. — As last, but Virtus stepping l. *B.M.C.* 290; *R.I.C.* 48 (a) ..	250
84	Fb. R. VIRTVTI AVGVSTI, as **83a.** *B.M.C.* 290 note; *R.I.C.* 49 (*perhaps misreading of last*)	
85	Ca ? R. — As last. *B.M.C.* p. 71; *R.I.C.* 49 note (*very doubtful*) ..	

SEPTIMIUS SEVERUS

193-211 A.D.

Lucius Septimius Severus was born on 11th April, 146 A.D., near Leptis Magna in Syrtica (N. Africa): his father being of a senatorial family. He became a soldier of outstanding ability, and held increasingly important commands until, at the death of Commodus, he was governor of Upper Pannonia and commander-in-chief of the armies in that area. Septimius expressed his allegiance to Pertinax, but on the latter's murder and the shameful elevation of Didius Julianus, which caused so much indignation in the provinces, he was proclaimed emperor by the troops at Carnuntum, on the Danube. He rapidly disposed of Didius and Pescennius Niger and later in 197 attacked and defeated Clodius Albinus, who had been hailed as emperor by the legions in Gaul, thus becoming undisputed master of the whole empire.

He made his elder son, Caracalla, joint emperor in 198 and in 209 raised his younger son, Geta, to the rank of Augustus.

He had many successful campaigns on the borders of the empire, and subdued the Parthians, the Arabians and the Adiabenians. In 208 he came to Britain, where there was much unrest, following a great invasion by the barbarians of the north in 197. He had Hadrian's Wall repaired, as it had been partly destroyed, and he invaded Caledonia, but without much success. The strains of this campaign affected the health of the elderly Septimius and he died at Eboracum (York) on 4th February, 211 A.D.

Septimius had two wives; the first was Marcia, who died before he became emperor, the second was Julia Domna by whom he had his two sons.

Obverse legends.

During the Wars of the Succession

A.	IMP . CAE . L . SEP . SEV . PERT . AVG.		193-195 A.D.
B.	,, ,, ,, ,, ,, ,,	COS.	193
BI.	,, ,, ,, ,, ,, ,,	,, I.	193
BII.	,, ,, ,, ,, ,, ,,	,, II.	194
C.	L . SEPT . SEV . PERT . AVG . IMP.		193
CI.	,, ,, ,, ,, ,, ,,	I.	193
CII.	,, ,, ,, ,, ,, ,,	II.	194
CIII.	,, ,, ,, ,, ,, ,,	III.	194
CIV.	,, ,, ,, ,, ,, ,,	IV.	194-195
CV.	,, ,, ,, ,, ,, ,,	V.	195
CVI	,, ,, ,, ,, ,, ,,	VI.	195
CVII.	,, ,, ,, ,, ,, ,,	VII.	195-196
CVIII.	,, ,, ,, ,, ,, ,,	VIII.	196-197
CVIIII.	,, ,, ,, ,, ,, ,,	VIIII.	197
CX.	,, ,, ,, ,, ,, ,,	X.	197-198

With Caracalla and later with Geta also

D.	L SEP . SEVERVS PER . AVG . P . M . IMP . XI.	198
E.	L . SEPT . SEV . AVG . IMP . XI . PART . MAX.	198-202
F.	SEVERVS AVG . PART . MAX.	200-201
G.	,, ,, ,, ,, P . M . TR . P . VIIII.	201
H.	SEVERVS PIVS AVG.	201-210
I.	,, ,, ,, BRIT.	210-211

After his death

J.	DIVO SEVERO PIO

Obverse type:

Laureate head, bearded r., unless otherwise stated in text, except with legend J. when the head is bare.

References.

In the British Museum Catalogue this reign is covered in three separate sections, with the numbering starting again from 1 in each.

Wars of the Succession, A.D. 193-198, which covers *B.M.C.* pp. 20-117. Here we have prefixed the *B.M.C.* number with a ' W '.

Joint Reign of Septimius Severus and Caracalla, A.D. 198-209. No prefix letter and covers pp. 156-306.

Joint Reign of Septimius Severus, Caracalla and Geta, A.D. 209-211, which covers pp. 356-386. Here we have prefixed the *B.M.C.* number with a ' G '.

Those struck after his death, during the joint reign of Caracalla and Geta, have the *B.M.C.* number prefixed with a ' C '.

Mints.

Both the *B.M.C.* and *R.I.C.* attribute all the denarii to Rome except the following:

Alexandria ? *B.M.C.* W319-W328 (pp. 83-6); *R.I.C.* 343-350к (pp. 135-6).

Emesa ? *B.M.C.* W335-W411 (pp. 87-102); *R.I.C.* 351a-436a (pp. 137-150).

Laodicea ad Mare ? *B.M.C.* W425-W457 (pp. 105-114), 625-35 (pp. 280-2), 650-81 (pp. 285-9), 712-4, 725-6 (pp. 297-8), 732-3; *R.I.C.* 437-526 (pp. 150-163).

Uncertain mint. *B.M.C.* W468 (p. 117).

Cistophoric tetradrachms struck in Asia. *B.M.C.* 758-60 (pp. 304-5); *R.I.C.* 527-33 (pp. 163-4).

Barbarous and Irregular. *B.M.C.* G126-149 (pp. 379-83); *R.I.C.* 337a-342a (pp. 133-4).

1 bis Denarius. F, but IVERVS. Ŗ. ABVNDANTIA AVG., Abundantia stg. l., emptying cornucopiae (Hy.; *rev. of Elagabalus*). *B.M.C.* p. 619, A171 (*Ashmolean*) .. ..

1   14

1   H. Ŗ. ADVENT . AVGG., Septimius, in military dress, on horse prancing l., raising r. hand and holding spear; on l., a soldier, holding vexillum and leading the horse. *B.M.C.* 304-6; *R.I.C.* 248 .. .. .. £45

4   ? Ŗ. ADVENTVI AVG . FEL., Septimius on horseback l. (*very doubtful*) ..

6   CVIII. Ŗ. ADVENTVI AVG . FELICISSIMO, Septimius, in military dress, on horse pacing r., raising r. hand. *B.M.C.* W151-6; *R.I.C.* 74 40

11   H. Ŗ. ADVENTVS AVG., Septimius on horseback .. ..

12   ? Ŗ. — Septimius on horseback preceded by soldier .. .. ..

13   ? Ŗ. — The three emperors on horseback .. ..

    N.B.—*Nos.* 11, 12 *and* 13 *all very doubtful.*

14   I. Ŗ. ADVENTVS AVGVSTI, Septimius, in military dress, with cloak floating behind, on horse pacing l., raising hand and holding spear. *B.M.C.* G50; *R.I.C.* 330 60

15   H Ŗ — As last (Hy.). *B.M.C.* 304 note; *R.I.C.* 249 .. .. ..

15a Denarius. A, but CAES. R. AEQVIT . AVG . TR . P . COS . II., Aequitas
stg. l., holding scales and cornucopiae (Hy.; *rev. of Pertinax*). *B.M.C.*
p. 24 (*probably ancient forgery*); *R.I.C.* p. 92, * .. ..

16 A. R. AEQVITAS AVG., as last. *B.M.C.* W319 note; *R.I.C.* 343 .. ..

17 F. R. AEQVITAS AVGG., Septimius seated on curule chair l.; before him,
Aequitas stg. r., holding scales and cornucopiae. *B.M.C.* p. 191, *;
R.I.C. 154 .. .. £85

18 A. R. AEQVITAS II, as **15a.** *B.M.C.* W319; *R.I.C.* 344 40

19 D, but IMP . X . PART or more probably IMP . XI . ART. R. AEQVITATI AVGG.,
as **15a.** *B.M.C.* p. 63; *R.I.C.* p. 103, † .. ..

21   39

21 E. R. — As last. *B.M.C.* 122-6 and 650-1; *R.I.C.* 122 (c) and 500 .. 25

21a E. Drapery on l. shoulder. R. — As last. *B.M.C.* 122 note; *R.I.C.*
122 (d) (*Tinchant cat.*) 35

21b E. Laur. bust cuir. with aegis (?) half-length. R. — As last. *B.M.C.*
p. 618 (*Oldroyd*) 55

22 E. Laur. bust dr. R. — As last. *B.M.C.* 122 note; *R.I.C.* 122 (b) .. 45

22a E. Laur. bust dr. and cuir. R. — As last (*G. R. Arnold*) 45

24a Cistophoric tetradrachm (= three denarii). IMP . L . CAES . SEPT .
SEV . PERT . AVG . TR . P . VI. R. AETERNITAS AVG., crescent and seven stars.
B.M.C. p. 304, *; *R.I.C.* 527 750

25 Denarius. H. R. AFRICA, Africa, wearing elephant-skin head-dress, stg.
r., holding out corn-ears or more probably scorpion in her robe; at her
far side, lion r. *B.M.C.* 309; *R.I.C.* 253 40

31 H. R. — Africa, as last, reclining l. against rock and/or lion, holding
scorpion and cornucopiae; before her, basket of corn-ears. *B.M.C.*
310-11; *R.I.C.* 254 45

36 Cv. R. ANNONAE AVG., Annona stg. l., foot on prow, holding two corn-
ears and cornucopiae. *B.M.C.* p. 39, * (*hydrid and ancient forgery?*);
R.I.C. 57 .. ..

36a CVIII. R. — As last. *B.M.C.* p. 49 (*very doubtful*); *R.I.C.* 75.. ..

37 Cx. R. ANNONAE AVGG. (*Cohen* AVG. *in error*), as last. *B.M.C.* W239-43;
R.I.C. 107 25

38 E, but IMP . X. R. — As last. *B.M.C.* p. 63; *R.I.C.* p. 103, † (*very
doubtful*) .. ..

39 E (*Cohen has* PERT. *after* SEV. *in error*). R. — As last. *B.M.C.* p. 175, †
and 652; *R.I.C.* 123 and 501.. 25

39a F. R. — As last. *B.M.C.* 185 note 25

40 E. R. — Annona seated r. before modius filled with corn-ears (Hy.?).
B.M.C. p. 180, (a); *R.I.C.* 124 .. ..

41 F. R. — As last. *B.M.C.* 185-6; *R.I.C.* 156 25

42 CIIII. R. APOLLINI AVGVSTO, Apollo, laur. and wearing long robe, stg.
front, hd. l., holding patera and lyre. *B.M.C.* W78-9; *R.I.C.* 40 .. 25

42a A. R. — As last. *B.M.C.* W320; *R.I.C.* 345 30

43 C, but without IMP. R. — As last (*most improbable*)

47a A. R. ARAB . ADIAB . COS . II . P . P., Victory advancing l., holding wreath
and trophy. *B.M.C.* W326; *R.I.C.* 346 30

48 Cv R. — As last. *B.M.C.* W107-9; *R.I.C.* 58 25

48a Cvi. ℞. — As last, *B.M.C.* p. 41, *; *R.I.C.* 63A (*R. D. hoard*). *The only recorded coin with* IMP . VI £50
50 Cvii. ℞. — As last. *B.M.C.* W131-3; *R.I.C.* 64 25
51 Cviii. ℞. — As last. *B.M.C.* W157-8; *R.I.C.* 76 25
52 Cvii. ℞. ARAB . ADIABENIC., as last. *B.M.C.* p. 110, §; *R.I.C.* 466 .. 30
52a SEP . SEVERVS PERT . AVG . IMP . XI . PARP . M[AX]. ℞. AR . AD . TR . P . VI . COS . II . P . P., as last. *B.M.C.* p. 280, *; *R.I.C.* 494A (*R. D. hoard*) .. 30
52b L . SEP . SEVERVS PER . AVG . P . V . IMP . XI . PAR . P . M. ℞. — Two captives seated back to back at base of trophy. *B.M.C.* p. 280, †; *R.I.C.* 494B (*R. D. hoard*) 30
The last eight coins refer to victories in the Arabian-Adiabenian War.

55   58

55 **Tetradrachm.** IMP . C . L . SEP . SEVERVS P . AV (or A͡V). ℞. AVGVS / TORVM across field and split up by legionary eagle between two standards. *B.M.C.* 758; *R.I.C.* 528 650
55a **Denarius.** Bii, but L. omitted. ℞. BAN EVENT, Bonus Eventus stg. front, hd. l., holding plate of fruit and two corn-ears. *B.M.C.* W343 note; *R.I.C.* 368 note (*R. D. hoard*) 40
55b Bii. ℞. BONA SEPS., Spes advancing l., holding up flower and lifting skirt. *B.M.C.* W340 note; *R.I.C.* 364 note (*Lawrence*) 30
55c Bii, but II . CO . for COS . II. ℞. BONA SPEI, as last. *B.M.C.* W341 note; *R.I.C.* 365 (*Lawrence*).. 30
55d Bii. ℞. — As last (*Tinchant cat.*) 30
55e B. ℞. — As last. *B.M.C.* p. 617 (*Oldroyd*) 30
55f Cii, but PERTE. ℞. — As last. *B.M.C.* W425 note; *R.I.C.* 445 .. 30
56 C, but PERTE. ℞. BONA SPES, as last. *B.M.C.* p. 105, *; *R.I.C.* 437 .. 30
57 Cii. ℞. — As last, *B.M.C.* W425 note; *R.I.C.* 444 (a) 30
57a Cii, but PERTE. ℞. — As last. *B.M.C.* W425; *R.I.C.* 444 (b) 30
58 Bii. ℞. — As last. *B.M.C.* W340; *R.I.C.* 364 30
58a Bii, but CEV. ℞. — As last. *B.M.C.* G126 (*base and irregular*); *R.I.C.* 338 (*gives* SEV.; *barbarous*) .. ..
59 Cviii (*Cohen has* SEP. *for* SEPT., *possibly in error*). ℞. — As last. *B.M.C.* p. 111, †; *R.I.C.* 472 30
59a Bii. ℞. — Bonus Eventus, as **55a.** *B.M.C.* p. 617 (*Ashmolean*) .. 40
60 Bii, but II . CO. for COS . II. ℞. BONAE SPEI, Spes advancing l., as **55b.** *B.M.C.* W341; *R.I.C.* 366 (a) 35
61 Bii. ℞. — As last. *B.M.C.* W341 note; *R.I.C.* 366 (b) 30
61a Bii, but C. for COS. ℞. — As last. *B.M.C.* W341 note; *R.I.C.* 366 (c) (*R.D. hoard*) 35
61b A. ℞. — As last. *B.M.C.* p 87, †; *R I C* 351A 35
62 Bii, but CA. and PER. ℞. BONI SPES, as last. *B.M.C.* W342 note; *R.I.C.* 367 .. ..
62a Bii. ℞. — As last. *B.M.C.* W342; *R.I.C.* 367 30
62b Cii, but PERTE. ℞. — As last. *B.M.C.* W426; *R.I.C.* 446 30

63 Denarius. CVII. ℞. BON . EVENT., Bonus Eventus stg. front, hd. l., holding plate of fruit and two corn-ears. *B.M.C.* W437 note; *R.I.C.* 467   £30

64 CVIII. ℞. BONI EVENT., as last. *B.M.C.* W440; *R.I.C.* 473   30

65 A. ℞. — As last. *B.M.C.* p. 88, *; *R.I.C.* 351B   30

65a BII. ℞. — As last. *B.M.C.* W343 note; *R.I.C.* 368   30

65b BII. ℞. BONI EVENTV., as last. *B.M.C.* W343 note; *R.I.C.* 369 note (*R.D. hoard*)   30

65c BII. ℞. BONI EVENTVIC, as last. *B.M.C.* W343 note; *R.I.C.* 369 note (*R. D. hoard*)   30

66 A. ℞. BONI EVENTVS., as last. *B.M.C.* W321 and p. 88, * note; *R.I.C.* 347 and 352   30

67 CII. ℞. — As last. *B.M.C.* W427 note; *R.I.C.* 447   30

67a CVII. ℞. — As last. *B.M.C.* W437; *R.I.C.* 468   30

67b CVIII. ℞. — As last. *B.M.C.* W440; *R.I.C.* 474   30

67c CII, but PERET. ℞. — As last. *B.M.C.* W427   30

68 BII. ℞. — As last. *B.M.C.* W343-4; *R.I.C.* 369   25

68a BI. ℞. — As last (*Tinchant cat.*)   30

68b A. ℞. BONI EVENTVS COS . II., as last. *B.M.C.* W343 note; *R.I.C.* 369 note (*R. D. hoard*)   35

On a few of the pieces from 63 Bonus Eventus may be stg. l., as in Cohen.

68c BII, but C . II . C. instead of COS . II. ℞. BONI EVENTVS, corn-ear between two crossed cornuacopiae. *B.M.C.* p. 91, *; *R.I.C.* 369A   ..   45

68d BII. ℞. CERER . ERVG., Ceres stg. l., or front with hd. l., holding two corn-ears and long torch. *B.M.C.* p. 617 (*Oldroyd*)   35

68e CVIII. ℞. CERER . ERVGIF., as last. *B.M.C.* W441; *R.I.C.* 475 note   ..   35

69 BII. ℞. CERER . FRVG., as last. *B.M.C.* W345; *R.I.C.* 370   ..   30

69a BII. ℞. CERERI FRVG., as last. *B.M.C.* W345 note; *R.I.C.* 371   30

69b BII. ℞. CERER . FRVG . II . COS., as last. *B.M.C.* W345 note, *R.I.C.* 370A   40

69c BII, but II . C for COS . II . ℞ CERER FRVGIF . COS., as last. *B.M.C.*, W345 note; *R.I.C.* 370B   40

70 CVIII. ℞. CERER . FRVGIF., as last. *B.M.C.* W441 note; *R.I.C.* 475 ..   30

70a CVIII. ℞. CERER . FRVIFER., as last. *B.M.C.* W441 note; *R.I.C.* 476 ..   30

71 H. ℞. CONCORDIA, Concordia stg. l., sacrificing from patera over altar and holding double cornucopiae, star on l. (Hy.; *rev. of Aquilia Severa*) *B.M.C.* p. 225, 1; *R.I.C.* 313   ..   ..

72 H. ℞. — Concordia stg. l., holding patera and cornucopiae (Hy.; *rev. of Crispina*). *B.M.C.* p. 225, 2; *R.I.C.* 314   ..   ..   ..

73a H. ℞. CONCORDIA AVGVSTORVM, Caracalla and Geta stg., holding Victory on globe between them. *B.M.C.* p. 619, A172 (*Oldroyd; cast from N*) ..

76 Cx. ℞. CONCORDIAE MILITVM, Concordia stg. front, hd. l., holding in each hand a standard. *B.M.C.* W244; *R.I.C.* 108   40

78 E. Laur. but dr. and cuir. r. ℞. — As last. *B.M.C.* 654 note; *R.I.C.* 502 (a). (*This is probably a mistake for the next*) ..   ..

78a E. ℞. — As last. *B.M.C.* 654; *R.I.C.* 502 (b)   30

80 J. R. CONSACRATIO, Septimius, veiled, stg., holding olive-branch. *R.I.C.* p. 239, † (*possibly a mistake of Cohen for 82*) .. .. ..

80a J. R. — Eagle on globe (*base or Æ*). *B.M.C.* C21 note; *R.I.C.* 191c note

82 J. R. CONSECRATIO, eagle stg. front on thunderbolt, looking l. *B.M.C.* C24; *R.I.C.* 191B (*Illustrated with 84 at bottom of last page*) £90

84 J. R. — Eagle stg. front on globe, looking l. *B.M.C.* C21-3; *R.I.C.* 191c 85

84a J. R. — Eagle stg. r. on globe, looking l. (*Tinchant cat.*) 90

84b Cviii. R. — As **84.** *B.M.C.* p. 114 (*in B.M., ex Trau; base, probably ancient forgery*) .. ..

85 J. R. — Eagle on globe (*base or Æ*). *B.M.C.* C21 note; *R.I.C.* 191c note

86 J. R. — Eagle stg. front or half-right on cippus or altar, looking l. *B.M.C.* C20; *R.I.C.* 191D 90

87 89

87 J. R. — Wreath on throne, footstool below. *B.M.C.* C25; *R.I.C.* 191E 95

89 J. R. — Funeral pyre with facing quadriga on top. *B.M.C.* C27; *R.I.C.* 191F 90

92 **Quinarius.** H. R. COS . II., Victory advancing l., holding wreath and palm. *B.M.C.* p. 215, *; *R.I.C.* p. 123, * (*curious style, Eastern?*) .. 130

94 Ciiii. R. COS . II . P . P., similar, but Victory advancing or running r. *B.M.C.* W80 (*this could be as next*); *R.I.C.* 42 120

94a Cvii. R. — As last (*Rome*) 120

95 Cx. R. — Victory l., as **92.** *B.M.C.* p. 60, *; *R.I.C.* 109 120

95a E, but IMP . X. Laur. bust dr. and cuir. r. R. — As last (*Tinchant cat.*) 150

96 **Denarius.** E. R. — As last. *B.M.C.* p. 176, * and 655-6; *R.I.C.* 125 (a) and 503 (a) 25

97 **Quinarius.** E. R. — As last. *B.M.C.* p. 176, * note; *R.I.C.* 125 (a) 120 *On the last two Cohen has* PERT. *after* SEV. *on obv. in error.*

97a F, Laur. bust dr. (and/or dr. and cuir.) r. R. — As last. *B.M.C.* p. 192, *; *R.I.C.* 158 (*Vautier*) 150

98 **Denarius.** G. R. — As last. *B.M.C.* 725-6; *R I.C.* 523 30

99 G. R. — As last (*base or Æ*). *B.M.C.* 725 note; *R.I.C.* 523 note ..

100 E. R. COS . III . P . P., as last. *B.M.C.* 657-9; *R.I.C.* 504 25

102 H. R. — As last. *B.M.C.* 732-3; *R.I.C.* 526 25

103 **Quinarius.** H. R. — As last. *B.M.C.* 318; *R.I.C.* 258 110

103 104

104 **Denarius.** H. R. — Triumphal arch of Septimius of four columns and three doors or arches; on top, facing chariot with six horses between two equestrian statues. *B.M.C.* 320; *R.I.C.* 259 450

109 Denarius. H. R. COS . III . LVDOS SAECVL . FEC., Liber (*Bacchus*) stg. half-right, naked except for leopard's skin, holding cup or jug and thyrsus; on l., leopard stg. l., head turned back to catch drips from cup; facing him, Hercules, naked, stg. half-left, holding club on ground and with lion's skin over arm. *B.M.C.* 315-7; *R.I.C.* 257 .. .. £200

115 CIII. R. DIS . AVSPICIB . TR . P . II. around, COS . II . P . P. in ex., somewhat as last, but both figures stg. half-left, with Hercules on l. and leopard between them. *B.M.C.* W63 note; *R.I.C.* 31 (*does it exist in* Æ ?) ..

133 IMP . CAE . L . SEP. (*or* SEPT.) SEVER . AVG. R. ET IA II, Roma (?) seated l., holding palladium and sceptre. *B.M.C.* p. 83, *; *R.I.C.* 348 (*obv.* A) .. 45

133a A ? R. FEIICT . TEMPOR, corn-ear between two crossed cornuacopiae. *B.M.C.* p. 617 (*Caister Treasure Trove*) 60

134 H. R. FELICITAS above, SAECVLI in ex., Septimius, Caracalla and Geta seated r. on platform; stg. before them, attendant; on r. below platform, citizen stg. l.; on r. of platform an urn. *B.M.C.* 326; *R.I.C.* 263. *Showing one of the ceremonies before the Secular Games* 300

135 H. R. FELICITAS AVGG, Felicitas stg. l., holding caduceus and cornucopiae. *B.M.C.* 322-5; *R.I.C.* 261 25

136 H. R. FELICITAS AVG., as last (*base or* Æ) *B.M.C.* 322 note; *R.I.C.* 261 note .. ..

137 H. R. FELICITAS PVBLICA, as last. *B.M.C.* p. 217, *; *R.I.C.* 262 .. 35

137a I. R. — As last. *B.M.C.* p. 368 and p. 619 (*Oldroyd*); *R.I.C.* 331 .. 35

140 BII, Laur. hd. l. R. FELICITAS TEMPOR., vase-shaped basket containing fruits and corn-ears. *B.M.C.* W346 note and p. 617 (*Oldroyd*); *R.I.C.* 376 150

141 A. R. — Corn-ear between two crossed cornuacopiae. *B.M.C.* p. 88, ‡; *R.I C* 354 35

141a BII. R. FELICITAS TEMPO, as last. *B.M.C.* W351; *R.I.C.* 374 35

141b BII. R. FELICITAS TEMPOR., as last. *B.M.C.* W347 note (*Lawrence*); *R.I.C.* 374A 35

142 BII R. FELICIT . TEMPO, as last. *B.M.C.* W347 note; *R.I.C.* 372 .. 30

142a BII. R FELICIT TEMPOM, as last. *B.M.C.* W350; *R.I.C.* 373 note .. 35

142b BII. R. FELICIT . TEMPOR, as last. *B.M.C.* W347-9; *R.I.C.* 373 .. 30

143 A. R. FELICIT . TEMPOR, basket of fruit as **140**. *B.M.C.* p. 88, †; *R.I.C.* 353 85
Cohen has SEPT. *for* SEP. *in error in* **142-4,** *and missed out* SEV. *in next.*

144 BII. R. — As last. *B.M.C.* W346; *R.I.C.* 375 85

146 A. R. FIDEI LEG . TR . P . COS., Fides stg. half-left, holding Victory and standard (vexillum). *B.M.C.* W6 and p. 83, †; *R.I.C.* 1 and 349 .. 45

149 A. R. FIDEI LEG . TR . P . COS . II., as last. *B.M.C.* W6 note and 327; *R.I.C.* 1 note and 349 note (*Cohen has* SEPT. *for* SEP. *in error*) .. 45

153a L . . VS AAVG IMT I R. FIDES MILITVM, Fides stg. front, hd. r., holding two standards. *B.M.C.* G127 (*plated; ancient forgery, possibly British*); *R.I.C.* 339; *C.R.B.* 58 .. ..

N.B.—*In the types where Fortuna holds a rudder, it is sometimes on a globe.*

153b BII. R. FORETVN . REDVC., Fortuna or Hilaritas stg. front, hd. l., holding long palm and cornucopiae. *B.M.C.* W357 note; *R.I.C.* 382A (*R. D. hoard*) 30

153c BII. R. FORNI . REDVC., Fortuna stg. half-left, holding rudder and cornucopiae. *B.M.C.* p. 617 (*Caister Treasure Trove*) 35

153d CI, but PERET. R . FORT . RDEVC, Fortuna stg. l., holding sceptre and cornucopiae. ‧ *B.M.C.* p. 106, (a) variety; *R.I.C.* 440 note (*R.D. hoard*) .. £35
153e CII. R . — As last. *B.M.C.* p. 107, * note; *R.I.C.* 449A 35
153f CII, but PERTE. R . — As last. *B.M.C.* p. 107, * note; *R.I.C.* 449 note 35
153g CII, but PERTE. R . — Fortuna seated l., holding cornucopiae and sceptre.
B.M.C. W430; *R.I.C.* 450 35
153h CII, but PERTE. R . FORT . RDVC., as **153b**. *B.M.C.* p. 108, † note; *R.I.C.*
453 note 35
153i C. II, but PERTE. R . FORT. REDEVC. Fortuna seated l., holding cornucopiae in each hand. (*G. R. Arnold*) 35
154 I. R . FORT . RED . P . M . TR . P . XIX . COS . III . P . P., Fortuna seated l.,
holding rudder on globe and cornucopiae, wheel under throne. *B.M.C.*
G109-10; *R.I.C.* 246 45
155a I. R . As last, but without the P.M. or wheel. *B.M.C.* G109 note;
R.I.C. 247A .. .. ‾ .. .. ..
156 CI. R . FORT . REDVC, Fortuna (?) stg. l., holding cornucopiae and sceptre.
B.M.C. p. 106, (b); *R.I.C.* 439 (*doubtful*) ..
156a C or CI, two dots below bust. R . — Fortuna or Hilaritas as **153b**.
B.M.C. p. 106, (c); *R.I.C.* 440 note (*Both references have* RDVC, *but this is
corrected,* B.M.C p 622) 35
157 CII. R . — As last. *B.M.C.* p. 108, †; *R.I.C.* 453 35
157a CII, but PERET. R . — As last. *B.M.C.* p. 108, † note; *R.I.C.* 453 note
(*Lawrence*) 35
157b CVIII. R . — As last, but long branch for palm. *B.M.C.* p. 112, †;
R.I.C. 479A (b) 40
158 IMP . CA . L . SE . SEVER . AG . COS . II. R . — As **156a**. *B.M.C.* W357 note;
R.I.C. 382 note .. ..
159 CII, but CA. and PER. R . — As **156**. *B.M.C.* p. 93, ‡; *R.I.C.* 388 .. 35
159a CII, but PERTE. R . — As **156**. *B.M.C.* p. 108, *; *R.I.C.* 449 35
160 CII. R . — Fortuna, wearing polos on hd., stg. front, hd. l., holding
rudder and cornucopiae. *B.M.C.* W428 note; *R.I.C.* 448 (a) 30
160a CII, but PERTE. R . — As last. *B.M.C.* W428; *R.I.C.* 448 (b) 30
160b CII, but PERET. R . — As last. *B.M.C.* W429 30
161 CI. R . — As last. *B.M.C.* p. 106, (a); *R.I.C.* 440 30
161a BII. R . — As last. *B.M.C.* W352 note; *R.I.C.* 376B (*Third Dura hoard*) 30
162 CVI. R . — As last. *B.M.C.* p. 110, †; *R.I.C.* p. 154, * (*doubtful*) ..
163 CVII. R . — As last. *B.M.C.* p. 111, *; *R.I.C.* 469 30
164 CVIII. R . — As last. *B.M.C.* p. 111, ‡; *R.I.C.* 477 30
165 CVII. R . — As **160**, but Fortuna seated. *B.M.C.* W438; *R.I.C.* 470 .. 30
166 CVIII. R . — As last. *B.M.C.* W442-3; *R.I.C.* 478 30
167 CVIIII (*Cohen has* VIII *in error*). R . — As last. *B.M.C.* p. 116, (a);
R.I.C. p. 158, * 30
167a CVIII. R . — Fortuna stg. l., holding cornucopiae in each hand. *B.M.C.*
p. 112, *; *R.I.C.* 477A (*R.D. hoard*) 45
168 CII. R . FORT . RDEVC, as **165**. *B.M.C.* p. 108, *; *R.I.C.* 451 30
168a BII. R . — Fortuna or Pietas stg. half-left, sacrificing out of patera
before altar and holding cornucopiae. *B.M.C.* W363 note; *R.I.C.* 385
note (*R. D. hoard*) 35
For others with this rev. legend see **153d-g.**
168b CII. R . FORT . REDEVC, as **165**. *B.M.C.* p. 108, * note; *R.I.C.* 451A
(*R. D. hoard*) 30
168c CVIII. R . FORT . REDVC., as **168a**, but Fortuna stg. front, hd. l. *B.M.C.*
W444; *R.I.C.* 479B (*R. D. hoard*) 35
168d C. R . — As **168a**, but modius on hd. *B.M.C.* p.105, †; *R.I.C.* 437A .. 35
169 A. R . FORT . REDVG., Fortuna or Hilaritas stg. l., holding long palm .
and cornucopiae. *B.M.C.* p. 88, §; *R.I.C.* 355 35
169a CVIII. R . — As last, but long branch for palm. *B.M.C.* p. 112, † note;
R.I.C. 479A (a) (*R.D. hoard*) 35

170 Denarius. Cviii. ℞. FORTA . REDVC., Fortuna, with modius on hd., seated l., holding rudder and cornucopiae. *B.M.C.* W442 note; *R.I.C.* 479   £35

172 Cii, but PERTE. ℞. FORTV . REDVC., as last. *B.M.C.* p. 108, * note; *R.I.C.* 452 30

172a Bii. ℞. — As last. *B.M.C.* W354 note; *R.I.C.* 378A (*Tinchant cat.*) .. 30

172b Bii. ℞. FORTVI . REDVC., Fortuna or Hilaritas stg. l., holding long palm and cornucopiae. *B.M.C.* W357 note; *R.I.C.* 383B (*R.D. hoard*) 35

172c Bii. ℞. FORTVN . AVG., Fortuna stg. l., holding rudder and cornucopiae. *B.M.C.* p. 92, *; *R.I.C.* 376A (*R.D. hoard*) 35

172d Bii. ℞. FORTVN . REDV., as **172b.** *B.M.C.* W357 note; *R.I.C.* 382 .. 35

173 Bi. ℞. FORTVN . REDVC, as **170.** *B.M.C.* p. 89, (b); *R.I.C.* p. 138, (1) .. 30

173a Bii. ℞. — As last. *B.M.C.* W354-6; *R.I.C.* 379 25

174 Bi. ℞. — Similar, but Fortuna stg. *B.M.C.* p. 89, (a); *R.I.C.* p. 138, (2) 30

174a Bii. ℞. — As last. *B.M.C.* W352-3; *R.I.C.* 377 25

175 Bi. ℞. — Fortuna or Hilaritas, with modius on hd., stg. l. (or front, hd. l.), holding long palm and cornucopiae. *B.M.C.* p. 89, (c); *R.I.C.* p. 138, (3) 35

175a Bii. ℞. — As last. *B.M.C.* W357-61; *R.I.C.* 383 25

175b Bi. ℞. — As last, but Fortuna seated. *B.M.C.* p. 89, (d); *R.I.C.* p. 138, (3A) 35

176 Bi. ℞. — Fortuna or Pax, with modius on hd., seated l., holding branch and cornucopiae. *B.M.C.* p. 89, (e); *R.I.C.* p. 138, (4) 35

177 Bii. ℞. — As last. *B.M.C.* p. 93, †; *R.I.C.* 386 30

Some of the Bi *from* **173** *may not really exist and may be misreadings of* Bii.

177a Bii. ℞. — Fortuna or Pietas stg. half-left, sacrificing out of patera over lighted altar and holding cornucopiae. *B.M.C.* W363 note; *R.I.C.* 385 note (*R.D. hoard*) 40

177b Bii. ℞. FORTVN . REDVG, as **175.** *B.M.C.* W357 note; *R.I.C.* 383A (*R. D. hoard*) 35

177c Cii, but PERET. ℞. FORTVNA AEDVC., Fortuna stg. l., holding cornucopiae and sceptre. *B.M.C.* p. 107, * note; *R.I.C.* 450A (*R. D. hoard*) 35

179 Quinarius. H. Laur. bust dr. and cuir. r. ℞. FORTVNA REDVX, Fortuna seated l., holding rudder and cornucopiae, wheel under throne. *B.M.C.* 327 note; *R.I.C.* 264 (b) 140

180 Denarius. Bii (*Cohen has* SEPT. *for* SEP. *in error*). ℞. — As last. *B.M.C.* W354 note; *R.I.C.* 380 .. .. ..

181   185

181 H. ℞. — As last. *B.M.C.* 327-9; *R.I.C.* 264 (a) 25

181a H. ℞. — As last, but rudder on globe. *B.M.C.* 327 note; *R.I.C.* 264 (a) 30

181b H. ℞. — As **181,** but without the wheel (*Brussels and Mazzini cat.*) .. 30

185 Bii. ℞. FORTVNA REDVCI, Fortuna or Pietas sacrificing, as **177a.** *B.M.C.* W363 note; *R.I.C.* 385 30

185a Bii. ℞. — Fortuna seated l., holding rudder and cornucopiae. *B.M.C.* W354 note; *R.I.C.* 381 30

185b Bɪɪ. ℞. — Fortuna or Hilaritas, with modius on hd., stg. front, hd. l., holding long palm and cornucopiae. *B.M.C.* W362; *R.I.C.* 384.. .. £30

185c Bɪɪ. ℞. — Fortuna or Pax stg. l., holding branch and cornucopiae. *B.M.C.* p. 93, *; *R.I.C.* 385 (a) (*R. D. hoard*) 35

185d Bɪ. ℞. FORTVNAE REDVCI, as **185**. *B.M.C.* W339; *R.I.C.* p. 138, 5 .. 30

186 Bɪɪ, but without cos. ℞. — Fortuna, with modius on hd., stg. l., holding rudder or branch and cornucopiae. *B.M.C.* W352 note; *R.I.C.* 378 .. 30

186a Bɪɪ. ℞. — As last. *B.M.C.* W352 note; *R.I.C.* 378 note (*R. D. hoard*) 30

186b Bɪɪ. ℞. — As **185**. *B.M.C.* W363 note; *R.I.C.* 385 note (*R. D. hoard*) 30

188 Cvɪɪɪ. ℞. — Fortuna seated l., holding rudder and cornucopiae, wheel under seat. *B.M.C.* W161-2; *R.I.C.* 78 (a) 25

188a H. ℞. — As last. *B.M.C.* 327 note; *R.I.C.* 264A 30

194a Bɪɪ. ℞. FORTVNAE REREDVC., Fortuna seated l., holding poppy and corn-ears (or small rudder on globe) and cornucopiae. *B.M.C.* W364; *R.I.C.* 387 (*misdescribed*) 30

195 E. ℞. FORTVNAE AVGG., Fortuna, with modius on hd., stg. front, hd. r., holding cornucopiae and long rudder; on l., prow. *B.M.C.* 127-8; *R.I.C.* 126 (a) 25

195a E. ℞. — As last, but without modius on hd. (*Brussels*) 30

197 Cvɪɪɪ. ℞. — As **188**, but rudder on globe. *B.M.C.* W161 note; *R.I.C.* 77 30

198 Cx. ℞. — As last. *B.M.C.* W245; *R.I.C.* 110.. 25

199 E. ℞. — As last (Hy. ?). *B.M.C.* p. 180, (b); *R.I.C.* 127 ..

200 H. ℞. FORTVNE AVG., Fortuna stg. l., holding wand and cornucopiae. *B.M.C.* p. 49 and p. 226, 4; *R.I.C.* p. 124, * (*very doubtful*) .. ..

201 Cvɪɪɪ. ℞. — As last. *B.M.C.* p. 49; *R.I.C.* p. 100 note (*doubtful*) ..

201a Bɪɪ. ℞. FORVN . REDVC., Fortuna seated l., holding rudder and cornu-copiae. *B.M.C.* W354 note; *R.I.C.* 378A note (*R. D. hoard*) 30

205 209

203 F. ℞. FVNDATOR PACIS, Septimius, veiled, stg. half-left, holding branch and roll. *B.M.C.* 190-1; *R.I.C.* 160.. .. ,. 25

204 E. ℞. — As last (Hy. ?). *B.M.C.* p. 180, (d); *R.I.C.* 129 .. ..

205 H. ℞. — As last. *B.M.C.* 330-1; *R.I.C.* 265 25

206 ? ℞. — As last (*base or Æ*). *B.M.C.* 331 note; *R.I.C.* 265 note ..

207 E. ℞. FVNDAT . PACIS, as last. *B.M.C.* p. 180 (c); *R.I.C.* 128 .. ..

207a H. ℞. — As last. *B.M.C.* 331 note (*in B.M., curious style, probably ancient forgery*).. .. ..

208 H. ℞. FVRTVNAE FELICI, Fortuna stg. l., holding rudder and cornucopiae (Hy.; *rev. imitated from J. Domna*). *B.M.C.* p. 226, 5; *R.I.C.* 315 ..

208a Cɪɪ. ℞. GENIVS P . R., Genius stg. half-left, sacrificing out of patera over altar and holding cornucopiae. *B.M.C.* W59; *R.I.C.* 26 35

209 ·Cɪɪɪɪ. ℞. — As last. *B.M.C.* W81; *R.I.C.* 43 25

210 Cvɪɪɪ. ℞. HERCVLI DEFENS., Hercules stg. half-right, resting on club, holding bow, lion's skin over arm. *B.M.C.* p. 47, * and W451; *R.I.C.* 79 and 488 25

212 Cvɪɪɪɪ. ℞. — As last. *B.M.C.* W218-20; *R.I.C.* 97 25

214 Cx. ℞. — As last. *B.M.C.* W246; *R.I.C.* 111 30

214a As one of the last (*plated*), *Seaby's Bull.*, Feb. 1938, 46429 .. ..

215 **Tetradrachm.** IMP . C . L . SEP . SEVERVS AVG. ℞. IMPE . C . L . SEP .
SEVERVS P . AVG., in laurel-wreath. *B.M.C.* p. 304, † note; *R.I.C.* 529 (a) £750
215a As last, but *obv.* legend ends P . AV. *B.M.C.* p. 304, †; *R.I.C.* 529 (b) .. 750
215b As **215,** but *rev.* ends P . P . AVG. (*Tinchant cat.*) 750

215c As last, but obv. legend ends P . AV. (*B.M.*)   750
215d **Denarius.** BII, but AV. ? ℞. IMP . VI RIB (or V . IRIB) . POT . IIII . CO ...,
  captive, wearing peaked cap, seated on ground r. *B.M.C.* W411; *R.I.C.* 436   45
216 CVIII. ℞. INDVLGENTIA AVG., Indulgentia seated l., holding patera and
  sceptre. *B.M.C.* W163-5; *R.I.C.* 80   30
219 H. ℞. INDVLGENTIA AVGG. around, IN CARTH. in ex., the Dea Caelestis,
  with elaborate head-dress, looking front, riding r. on lion, holding drum;
  below, water gushing from rocks on l. *B.M.C.* 334 note; *R.I.C.* 267A .. 45
219a H. ℞. — As last, but she holds drum and sceptre. *B.M.C.* 334; *R.I.C.*
  267 (a) 40

222 H. ℞. — As last, but she holds thunderbolt and sceptre. *B.M.C.* 335-8;
  R.I.C. 266   35
222a H. ℞. — As last, but she only holds thunderbolt. *B.M.C.* 335 note;
  R.I.C. 267B   40
228 H. ℞. INDVLGENTIA AVGG . IN ITALIAM, Italia, towered, seated l. on
  globe, holding cornucopiae and sceptre. *B.M.C.* 339; *R.I.C.* 268   .. 150

              229   236

229 H. ℞. INVICTA VIRTVS,e Septimius on horse prancing r., brandishing
  javelin at prostrate foe. *B.M.C.* 340; *R.I.C.* 269 65
230 CI (or perhaps CII). ℞. INVICTO IMP., captive seated r., in attitude of
  sadness, at base of trophy. *B.M.C.* p. 106, (d); *R.I.C.* 441   35
231 BII. ℞. — As last   ..   ..
232 BII. ℞. — Trophy with captured arms below. *B.M.C.* W365-6;
  R.I.C. 389   30
232a BII, but COS . V. ℞. —· As last. *B.M.C.* W365 note; *R.I.C.* 389 note
  (*R. D. hoard*) 35
232b CI. ℞. — As last. *B.M.C.* p. 106, (e); *R.I.C.* 441A (*Fourth Dura hoard*) 35
232c CII. ℞. INVICTO IMPE., as last. *B.M.C.* p. 617 (*Caister T. T.*) 35
232d BII. ℞. INVICTO IMP. I (or II), as last. *B.M.C.* W367; *R.I.C.* 390   .. 35
233 A. ℞. INVICTO IMP . TROPAEA, as last. *B.M.C.* W335; *R.I.C.* 356   .. 35
233a BII. ℞. — As last (*Tinchant cat.*) 35

234 Bii. R. invicto imp . tropae., as last. *B.M.C.* W368 note; *R.I.C.* 391   £35
235 Bii, but ii . co. for cos . ii. R. — As last. *B.M.C.* W368 note; *R.I.C.* 392   35
235a Similar, but tropea. *B.M.C.* W368 note; *R.I.C.* 393   35
235b Similar, but tropei. *B.M.C.* W368 note; *R.I.C.* 394   35
235c Similar, but tropaea. *B.M.C.* W368 note; *R.I C.* 392a (*R. D. hoard*) ..   35
235d Similar, but tropaea ii. *B.M.C.* W368; *R.I.C.* 395   35
236 Cx. R. iovi conservatori, Jupiter, naked to waist, seated l. on throne, holding Victory and sceptre. *B.M.C.* W247; *R.I.C.* 111a   40
237 E (*Cohen has* xii *in error*). R. — As last. *B.M.C.* 129-31 and p. 286, *; *R.I.C.* 130 and 504a (*Lawrence*)   30
238a H. R. — Bust of Jupiter, wreathed, with touch of drapery, r. (*Basle*)   250
239 Cviii, but sever. R. iovi invicto, Jupiter seated l., holding Victory and sceptre. *B.M.C.* p. 112, ‡ note; *R.I.C.* 480 (b)   40
239a Cviii. R. — As last. *B.M.C.* p. 112, ‡; *R.I.C.* 480 (a) (*Vienna*) ..   40
240 Bi. R. iovi prae . orbis (Governor of the World), Jupiter, naked to waist, seated l. on low seat, holding Victory and sceptre; at feet l., eagle stg. half-left, hd. r. *B.M.C.* p. 89, (f); *R.I.C.* p. 139 (6)   50
242 Bii. R. — As last. *B.M.C.* W370; *R.I.C.* 396   50

243   251

243 E (*Cohen has* sep. *in error ?*). R. iovi propvgnatori, Jupiter, naked except for cloak over l. arm, advancing r., brandishing thunderbolt and raising l. hand. *B.M.C.* 132 (*cast ?*); *R.I.C.* 131   30
244 Similar (*base or* Æ *forgery*). *B.M.C.* 132 note .. ..
244a H. R. — As last. (Hy.; *plated*). *B.M.C.* p. 226, 6; *R.I.C.* 270 (*Lawrence*)
244b F. R. — As last, but Jupiter (?) in long robe and helmeted. *B.M.C.* p. 195 (*in B.M., ex Lawrence; an ancient forgery ?*).. .. .. ..
245 H. R. iovi, in ex., sospitatori, around, Jupiter stg. facing in shrine with flat roof, holding patera and sceptre. *B.M.C.* 341; *R.I.C.* 271 ..   125
247 Cii, but perte. R. iovi vict., Jupiter seated, holding Victory and spear. *B.M.C.* W431 note; *R.I.C.* 454   35
247a Similar, but iobi vict. *B.M.C.* W431 note; *R.I.C.* 454 note   35
247b Cii, but peret. R. iovi vict., Jupiter, naked to the waist, seated l. on low seat, holding Victory and sceptre. *B.M.C.* p. 617 (*Ashmolean*) ..   35
248 H. R. iovi vict. in ex., p . m . tr . p . xv . cos . iii . p . p. around, Jupiter in quadriga galloping r., hurling thunderbolt at two giants. *B.M.C.* p. 262, *; *R.I.C.* 204   350
249a Ci (or perhaps ii). R. iovi victori, Jupiter seated l., holding Victory and sceptre. *B.M.C.* p. 106 (f); *R.I.C.* 441b   35
249b Cii, but peret. R. — As **247b.** *B.M.C.* 431   35
250 **Medallion.** l . sept . severvs pivs avg . imp . xi . part . max, laur. bust cuir., with aegis, r. R. iovi victori in ex., p . m . tr . p . xv . cos . iii . p . p. around, Jupiter in quad. r., hurling thunderbolt at two giants on ground .. ..   *Excessively rare, if genuine*
250a **Denarius.** H. R. ivno avgvstae, Juno seated l., holding flower (?) and child in swaddling clothes (Hy.; *rev. of Julia Mamaea*). *B.M.C.* p. 226, 7 and G128; *R.I.C.* 316.. .. ..
251 E. R. ivstitia, Justitia seated l., holding patera and sceptre. *B.M.C.* 660-1; *R.I.C.* 505   25
252 H. R. laetitia avgg., Laetitia stg., holding wreath and rudder. *B.M.C.* p. 226, 8; *R.I.C.* 317 .. ..

253 **Denarius.** H. ℞. LAETITIA above, TEMPORVM below a ship, from which
a variety of animals run; above, in background, four quadrigae. *B.M.C.*
343-4; *R.I.C.* 274 .. .. £225
253a As last, but only two quadrigae (*Tinchant cat.*) 225

256   262

255 A. ℞. TR . P . COS in ex., LEG . ITALICA around legionary eagle on low
perch l., between two standards. *B.M.C.* p. 21, †; *R.I.C.* 3 note ..
256 A. ℞. — LEG . I . ADIVT around, as last. *B.M.C.* W7; *R.I.C.* 2 .. 120
257 A. ℞. — LEG . I . ITAL. — *B.M.C.* p. 21, †; *R.I.C.* 3 .. .. ..
259 A. ℞. — LEG . I MIN. — *B.M.C.* p. 21, ‡; *R.I.C.* 4 140
260 A. ℞. — LEG . II . ADIVT — *B.M.C.* W8; *R.I.C.* 5 100
261 A. ℞. — LEG . II . ITAL. — *B.M.C.* W9; *R.I.C.* 6 100
262 A. ℞. — LEG . III . ITAL.— *B.M.C.* W10; *R.I.C.* 7 120
263 A. ℞. TR . P . C. in ex., LEG . III . IT. around, as **255.** *B.M.C.* W10 note
(*very doubtful*); *R.I.C.* 7 note .. ..
264 A. R. TR . P . COS in ex., LEG . IIII . FL. around, as **255.** *B.M.C.* p. 616
(*Oldroyd*); *R.I.C.* 8 100
265 A. ℞. — LEG . V . MAC. — *B.M.C.* W11; *R.I.C.* 9 120
266 A. ℞. — LEG . VII . CL. — *B.M.C.* W12; *R.I.C.* 10 120
267 A. ℞. — LEG . VIII . AVG. — *B.M.C.* W14-5 and 336; *R.I.C.* 11 and 357 90
268 A. ℞. — LEG . XI . CL. — *B.M.C.* W16; *R.I.C.* 12 100
269 A. ℞. — LEG . XIII . GEM. — *B.M.C.* W17; *R.I.C.* 13 120
269a A. ℞. — LEG . XIII . GEM . M . V. — *B.M.C.* W17 note; *R.I.C.* 13 note
(*R. D. hoard*) 130
270 A. ℞. — LEG . XIIII . GEM. — *B.M.C.* W19 note; *R.I.C.* 14 note ..
272 A. ℞. — LEG . XIIII . GEM . M . V. — *B.M.C.* W19-22; *R.I.C.* 14 .. 75
274 BII. ℞. — As last. *B.M.C.* W371; *R.I.C.* 397 140
276 A. ℞. — LEG . XXII — *B.M.C.* W23-4; *R.I.C.* 15 120
277 A. ℞. — LEG . XXII . PRI. — *B.M.C.* W23 note; *R.I.C.* 16 140
278 A. ℞. — LEG . XXX . VLP. — *B.M.C.* W25; *R.I.C.* 17 120
278a A. ℞. — LEG . XXX . VL. — *B.M.C.* W25 note; *R.I.C.* 17 120

279b   296

279 CI, but PERET. R. LIBER . AVG., Liberalitas stg. half-left (or front, hd. l.) holding abacus (*counting-board*) and cornucopiae. *B.M.C.* p. 106, g; *R.I.C.* 442 (*possibly a misreading of* 279b) £35

279a BII. R. — As last. *B.M.C.* W373-4; *R.I.C.* 398 30

279b CII, but PERET. R — As last. *B.M.C.* W432 note; *R.I.C.* 455 (b), (*Lawrence*). *Illustrated at bottom of last page* 35

279c CII, but PERTE. R. — As last. *B.M.C.* W432; *R.I.C.* 455 (a) 35

281 A. R. LIBERAL . AVG . COS., as last. *B.M.C.* W2-3; *R.I.C.* 18 25

281a CII. R. — As last (Hy.). *B.M.C.* p. 30, (a); *R.I.C.* 27 (*Lawrence*) .. 40

282 IMP . CAE . L . SEPT . SEV . PERT . AVG . II. R. LIBERA . AVG., as last (Hy. or *misreading of next*). B M.C. W375 note; *R.I.C.* 399 note .. ..

283 BII (*Cohen has* SEPT. *in error*). R. LIBERA . AVG., as last. *B.M.C.* W375; *R.I.C.* 399 .. .. ‾ 25

283a As last, but LIBERAL. *B.M.C.* W373 note; *R.I.C.* 400 30

283b As last, but LIBERT. *B.M.C.* W373 note; *R.I.C.* 400 note 30

283c CII, but PERTE. R. — As last. *B.M.C.* p. 617 (*Ashmolean*) 35

287 BII (*Cohen has* SEPT. *in error*). R. LIBER . AVG., Liberalitas seated l., holding abacus and cornucopiae. *B.M.C.* W376 note and p. 617 (*Oldroyd*); *R.I.C.* 401 30

287a As last, but LIBERAL. *B.M.C.* W376; *R.I.C.* 403 30

287b BII. R. LIBERA . AVG., as last. *B.M.C.* W376 note; *R.I.C.* 402.. .. 30

  N.B.—*On some of the Liberalitas pieces, she wears polos (small modius) on head.*

288 CVIII. R. LIBER . AVG., as **279**. *B.M.C.* W445; *R.I.C.* 481 30

288a CVIII. R. LIBERTA . AVG., at last. *B.M.C.* W446-7; *R.I.C.* 482 .. 30

290 CVIII. R. LIBERALITAS AVG . II, as last. *B.M.C.* W166-7; *R.I.C.* 81a (*Cohen has* dr. and cuir. *in error*) 25

291 H. R. LIB . AVG . III . P . M . TR . P . X . COS . III . P . P., as last. *B.M.C.* 381-2; *R.I.C.* 182 25

292 H. R. LIBERALITAS AVG., as last. *B.M.C.* 345 note; *R.I.C.* 275 (*doubtful*)

293 H. R. IIII . LIBERALITAS AVGG., as last. *B.M.C.* 345; *R.I.C.* 276 .. 30

296 H. R. LIBERALITAS AVGG . V, as last. *B.M.C.* 347; *R.I.C.* 277. *Illustrated at bottom of last page* 25

298 H. R. LIBERALITAS AVG . VI, as last. *B.M.C.* 349-51; *R.I.C.* 278 (a) .. 25

299 As last (*base or Æ*). *B.M.C.* 350 note; *R.I.C.* 278 (a) note .. ..

299a As last (*plated*). *B.M.C.* G129 .. ..

300a CII. R. LIBERO PATRI, Liber (Bacchus) stg. half-left, cloak or skin over l. shoulder, holding oenochoe and thyrsus; on l., panther stg. l., head turned back to catch drips from the jug. *B.M.C.* W60; *R.I.C.* 27A 35

301 CIII. R. — As last. *B.M.C.* W64-5; *R.I.C.* 32 25

301a As last, but ? bunch of grapes in place of oenochoe. *B.M.C.* W66 .. 35

302 CIIII. R. — As **300a**. *B.M.C.* p. 34, *; *R.I.C.* 44 35

302a CVIII. R. — As next. *B.M.C.* p. 616 (*Ashmolean*) 35

304 CVIIII. R. — Liber stg. front, hd. l., crowning himself and holding thyrsus; at his feet, panther. *B.M.C.* W222-3; *R.I.C.* 99 25

305 Cx. R. — As last. *B.M.C.* W248-9; *R.I.C.* 112 (a) 30

306 E (*Cohen has* SEP. *in error for* SEPT.). R. LIBERTAS AVGG., Libertas stg. half-left, holding pileus and rod. *B.M.C.* p. 177, † and 663-4; *R.I.C.* 133 and 507 25

307 H. R. LIBERTAS AVG. *B.M.C.* p. 226, 9; *R.I.C.* 280 (C. L. Clay coll.) .. 40

307a BII. R. LIR . AVG., Liberalitas stg. holding abacus and cornucopiae.. *B.M.C.* W376 note; *R.I.C.* 403A (*Third Dura hoard*) .. .. ..

307b IMP . CE . L . SEP . SEV . PERT . AVG . CO. R. MANET . AVG., Moneta stg. l., holding scales and cornucopiae. *B.M.C.* p. 90, (j) var.; *R.I.C.* p. 139, (6A) (*R. D. hoard*) .. ..

308 **Denarius.** Cɪɪɪ. ℞. MARS PACATOR, Mars, helmeted, naked except for
cloak over l. shoulder, stg. half-left, holding branch and spear (or sceptre).
B.M.C. p. 31, *; *R.I.C.* 33 ..   ..   £30

309 Cɪɪɪɪ. ℞. — As last. *B.M.C.* W82-3; *R.I.C.* 45   25

310 Cvɪɪɪɪ. ℞. — As last. (Hy.; *ancient forgery* ?). *B.M.C.* p. 58; *R.I.C.*
p. 103, *   ..   ..

311 Cɪɪɪ. ℞. MARS PATER, Mars, as before, but cloak floating out from waist,
advancing r., holding trophy over shoulder and spear. *B.M.C.* W84; *R.I.C.*
46   25

314a Bɪɪ, but CA. ℞. MAREI . VICT., as last. *B.M.C.* W378 note; *R.I.C.* 405ʙ   30

315 Cx. ℞. MARTI PACIFERO, Mars stg. l., foot on helmet or cuirass, holding
branch and spear. *B.M.C.* 250-1; *R.I.C.* 113   25

316 E. ℞. — As last (Hy. ?). *B.M.C.* p. 180, (e); *R.I.C.* 133ᴀ   30

317 As last (*base or Æ*)   ..   ..

318a B ? ℞. MARTI . VICT., Mars adv. r., holding spear and trophy. *B.M.C.*
p. 89, (g); *R.I.C.* p. 139, (6ʙ) (*R. D. hoard*)   ..   ..   ..

318b Bɪ. ℞. — As last. *B.M.C.* p. 617 (*Oldroyd*)   30

318c Bɪɪ ? ℞. — As **311**. *B.M.C.* W377; *R.I.C.* 405   30

318d Cɪɪ. ℞. — As **318a**. *B.M.C.* p. 108, ‡ note; *R.I.C.* 457ᴀ (*R. D. hoard*)   30

318e Bɪɪ, but CA. ℞. MARTI VICTO., as last. *B.M.C.* W378 note; *R.I.C.* 405ᴀ
(*R. D. hoard*)   30

319 Cx. ℞. MARTI VICTORI, Mars, naked to waist, stg. half-right, holding
shield and spear. *B.M.C.* W252 note; *R.I.C.* 114   30

319a Cx. ℞. — As last, but captive below shield. *B.M.C.* W252; *R.I.C.*
114 note   30

319b Cx. ℞. — As last, with captive, but Mars half-left. *B.M.C.* W252 note;
R.I.C. 114ᴀ (*Tinchant cat.*)   35

319c Cvɪɪɪɪ. ℞. — As **319**. *B.M.C.* p. 117 (b); *R.I.C.* 158, * (*R. D. hoard*)   35

319d G. ℞. — As last (Hy ?). *B.M.C.* p. 202; *R.I.C.* 151c   35

319e G. ℞. — Mars stg. front, hd. r., resting on shield set on low base and
holding spear. *B.M.C.* p. 298, *; *R.I.C.* 523ᴀ (*Lawrence*)   ..   35

320 E. ℞. — As **319**. *B.M.C.* 667 (?); *R.I.C.* 508   30

321 E. ℞. — As **319a**. *B.M.C.* 665-6; *R.I.C.* 509   25

321a E. ℞. — As last, but shield rests on small round object, perhaps
foeman's hd. or helmet. *B.M.C.* 133; *R.I.C.* 134   25

322 Cɪ. ℞. MART . VICTO., Mars, naked except for cloak flying behind,
advancing r., holding trophy over shoulder and spear. *B.M.C.* p. 106, (h);
R.I.C. 443   35

323 Cɪɪ. ℞. MART . VICT., as last. *B.M.C.* p. 108, ‡; *R.I.C.* 456 ..   30

323a Cɪɪ. ℞. MART . VICTOR., as last. *B.M.C.* p. 108, note, *R.I.C.* 457 ..   30

324 Bɪɪ, but CA. and PER. ℞. MART . VICT., as last. *B.M.C.* W378 note;
R.I.C. 404 (a)   30

324a Bɪɪ, but PER. ℞. — As last. *B.M.C.* W378 note; *R.I.C.* 404 (c) (*R. D.
hoard*)   30

324b Bɪɪ, but ɪɪ . CO. for COS . ɪɪ. ℞. — As last. *B.M.C.* W378 note; *R.I.C.*
404 (b) (*R. D. hoard*)   30

324c Bɪɪ. ℞. MART . VICTOR., as last. *B.M.C.* W378 note; *R.I.C.* 406 (a)
(*Lawrence*)   30

324d Bɪɪ. Laur. hd. l. ℞. — As last. *B.M.C.* W378 (*Orpington hoard*) ..   150

324e Bɪɪ, but CA. and PER. ℞. — As last. *B.M.C.* W378 note; *R.I.C.* 406 (b)   30

324f A, but PERTI . AVG . IIII. ℞. MARTI VLTORI, as last. *R.I.C.* 339ᴀ
(*barbarous*)   ..   ..

324g L . SEP . SEV . PERT . AV . COS . II. ℟. MINER . AVG., Minerva stg. front, hd.
l., holding oval shield set on ground and spear. *B.M.C.* W379 .. .. £35
324h CII, but PERTE. ℟. — Minerva stg. l., resting r. hand on shield and
holding spear. *B.M.C.* p. 108, §; *R.I.C.* 458 (*not in* B.M., *as it says*) ..
325 H. ℟. MINERVA SANCT., Minerva stg. l., holding shield and spear reversed
(Hy.; *rev. of Geta*). *B.M.C.* p. 226, 11; *R.I.C.* 319 .. .. ..
326 BI. ℟. MINER . VICT., Minerva advancing, brandishing javelin and
holding shield. *B.M.C.* p. 90, (h); *R.I.C.* p. 139, (7) .. .. ..
326a BI. ℟. — Roma seated on shield. *B.M.C.* p. 90, (i); *R.I.C.* p. 139, (7A)
327 BII, but CA. (*Cohen omits* PERT *in error*). ℟. — As **325**. *B.M.C.* p. 96, *;
R.I.C. 408 30
327a As last, but VICTRIC. *B.M.C.* p. 96, * note; *R.I.C.* 409 30
B.M.C. and R.I.C. give these last two as stg. l., brandishing javelin.
327b BII. ℟. MINER . VICT., Minerva stg. l., resting r. hand on shield, l. hand
at side. *B.M.C.* p. 96, †; *R.I.C.* 409B (*Third Dura hoard*) 30
327c BII. ℟. MINER . VICTRIC., as last, but spear in l. hand. *B.M.C.* p. 96, ‡;
R.I.C. 410 30
327d BII. ℟. MINER . VICT., Minerva stg. l., holding Victory and spear, shield
at feet. *B.M.C.* p. 96, §; *R.I.C.* 409A (*Lawrence*) 30
327e BII. ℟. MINER . VICT., Minerva stg. l., holding spear in r. hand, l. hand
on hip (*G. R. Arnold; mint of Emesa*) 30
328 CVIII, but SEVER.? ℟. MINER . VICTRIC., as **325**. *B.M.C.* p. 113, *; *R.I.C.*
483 30

328a H. ℟. — Minerva stg. r. by trophy, holding Victory and spear, shield
at feet (Hy., *plated; rev. of Caracalla*). *B.M.C.* p. 226, 10; *R.I.C.* 318 ..
N.B.—*On the following twenty-eight denarii* Moneta *often wears polos*
(modius) *on her hd.*
328b BII. ℟. MONE . AVG., Moneta stg. l. (or front, hd. l.), holding scales and
cornucopiae. *B.M.C.* W380 note; *R.I.C.* 411 note 30
329 A. ℟. MONET . AVG., as last. *B.M.C.* p. 88, ‖; *R.I.C.* 359 30

330   334a

330 BII. ℟. — As last. *B.M.C.* W380-2, 384-6; *R.I.C.* 411 (a) 25
330a BII, but SPE. for SEP. ℟. — As last. *B.M.C.* W383 25
330b BII, but II . C. for COS . II. ℟. — As last. *B.M.C.* W380 note; *R.I.C.*
411 (b) (*R. D. hoard*) 30
331 CII, but PERTE. ℟. — As last. *B.M.C.* p. 109, *; *R.I.C.* 459 30
331a CII, but PERET. ℟. — As last. *B.M.C.* p. 109, *note; *R.I.C.* 459 note
(*R. D. hoard*) 30
332 CVIII (*Cohen has* SEVER, *perhaps in error*). ℟. — As last. *B.M.C.* W448-9;
R.I.C. 484 (a) 25
333 B, but CA. and OCS. ℟. — As last. *B.M.C.* W380 note; *R.I.C.* 411 note
334a BI. ℟. — Moneta seated l. on stool, holding scales and cornucopiae
(*G. R. Arnold; mint of Emesa*) 35
338a IMP . CAE . L . SEP . SE . PER ℟. MONETA, as last. *B.M.C.* p. 83, ‡ note;
R.I.C. 350A note .. ..

339 **Denarius.** CII. ℞. MONETA AVG., Moneta stg. l. (or front, hd. l.), holding
scales and cornucopiae. *B.M.C.* p. 109, note*; *R.I.C.* 460 (a) £30
339a CII, but PERET. ℞. — As last. *B.M.C.* p. 109, * note; *R.I.C.* 460 (b) 30
339b CII, but PRTE. ℞. — As last. *B.M.C.* p. 109, * note; *R.I.C.* 460 (c) .. 30
339c A, but SEPT. ℞. — As last. *B.M.C.* p. 83, ‡; *R.I.C.* 350A (*Vienna*) .. 30
340 CVI. ℞. — As last. *B.M.C.* p. 110, ‡; *R.I.C.* p. 154, * .. ..
342 E. ℞. MONETA AVGG., as last. *B.M.C.* p. 177, ‡; *R.I.C.* 135 25

343   348-9

343 F. ℞. — As last. *B.M.C.* 194-5; *R.I.C.* 162 25
344 F. ℞. — As last, but Moneta seated l. *B.M.C.* 196; *R.I.C.* 163 (*in
Cohen the rev. has become separated from the obv. by* 345 *being inserted in
wrong place*) 25
345 E. ℞. — As last. *B.M.C.* p. 177, ‡ note and 669-70; *R.I.C.* 135A (b)
and 510 (a) 25
345a H. ℞. — As last. *B.M.C.* p. 227, 12; *R.I.C.* 280A (*Lawrence*).. .. 30
346 BII (*Cohen omits* SEP.). ℞. MONETA II . AVG., as last. *R.I.C.* 412 (*doubtful*)
347 IMP . CAE . L . SEV . PERT . AVG . N . C. (*possibly the same obv. as* **330b**). ℞.
MONETAE AVG., as **339.** *B.M.C.* W380 note; *R.I.C.* 411 note 30
347a BII, but CO. for COS. ℞. — As last. *B.M.C.* W380 note; *R.I.C.* 412A 30
347b A. ℞. — As last. *B.M.C.* p. 88, ‖ note; *R.I.C.* 359A (*R. D. hoard*) .. 30
347c BI. ℞. — As last. *B.M.C.* p. 90, (j); *R.I.C.* p. 139, (7B) 30
347d B, but CE. and CO. ℞. — As last. *B.M.C.* p. 90, (j) variant; *R.I.C.* p. 139,
(7B) (*R. D. hoard*) 30
348 CVIII. ℞. MVNIFICENTIA AVG., elephant walking r., perhaps cuir.
B.M.C. W168-9; *R.I.C.* 82 45
349 CVIIII. ℞. — As last. *B.M.C.* W224-5; *R.I.C.* 100 45
353 H. ℞. NCBILITAS, Nobilitas stg. r. (or stg. front, hd. r.), holding sceptre
and palladium (Hy.; *type of Geta*). *B.M.C.* p. 227, 13; *R.I.C.* 320 ..
353a H. ℞. NOBILITAS, as last (*base, and rather barbarous*). *B.M.C.* G131;
R.I.C. 320 note .. ..
354 **Quinarius.** H. ℞. — As last (Hy.). *B.M.C.* G131 note and p. 227,
13 note; *R.I.C.* 320 (*Rome*) .. ..
354a **Denarius.** CII, but PERET. ℞. ORT . REDVC., Fortuna stg. l., holding
cornucopiae and sceptre. *B.M.C.* p. 107, * note; *R.I.C.* 451 note (*R. D.
hoard*) 30

356 H. ℞. PACATOR ORBIS, rad. bust of young Sol dr. r. *B.M.C.* 354; *R.I.C.*
282 90

357 Cx. ℞. PACI AETERNAE, Pax seated l. on throne, holding branch and sceptre. *B.M.C.* W253-4; *R.I.C.* 118 .. .. £25

357a Cx. ℞. — As last, but cornucopiae for sceptre. *B.M.C.* W253 note; *R.I.C.* 118A 30

359 CIII. ℞. PACI AVGVSTI, as last (*Cohen has it as* **357**, *in error*). *B.M.C.* W70-1; *R.I.C.* 37 25

359a CIIII. ℞. — As last. *B.M.C.* W85; *R.I.C.* 54 (*R. D. hoard*) 35

359b CVIII. ℞. — As last (Hy.; *ancient forgery ?*). *B.M.C.* p. 48, *; *R.I.C.* 89

359c L . S . SEVER . . . . . ℞. PAET MA . . . MT VP . VOI., Moneta stg. l., holding scales and sceptre (Hy., *plated*). *B.M.C.* G133 (*local British work?*); *R.I.C.* 340; *C.R.B.* 56 50

359d D. ℞. PAR . ARAB . TR . P . VI around, COS . II . P . P in ex., two captives seated back to back at foot of trophy. *B.M.C.* 627 note; *R.I.C.* 496 (a) note 35

359e D. ℞. PAR . ARAB . . . P . COS . I . P . P., Victory advancing l., holding palm over l. shoulder and wreath. *B.M.C.* G135 (*irregular Eastern mint?*) 40

360 D. ℞. PAR . AR . AD., trophy, as **359d**. *B.M.C.* 627 note; *R.I.C.* 49 (b) note .. ..

361 D. ℞. PAR . AR . AD . TR . P . VI . COS . II . P . P., Victory, as **359e**. *B.M.C.* 625-6; *R.I.C.* 495 25

361a D, but AVГ . I . M. ℞. — As last. *B.M.C.* 625 note; *R.I.C.* 495 note .. 30

361b D. ℞. As **359d**, but AR . AD. *B.M.C.* 627-8; *R.I.C.* 496 (a) 30

362 Cv, but SEP. ℞. PAR . AR . ADIAB . COS . II . P . P., Victory, as **359e**. *B.M.C.* p. 40, *; *R.I.C.* p. 98, *

362a As last, but trophy for palm. *B.M.C.* p. 40, *; *R.I.C.* p. 98, * ..

361 373

363 Cv. ℞. PART . ARAB . PART . ADIAB. around, COS . II . P . P in ex., two captives seated back to back, each on a round shield and with their hands tied behind back. *B.M.C.* W118-9; *R.I.C.* 62 25

365 Cv. ℞. — As last, but trophy between the captives. *B.M.C.* W120-1; *R.I.C.* 63 25

369 D, but SEPT. ℞. PART . ARAB . TR . P . VI . COS . II . P . P., as last. *B.M.C.* 627 note; *R.I.C.* 496 (b) note 30

370 H. ℞. PART . MAX . P . M . TR . P . VIIII, as before, but the captives have their hands in front supporting their heads. *B.M.C.* 256-9; *R.I C.* 176 25

370a F. ℞. — As last. *B.M.C.* p. 202, †; *R.I.C.* 153 (*Lawrence*) 30

372 H. ℞. PART . MAX . P . M . TR . P . X, as last. *B.M.C.* 383-4; *R.I.C.* 184 25

373 H. ℞. PART . MAX . P . M . TR . P . X . COS . III . P . P., as last. *B.M.C.* 385-7; *R.I.C.* 185 25

374 CVIII. ℞. PART . MAX . PONT . TR . P . IIII, trophy and two captives (Hy.; *rev. of Caracalla; ancient forgery*). *B.M.C.* p. 45, ‡; *R.I.C.* 90 ..

374a H. ℞. — As last (Hy.; *rev. of Caracalla*). *B.M.C.* p. 227, 15 and G134 (*description is inaccurate, see pl. 63, 9, one captive has hands tied behind and one has hands in front*); *R.I.C.* 321 (*this is probably a genuine piece*) .. 40

374b F. ℞. As **374**, but TF . P. (Hy., *plated?*). *Seaby's Bull.*, Feb. 63, B1497

375 H. ℞. PAX AETERNA, Pax stg. l., holding branch and sceptre. *B.M.C.* p. 227, 16; *R.I.C.* 283 (*doubtful*) .. ..

375a Denarius. A. ℞. PIETAS, Pietas seated l., holding palladium, l. arm resting on side of throne (Hy.; *with rev. of J. Domna?*). *B.M.C.* W322; *R.I.C.* 350F £45

376 BII. ℞. PIETAT . AVG., Septimius, veiled, stg. half-left, sacrificing out of patera over tripod and holding roll. *B.M.C.* W387-8; *R.I.C.* 413 .. 35

377 CIIII. ℞. P . M . TR . P . COS . II . P . P., Septimius, in military dress, stg., holding globe and spear. *B.M.C.* p. 33; *R.I.C.* 50 note (*this could be* **386** *misdescribed*) 40

380 CIII. ℞. P . M . TR . P . II . COS . II . P . P., Jupiter, naked to waist, seated l., holding Victory and sceptre. *B.M.C.* W69; *R.I.C.* 34 25

380a CIIII. ℞. — As last. *B.M.C.* W74-5 (*text says* spear for sceptre, *but it looks like* W69) *and* 468 (*probably* spear); *R.I.C.* 48 *and* 464 25

381 CIII. ℞. — Minerva stg. half-left, holding spear and round shield. *B.M.C.* W76-7; *R.I.C.* 49 25

381a CIIII. ℞. — Apollo stg. l., holding patera and lyre. *B.M.C.* p. 32, ‡ (a); *R.I.C.* 47 .. ..

383 CIII. ℞. — Victory advancing l., holding wreath and palm. *B.M.C.* p. 32, *; *R.I.C.* 36 (*does it exist?*) .. ..

383a A. ℞. — As last. *B.M.C.* W325 note; *R.I.C.* 350B (*omits* P . P.) (*Vienna*) 40

384 F. ℞. — Victory flying l., holding in both hands open wreath over round shield set on base (Hy.?). *B.M.C.* p. 195 (*quite uncertain*); *R.I.C.* 173 (*hybrid; possibly a misdescription of* **454**) .. ..

385 ? ℞. — Fortuna stg., holding rudder and cornucopiae. (*Possibly* **404** *misread*) .. ..

386 CIIII. ℞. — Septimius stg., as **377**. *B.M.C.* p. 33; *R.I.C.* 50 40

388 CIIII. ℞. P . M . TR . P . III . COS . II . P . P., Apollo, in female attire, as **381a.** *B.M.C.* p. 38, † (a); *R.I.C.* 51 .. .. .. , ... 40

389 Cv. ℞. — As last. *B.M.C.* p. 39, †; *R.I.C.* 59 40

390   396

389a CIIII. ℞. — Minerva stg. half-left, as **381**. *B.M.C.* W106; *R.I.C.* 53.. 25

390 Cv. ℞. — As last. *B.M.C.* W114-7; *R.I.C.* 61 25

391 CVII. ℞. — As last. *B.M.C.* W124; *R.I.C.* 68 25

391a A. ℞. — As last. *B.M.C.* p. 86, *; *R.I.C.* W350E (*Lawrence*) .. 30

395 CIIII. ℞. — Mars, naked except for cloak floating out from waist, advancing r., holding spear and trophy over l. shoulder. *B.M.C.* W104-5; *R.I.C.* 52 25

396 Cv. ℞. — As last. *B.M.C.* W110-2 and p. 110, *; *R.I.C.* 52 and 465 25

396a Cv. Laur. bust dr. and cuir. r. ℞. P . M . TR . P . III . COS . II . P . P., as last. *B.M.C.* W113 (*Plevna hoard*) 55

397 CVII. ℞. — As last. *B.M.C.* W122-3; *R.I.C.* 67 25

397a A. ℞. — As last. *B.M.C.* W328; *R.I.C.* 350D 30

404 CVII. ℞. — Fortuna stg. half-left, holding rudder on globe and cornu-copiae. *B.M.C.* W125-30; *R.I.C.* 69 25

406a CIIII. ℞. — Roma seated l., holding Victory and spear. *B.M.C.* p. 38, † (b); *R.I.C.* 53A (*Lawrence*) 40

412 CVII. Laur. bust cuir. (*dr. and cuir.?*) r. ℞. P . M . TR . P . IIII . COS . II . P . P., Mars r., as **395**. *B.M.C.* p. 43, ‡; *R.I.C.* 70 (*possibly a misdescription of next or* **396a**) 55

412a CVII. ℞. — As last (*Tinchant*) 35

416   454

416 Cᴠɪɪ. ℞. — Minerva stg. half-left, as **381**. *B.M.C.* W134; *R.I.C.* 71   £25

417 Cᴠɪɪɪ. ℞. — As last. *B.M.C.* W138-9; *R.I.C.* 83   25

419 Cᴠɪɪɪ. ℞. — Victory advancing l., holding wreath and palm. *B.M.C.* W146-9; *R.I.C.* 86   25

423 Cᴠɪɪ. ℞. — Fortuna stg. half-left, as **404**. *B.M.C.* W137; *R.I.C.* 71ᴀ   25

424 Cᴠɪɪɪ. ℞. — As last. *B.M.C.* W140-1; *R.I.C.* 84   25

429 Cᴠɪɪɪ. ℞. — Pax seated l., holding branch and sceptre. *B.M.C.* W142-4; *R.I.C.* 85   25

432a Cᴠɪɪɪ. ℞. ᴘ . ᴍ . ᴛʀ . ᴘ . ᴠ . ᴄᴏs . ɪɪ . ᴘ . ᴘ., Sol, rad., naked except for cloak on l. shoulder, stg. half-left, raising r. hand and holding whip in l. *B.M.C.* p. 113, §; *R.I.C.* 489   30

433 Cᴠɪɪɪɪ. ℞. — As last. *B.M.C.* W227-8 and W463; *R.I.C.* 101 and 492   25

434 Cx. ℞. — As last. *B.M.C.* p. 58, *; *R.I.C.* 115   30

436 Cᴠɪɪɪ. ℞. — Genius, naked, stg. front, hd. l., sacrificing out of patera over lighted altar and holding two corn-ears. *B.M.C.* p. 55, *; *R.I.C.* 87   30

437 Cᴠɪɪɪɪ. ℞. — As last. *B.M.C.* W230-3; *R.I.C.* 105   25

440 Cx. ℞. — As last. *B.M.C.* W237-8; *R.I.C.* 116   25

442 Cᴠɪɪɪɪ. ℞. — Fortuna stg. half-left, holding rudder on globe and cornucopiae. *B.M.C.* W229 and W464; *R.I.C.* 104 and 493   25

442a Cᴠɪɪɪɪ. ℞. — As last, but no globe. *B.M.C.* W465 (*base*)   ..   ..

442b Cx. ℞. — As **442**. *B.M.C.* W236; *R.I.C.* 115ᴀ   30

444 Cᴠɪɪɪ. ℞. — Pax seated l., as **429**. *B.M.C.* W215-7 and W452-5; *R.I.C.* 88 (a) and 490 (a)   25

444a Cᴠɪɪɪ, but sᴠ. for sᴇᴠ. ℞. — As last. *B.M.C.* W452 note; *R.I.C.* 490 note   30

444b Cᴠɪɪɪ. ℞. — As **444**, but very curious and unusual style. *B.M.C.* W452 note; *R.I.C.* 490 note (*Lawrence*)   ..   ..

447 Cᴠɪɪɪɪ. ℞. — Concordia stg. l., holding patera and cornucopiae. *B.M.C.* p. 58; *R.I.C.* 103 note (*doubtful*)   ..   ..

449 Cx. ℞. ᴘ . ᴍ . ᴛʀ . ᴘ . ᴠɪ . ᴄᴏs . ɪɪ . ᴘ . ᴘ., Sol stg. half-left, as 432a. *B.M.C.* W263-5; *R.I.C.* 117   25

452 E. ℞. ᴘ . ᴍ . ᴛʀ . ᴘ . ᴠɪɪ . ᴄᴏs . ɪɪ . ᴘ . ᴘ., Fortuna (*Cohen gives* Abundantia), wearing modius on hd., stg. half-left before prow, hd. r., holding cornucopiae and long rudder. *B.M.C.* 151; *R.I.C.* 136   25

452a E. ℞. — Genius stg. l., sacrificing out of patera over altar and holding corn-ears. *B.M.C.* 151 note; *R.I.C.* 137   30

454 F. ℞. ᴘ . ᴍ . ᴛʀ . ᴘ . ᴠɪɪɪ . ᴄᴏs . ɪɪ . ᴘ . ᴘ., Victory flying l., holding open wreath in both hands over round shield set on low base. *B.M.C.* 175-7; *R.I.C.* 150   25

454a H. ℞. — As last (Hy., *plated*). *B.M.C.* p. 227, 14ᴀ   ..   ..   ..

454b E. ℞. — Fortuna stg. half-left, as **452**. *B.M.C.* p. 190, *R.I.C.* 136 note   30

455 E. ℞. — Fides, stg. front, hd. l., holding plate of fruit and two corn-ears. *B.M.C.* 712 note   35

455a E. ℞. ᴘ . ᴍᴀx . ᴛʀ . ᴘ . ᴠɪɪɪ . ᴄᴏs . ɪɪ . ᴘ . ᴘ., as last. *B.M.C.* 712-4; *R.I.C.* 511 (a)   25

455b E. Laur. hd. l. ℞. — As last. *B.M.C.* 712 note; *R.I.C.* 511 (b) (*R. D. hoard*)   150

457 F. ℞. ᴘ . ᴍ . ᴛʀ . ᴘ . ᴠɪɪɪɪ . ᴄᴏs . ɪɪ . ᴘ . ᴘ., Victory flying l., as **454**. *B.M.C.* 252; *R.I.C.* 152   25

461   475

461 **Denarius.** H. ℞. P . M . TR . P . XI . COS . III . P . P., Fortuna seated l.,
holding rudder and cornucopiae, wheel below seat. *B.M.C.* 432-3;
R.I.C. 189 (b) £25

461a H. ℞. — As last, but without wheel (*base*). *B.M.C.* 432 note (*in B.M.,
ancient forgery ?*) .. ..

462 H. ℞. — Genius stg. l., holding patera and double cornucopiae. *B.M.C.*
p. 240, *; *R.I.C.* 190. (*Probably* **504** *misread*) .. ..

463 **Quinarius.** H. ℞. — Victory walking l., holding wreath and palm.
B.M.C. p. 240, †; *R.I.C.* 191   120

464 **Denarius.** H. ℞. P . M . TR . P . XII . COS . III . P . P., Genius stg. half-left,
as **452a**. *B.M.C.* 467; *R.I.C.* 195   25

465 F. ℞. — As last (Hy.). *B.M.C.* 467 note (*in B.M., ancient forgery*) ..

466 H. ℞. — Fortuna seated l., as **461**. *B.M.C.* 467 note; *R.I.C.* 194 ..   30

466a H. ℞. — Salus seated l., feeding snake in arms. *B.M.C.* 467 note;
R.I.C. 195A (*Lawrence*)   35

469 H. ℞. P . M . TR . P . XIII . COS . III . P . P., Jupiter, naked except for
cloak over arm, stg. half-left, holding thunderbolt and sceptre, eagle at his
feet. *B.M.C.* 471-3; *R.I.C.* 196   25

470-1 H. ℞. — Roma (*Cohen gives* Pallas *and* Mars) stg. half-left, holding
Victory and spear reversed. *B.M.C.* 474; *R.I.C.* 197   25

472 H. ℞. — Annona stg. half-left, holding corn-ears over modius and
cornucopiae. *B.M.C.* 475; *R.I.C.* 198   25

472a H. ℞. — Salus seated l., feeding snake coiled around altar. *B.M.C.*
p. 250, *; *R.I.C.* 199   35

475 H. ℞. P . M . TR . P . XIIII . COS . III . P . P., Genius, naked, stg. front, hd. l.,
sacrificing out of patera over altar and holding two corn-ears. *B.M.C.*
493; *R.I.C.* 201   25

476 H. ℞. — Annona stg. front, hd. l., as **472**. *B.M.C.* 489-92, *R.I.C.*
200   25

477 As last (*base or Æ*). *B.M.C.* 489 note; *R.I.C.* 200 note .. .. ..

478 H. ℞. — Septimius on horse walking l., holding vertical spear and
statuette of Victory (?). *B.M.C.* 494; *R.I.C.* 203..   50

480 H. ℞. — Septimius on horse prancing or galloping r., holding spear
horizontally. *B.M.C.* 496; *R.I.C.* 202   45

487 H. ℞. P . M . TR . P . XV . COS . III . P . P., Genius l., as **475**. *B.M.C.*
p. 263, *; *R.I.C.* 209   30

488 **Quinarius.** H. ℞. — Victory advancing l., holding wreath and palm.
B.M.C. p. 264, *; *R.I.C.* 212   120

489 **Denarius.** H. ℞. — Victory stg., or possibly seated, r., foot on helmet
(or globe), inscribing shield set on palm-tree. *B.M.C.* 534-40; *R.I.C.* 211   25

490 H. ℞. — Annona stg., as **476**. *B.M.C.* 533; *R.I.C.* 208   25

491 H. ℞. — Salus seated l., feeding snake held in her arms. *B.M.C.* p. 263,
†; *R.I.C.* 210. (*This is quoted from the Paris coin which is an altered
specimen of* **531**) .. ..

493 H. R . — Africa, wearing elephant-skin head-dress, stg. half-right, holding out fold of drapery (*Cohen says* holds in her bosom a basket of fruit), lion at her feet. *B.M.C.* 531-2; *R.I.C.* 207 .. .. .. £35

493a H. R . — As last, but holding spear in l. hand (*the* spear *could be a* sceptre with a snake entwined around it). *B.M.C.* 530 40

493b H. R . — As last, but snake (?) in l. hand. *B.M.C.* 530 note; *R.I.C.* 207A. (*This could be a misdescription of* **493a**) 45

493c H. R . — As last, but uncertain object in l. hand, no lion. *B.M.C.* 530 note; *R.I.C.* 207 note (*Lawrence*) 45

494 H. R . — As **493** (*base or* Æ). *B.M.C.* 530 note; *R.I.C.* 207 note ..

495 H. R . — Septimius on horseback r., as **480**. *B.M.C.* p. 264, †; *R.I.C.* 213 50

495a H. R . — Septimius on horseback l., as **478**. *B.M.C.* p. 264, ‡; *R.I C.* 213A (*Lawrence*) 55

498 H. R . — trophy; to l., a captive seated l., in attitude of sadness; on r., a captive stg. r., hands tied behind his back. *B.M.C.* 541; *R.I.C.* 214 .. 35

499 H. R . — Galley with oarsmen l. *B.M.C.* p. 264, §; *R.I.C.* 215 .. 120

501 H. R . P . M . TR . P . XVI . COS . III . P . P., Jupiter, naked, stg. front, r. knee bent, looking r., brandishing thunderbolt and holding sceptre. *B.M.C.* 559; *R.I.C.* 216 25

501a As last, but of barbarous style, well struck on large flan. *Seaby's Bull.,* *April* 67 .. ..

502 H. R . — As **501**, but with cloak falling from shoulder. *B.M.C.* 560-1; *R.I.C.* 216 25

503 H. R . — Sol, rad., stg. l., raising r. hand and holding whip. *B.M.C.* p. 270, (a) (*perhaps doubtful*); *R.I.C.* 217 .. ..

504 H. R . — Genius, naked to the hips, stg. front, hd. l., holding patera and double cornucopiae. *B.M.C.* 564-5; *R.I.C.* 219 25

505 H. R . — As last, but on l. a lighted altar over which Genius holds the patera; the cornucopiae is single. *B.M.C.* 566-7; *R.I.C.* 220 25

508 **Quinarius.** H. R . — Victory advancing l., holding wreath and palm. *B.M.C.* p. 269, † note; *R.I.C.* 223 120

510 **Denarius.** H. R . — Victory seated r., holding palm and resting shield on l. knee; before her, trophy; under seat, shield. *B.M.C.* p. 269, ‡ note; *R.I.C.* 224 (a) (*Cohen says same as the aureus, which is* laur. hd. l.) ..

498   514

514 H. R . — Concordia (*Cohen,* Clementia?) seated l. on throne, holding patera and sceptre. *B.M.C.* 562-3; *R.I.C.* 218 25

515 H. R . — Concordia stg. l., holding patera and double cornucopiae. *B.M.C.* p. 270, (b) (*perhaps doubtful*); *R.I.C.* 219 note (*perhaps a poor specimen of* **504** *misdescribed*) .. ..

517 H. R . — Salus seated l. before altar, holding patera and sceptre. *B.M.C.* p. 270 (c); *R.I.C.* 221 30

518 H. R . — Septimius galloping r., holding spear horizontally. *B.M.C.* p. 269, *; *R.I.C.* 222 45

518a H. R . — As last, but galloping l. *Seaby's Bull.* Feb. 47, R1234 (*somewhat barbarous style*) 50

518b Denarius. H. ℞. P . M . TR . P . XVI . COS . III . P . P. Septimius on horse standing or walking l., holding spear and statuette of Victory (*B.M.*) £50

525   530

525 H. ℞. P . M . TR . P . XVII . COS . III . P . P., Jupiter, naked but for cloak over shoulder, stg. half-left, between two children (Caracalla and Geta ?); he holds thunderbolt and sceptre. *B.M.C.* G1-2; *R.I.C.* 226 .. .. **30**

526 As last (*base or Æ*). *B.M.C.* G1 note; *R.I.C.* 226 note .. .. ..

527 H. ℞. — As last, without the two small figures. *B.M.C.* G1 note; *R.I.C.* 227 .. .. **35**

529 H. ℞. — Neptune, naked but for cloak from shoulder, stg. half-left, foot on rock, holding trident and resting r. hand on knee. *B.M.C.* G3-4; *R.I.C.* 228 .. .. **25**

530 H. ℞. — Sea-god (Ocean or Triton, *Cohen says* Tiber ?), naked to waist, reclining r., resting l. elbow on rock or urn from which water gushes, holding horn-shaped shell and rudder (*Cohen*, cornucopiae ? and oar); at his feet, sea-horse. *B.M.C.* G5; *R.I.C.* 229 .. .. .. **90**

David Sear makes an interesting suggestion about this last coin. "The river-god on the reverse could easily be the Tyne in North Britain. Severus was on the Northern frontier in 209, when the coin was struck, and was engaged in repairing the Wall. The fort of Arbeia (South Shields), on the south bank of the Tyne, was the supply depot for the Scottish campaigns of Severus, which commenced in 209". I do not think this idea has been put forward before.

531 H. ℞. — Salus seated l., feeding serpent held in her lap. *B.M.C.* G5-9; *R.I.C.* 230 .. .. **25**

535 H. ℞. — Woman seated l., holding flower. *B.M.C.* p. 357, * note; *R.I.C.* 232 (*perhaps a mistaken description of the last*) **35**

535a H. ℞. — Somewhat as last (*base*). *B.M.C.* G132 (*who says,* Annona holding corn-ears and sceptre ?) .. ..

536 H. ℞. — Septimius galloping l., hurling javelin at prostrate foe. *B.M.C.* p. 357, *; *R.I.C.* 231 .. .. **50**

539 H. ℞. P . M . TR . P . XVIII . COS . III . P . P., Jupiter and two children, as **525**. *B.M.C.* G18; *R.I.C.* 233 .. .. **30**

540 I. ℞. — As last. *B.M.C.* G25; *R.I.C.* 240 .. .. .. **30**

541 As last (*base or Æ*). *B.M.C.* G25 note; *R.I.C.* 240 note ..

542 I. ℞. — Neptune stg. half-left, as **529**. *B.M.C.* G26; *R.I.C.* 241 .. **30**

543 H. ℞. — As last. *B.M.C.* G19; *R.I.C.* 234 .. .. .. **30**

547a H. ℞. — Pax (Felicitas ?) stg. l., holding branch and sceptre. *B.M.C.* p. 361 (a); *R.I.C.* 235 .. ..

548 H. ℞. — Salus seated l., as **531**. *B.M.C.* G20-1; *R.I.C.* 236 .. .. **30**

549 I. ℞. — As last. *B.M.C.* G27-8; *R.I.C.* 242 .. .. **30**

555 H. ℞. — Woman seated l., holding flower and resting elbow on chair. *B.M.C.* p. 361, (b); *R.I.C.* 239 (*probably the same as* **548**) .. ..

556 H. ℞. — Septimius galloping l., as **536**. *B.M.C.* G24; *R.I.C.* 238 .. **50**

563 I. ℞. P . M . TR . P . XIX . COS . III . P . P., Jupiter and two children, as **525.**
B.M.C. G111; *R.I.C.* 243 .. .. £45
563a H. ℞. — As last (Hy.; *base or* Æ). *B.M.C.* G111 note; *R.I.C.* 243 note
(*from Richborough*) .. ..
564 I. ℞. — Neptune stg. half-left, as **529.** *B.M.C.* G112; *R.I.C.* 244 .. 45
565 II. ℞. — Salus seated l., as **531.** *B.M.C.* p. 376, *; *R.I.C.* 245 .. 45
566a H. ℞. P . M . TR . P . XX . COS . III . P . P., Septimius on horseback l.,
holding vertical spear. *B.M.C.* p. 264, ‡ note; *R.I.C.* 213A note (XX *is an*
error for XV, *see no.* **495a**) .. ..
566b BII. ℞. POMA AETERNA, Roma seated l. on cuirass, holding Victory and
spear. *B.M.C.* p. 97, * note; *R.I.C.* 414 (*R. D. hoard*) .. .. ..
566c H. ℞. PONT . III . COS . II, Pietas stg. l., sacrificing over altar and holding
sceptre. *B.M.C.* p. 227, 17; *R.I.C.* 321A .. ..
566d H. ℞. PONTIF . COS . II., prince stg. l., sacrificing out of patera over altar
(Hy.; *rev. of Geta*). *B.M.C.* p. 227, 18; *R.I.C.* 321B .. .. ..
567 CIIII. ℞. PONTIF . TR . P . III, Caracalla (*Cohen*, Septimius) stg., holding
globe and spear. (Hy.; *rev. of Caracalla*) .. ..
567a H. ℞. PONTIF . TR . P . VII . COS . II, prince, in military dress, stg. l.,
holding Victory and reversed spear. (Hy.; *rev. of Caracalla*). *B.M.C.*
p. 227, 19; *R.I.C.* 321C (*R. D. hoard*) .. ..
568 H. ℞. PONTIF . TR . P . VIII . COS . II, Roma seated l., holding Victory and
sceptre (Hy.; *rev. of Caracalla*). *B.M.C.* p. 227, 20; *R.I.C.* 322.. ..
568a F. ℞. — As last. *B.M.C.* p. 227, 20 note; *R.I.C.* 322 note .. ..
568b H. ℞. PONTIF . TR . P . VIIII . COS . II., Mars stg. front, hd. l., resting
r. hand on shield and holding spear (Hy.; *rev. of Caracalla*). *B.M.C.* p.
228, 21; *R.I.C.* p. 132, * .. ..
568c As last. *B.M.C.* G138 (*base; ancient forgery*) .. ..
568d H. ℞. PONTIF . TR . P . X . COS . II, Mars stg. r., holding spear and leaning
on shield; to r., cuirass (Hy.; *rev. of Caracalla*). *B.M.C.* p. 228, 23;
R.I.C. 324 (*Dorchester*) .. ..
569 **Quinarius.** H. ℞. — (*Cohen has* COS . III *in error*) Victory advancing l.,
holding wreath and palm (Hy.; *rev. of Caracalla*). *B.M.C.* p. 228, 22 and
G136; *R.I.C.* 192 and 323 .. ..
569a As last (*base*). *B.M.C.* G137.. .. ..
570 H. ℞. PONTIF . TR . P . XI . COS . II (*Cohen has* COS . III *in error*), as **569**
(Hy.; *rev. of Caracalla*). *B.M.C.* p. 228, 24; *R.I.C.* 325-6 (*Dorchester*) ..

573   576

573 **Denarius.** H. ℞. PROF . AVGG. in ex., P . M . TR . P . XVI around, Septimius
riding r., holding spear, preceded by a foot-soldier, holding spear and
shield. *B.M.C.* 568; *R.I.C.* 225A 50
576 E. ℞. PROFECT . AVGG . FEL., Septimius, in military dress and cloak
floating out behind shoulder, on horse prancing r., holding spear. *B.M.C.*
134-5; *R.I.C.* 138 45
577 F. ℞. — As last. *B.M.C.* p. 193, †; *R.I.C* 165 (a) 50
578 CVIII ℞. PROFECTIO AVG., Septimius, in military dress, on horse walking
r., holding spear. *B.M.C.* W170-1; *R.I.C.* 91 45

580   599

580 Denarius. CVIIII. ℞. — As last. *B.M.C.* W234-5 and W466-7; *R.I.C.* 106 and 494 .. .. £45

586 F. ℞. PROVID . AVGG., Providentia stg. half-left, holding wand over globe and sceptre. *B.M.C.* 197-9; *R.I.C.* 166 25

587 E. ℞. — As last. *B.M.C.* 136; *R.I.C.* 139 25

588 As last (*base or* Æ). *B.M.C.* 136 note .. ..

588a H. ℞. — As last (Hy.). *B.M.C.* p. 228, 26 .. ..

588b H. ℞. — As last, but sceptre in r. hand and wand in l., globe at feet on r. (Hy.; *curious style, perhaps an irregular issue*). *B.M.C.* p. 228, 26 and G139; *R.I.C.* 284 .. ..

588c H, but SEVESVS. ℞. — As last (Hy.). *B.M.C.* p. 228, 26 note; *R.I.C.* 284 note (*R. D. hoard*) .. ..

588d H. ℞. PROVID . DEORVM., as **586** (Hy.; *rev. of Geta?*). *B.M.C.* p. 618, A173A .. ..

590 H. ℞. PROVIDENTIA, large hd. of Medusa facing, with curling hair (or serpents in hair) and wings. *B.M.C.* 356; *R.I.C.* 285. 250

591 H. ℞. — Small hd. of Medusa on aegis. *B.M.C.* 357; *R.I.C.* 286 .. 250

592 CVIII. ℞. PROVIDENTIA AVG., Providentia stg., as **586.** *B.M.C.* W172-3 and W456-7; *R.I.C.* 92 (a) and 491 (a) 25

593 CVIII. Laur. bust dr. and cuir. r., with aegis on breast. ℞. — As last. *B.M.C.* W172 note and W456 note; *R.I.C.* 92 (b) and 491 (b) 50

594 H. ℞. PROVIDENTIA DEORVM, as before (Hy.; *rev. of Geta?*) .. ..

595 F. ℞. PVDICITIA, Pudicitia, veiled, seated l., holding a sceptre in each hand. *B.M.C.* p. 298, §; *R.I.C.* 524 .. ..

596 H. ℞. RECTOR ORBIS, Sol (?) stg. l., holding globe and spear reversed (Hy.; *rev. of Caracalla*). *B.M.C.* p. 228, 27; *R.I.C.* 287 .. .. ..

596a F. ℞. RECTOR VRBIS, Septimius stg. l., holding globe and spear (Hy., *plated; rev. of Caracalla*). *B.M.C.* p. 195; *R.I.C.* 167 note (*Lawrence*) ..

597 H. ℞. RESTITVTORES VRBIS, helmeted bust of Roma r. (*G. R. Arnold*) .. 300

597   606

599 F. ℞. RESTITVTOR VRBIS, Septimius, in military dress, stg. half-left, sacrificing out of patera over lighted tripod and holding spear. *B.M.C.* 202-7; *R.I.C.* 167 (a) 25

600 E. ℞. — As last. *B.M.C.* p. 180, (f) and 671; *R.I.C.* 140 and 512A .. 30

602 H. ℞. — As last. *B.M.C.* 262 (*base, ancient forgery?*); *R.I.C.* 289 ..

606 H. ℞. — Roma seated l. on shield, holding palladium and sceptre. *B.M.C.* 59 25

606a H. ℞. — As before, but spear for sceptre. *B.M.C.* 360; *R.I.C.* 288 .. 25

606b H. Ⅰ. — As last, but spear reversed. *B.M.C.* 361. *I think Roma is sitting on a low stool, and the shield is at the side, also that it is difficult to distinguish between spear and sceptre* £25

612   628b

612 F. Ⅰ. RESTITVTORI VRBIS, as **599**. *B.M.C.* 203 note; *R.I.C.* 168 (a)   ..   30

612a Quinarius. E. Laur. bust dr. and cuir. Ⅰ. — As last. *B.M.C.* p. 180 (h); *R.I.C.* 140A   200

612b Denarius. CII. Ⅰ. ROI . EVENTVS, Bonus Eventus stg. l., holding plate of fruit and two corn-ears (Hy.). *B.M.C.* W427 note; *R.I.C.* 447 note (*R. D. hoard*) ..

613 Tetradrachm. IMP . C.L . SEPTI . SEVERVS P . P . AVG. Ⅰ. ROMAE around VRB[I ?] in ex., Roma seated l., sacrificing out of patera over altar and holding spear. *B.M.C.* 760; *R.I.C.* 531   750

614 Denarius. BII (*Cohen* SEPT. *in error*). Ⅰ. ROMAE AETERNAE, Roma seated l. on cuirass, holding Victory and spear. *B.M.C.* p. 97, *; *R.I.C.* 414   ..   35

615 A (*Cohen* SEPT. *in error*). Ⅰ. — As last, but Roma on low seat, round shield in front of seat. *B.M.C.* W323; *R.I.C.* 350G   40

619 H. Ⅰ. — Roma seated in hexastyle temple, surmounted by six statues; on the pediment, three figures (Hy. ?). *R.I.C.* 292

622 A. Ⅰ. SAEC . FRVGIF . COS, Saeculum Frugiferum (*Plentiful Age*), rad., naked to waist, stg. half-left, holding caduceus and trident. *B.M.C.* W4 note; *R.I.C.* 19   150

623a H. Ⅰ. SACRA SAECVLARIA, Caracalla, Sept. Severus and Geta sacrificing over altar before a temple. *B.M.C.* p. 222, ‡ note; *R.I.C.* 293A. (*I am indebted to Mr. Clay for the correct description of this coin*)   ..   500

627 A (*Cohen* SEPT. *in error*?). Ⅰ. SAEC . FELICIT, crescent and seven stars. *B.M.C.* p. 88, ¶; *R.I.C.* 360   35

628 BII. Ⅰ. SAECV . FELICIT., as last. *B.M.C.* W390 note; *R.I.C.* 416   ..   35

628a BII. Ⅰ. SAECVL . FELICIT., as last. *B.M.C.* W390-1; *R.I.C.* 417   ..   30

628b BII. Ⅰ. SAECVLI EELCI., as last. *B.M.C.* p. 617 (*Oldroyd*)   ..   35

628c BII. Ⅰ. SAECVLI FELICIT., as last. *B.M.C.* W390 note; *R.I.C.* 418   ..   35

628d BII, but CO . III. Ⅰ. SAECVLI FELICITAS, as last. *B.M.C.* W390 note; *R.I.C.* 418A   35

628e BII. Ⅰ. SAECVLL . FELICIT., as last. *B.M.C.* W392   35

628f BII. Ⅰ. SAECVLL . FELLCIT., as last. *B.M.C.* W392 note; *R.I.C.* 418B (*R. D. hoard*)   35

640a Tetradrachm. IMP . C . L . SEP . SEVERVS P . AV. Ⅰ. SALVTI AVG., lighted altar. *B.M.C.* p. 304, ‡; *R.I.C.* 530   650

641 Denarius. Cx. Ⅰ. SALVTI AVGG., Salus seated l., feeding out of patera a snake coiling up from altar, l. arm on side of throne. *B.M.C.* W255-6 (*text says* and holding sceptre *but is not clear on illustration; neither Cohen nor R.I.C. give sceptre*); *R.I.C.* 119A..   30

641a Cx. Ⅰ. SALVTI AVG., as last. *B.M.C.* W256 note; *R.I.C.* 119   ..   ..

641b E. Ⅰ. SALVTI AVGG., as last. *B.M.C.* p. 619 (*Ashmolean*)   ..   35

642 D. Ⅰ. — As last. *B.M.C.* 629-31; *R.I.C.* 497 (a)   25

642a D, but PAR . D . N after XI. Ⅰ. — As last. *B.M.C.* 632; *R.I.C.* 497 note   30

642b D, but XI . PART . MAX. Ⅰ. — As last (*G. R. Arnold*)   30

642c E, but SEVERVS PER . AVG . PIV. for SEV . AVG. Ⅰ. — As last. *B.M.C.* 629 note; *R.I.C.* 497 (b)   35

646 Denarius. C III. R. SECVRITAS PVBLICA, Securitas seated l. on
throne, holding globe. *B.M.C.* W87; *R.I.C.* 56 .. .. £30

647 C VIII. R. — As last. *B.M.C.* W174-6; *R.I.C.* 93. 25

651a H. R. SEVERI PII AVG . FIL., Caracalla stg. l., holding Victory and spear,
captive at feet (Hy., *plated*; *rev. of Caracalla*). *Seaby's Bull. Feb.* 63,
B1498 .. ..

652 B II. R. S . P . Q . R . OPTIMO PRINCIPI, Septimius, in military dress,
on horse walking l., holding spear. *B.M.C.* W389; *R.I.C.* 415 50

652a C I. R. — Septimius on horse r. (*G. R. Arnold; mint of Laodicea ad
Mare*) 65

652b IMP . EPT . SEV . PERET . AVG . COS . III. R. S . P . Q . R . OPTIMO PBINOPI,
as last (*Eastern fabric*). *Seaby's Bull. Apr.* 1937, 39732 .. ..

657 Quinarius. A. R. TR . P . COS., Victory advancing l., holding wreath
and palm. *B.M.C.* W26; *R.I.C.* 20 110

657a Denarius. C III. R. TR . P . IMP . III . COS . II . P . P., Roma (?) seated r.,
holding spear and parazonium. *B.M.C.* p. 109, †; *R.I.C.* 463A 40

657b B II. R. TR . P . III . IMP . COS . II. captive seated r., head bowed
forward, hands tied behind back; in front, bow, quiver and two oval shields.
B.M.C. W405; *R.I.C.* 433 note 35
On this and some of the following the last II *are from fractured punches
and look like,* ΓI, IΓ, ΓΓ *or* FI.

657c B II. R. — Captive seated r., propping hd. on l. hand, and resting r. hand
on ground, sword in ex. *B.M.C.* 409 note; *R.I.C.* 432 note (*Marnbach hoard*) 35

658 B II. R. TR . P . III . IMP . V . COS II, two captives seated back to back at
foot of trophy; the one on r. propping hd on r. hand, the other with hands
tied behind back. *B.M.C.* W410; *R.I.C.* 435 30

659 B II. R. — As **657b**. *B.M.C.* W406-7; *R.I.C.* 433 30

660 B II. R. — As **657c**, but nothing in ex. *R.I.C.* 432 30

660a B II. R. — As **557c**. *B.M.C.* W409; *R.I.C.* 432 30

661 B II. R. — Captive seated r., r. hand tied behind back, l. hand supporting
head; in front, shields and arms. *B.M.C.* 406 note; *R.I.C.* 434 35

662 B II. R. TR . P . III . IMP . VI . COS . II, as 658. *B.M.C.* p. 101, *; *R.I.C.*
435 note (*doubtful*) .. ..

664a C III. R. TR . P . V . IMP . COS . II . P . P., as 657a (*another reading of the
same coin*) .. ..

665a C V ? R. TR . P . VI . VI . IMP . II . COS . IIII, Libertas stg. l., holding
pileus and cornucopiae, shield (?) at her feet. *B.M.C.* G140 (*from the
Deanery Field, Chester—odd style; ancient forgery: British ?*); *C.R.B.* 57

667a A. R. VENERI VICTR., Venus stg. l., leaning against column, holding apple
and palm (Hy.; *rev. of J. Domna*). *B.M.C.* p. 84, *; *R.I.C.* 350K ..

667b B II. R. VENVP VICT., Venus stg. l., holding apple and sceptre. *B.M.C.*
p. 98, *; *R.I.C.* 419 ..

668 H. R. VENVS GENETRIX, Venus seated l., holding apple and sceptre;
before her, child (Hy; *rev. J. Domna*). *B.M.C.* p. 228, 28 .. ..

669 C VIII. R .VICT . AETERN., Victory inscribing shield (Hy.). *B.M.C.* p. 49,
*; *R.I.C.* 94 .. ..

660a 670

670 F. R. — Victory flying l., holding open wreath in both hands over round
shield set on low base. *B.M.C.* 209-10; *R.I.C.* 170 25

671 Cᴠɪɪɪ. Ꞧ. — As last (Hy.). *B.M.C.* p. 45, *; *R.I.C.* 95   ..   ..

671a ʟ . ꜱᴇᴠᴇʀᴠꜱ ᴀᴠɢᴠꜱᴛᴠꜱ. Ꞧ. — As last (*barbarous*). *B.M.C.* p. 619, A174

672 ᴇ. Ꞧ. ᴠɪᴄᴛ . ᴀᴇᴛᴇʀɴᴀᴇ, as last. *B.M.C.* p. 178, *; *R.I.C.* 141 ..   ..   £30

673 Bɪɪ. Ꞧ. ᴠɪᴄ . ᴀᴠɢ., Victory stg. l., holding palm and inscribing ᴀᴠɢ on shield set on column. *B.M.C.* p. 98, †; *R.I.C.* 420   45

673a ᴅ. Ꞧ. ᴠɪᴄ . ᴀᴠɢɢ . ᴄᴏꜱ . ɪɪ . ᴘ . ᴘ., Victory walking l., holding wreath and palm. *B.M.C.* 633; *R.I.C.* 98   30

673b Bɪɪ. Ꞧ. ᴠɪᴄᴛ . ᴀᴠɢ., as **673**. *B.M.C.* p. 98, † note; *R.I.C.* 420 note ..   45

674 Bɪɪ. Ꞧ. — Victory walking r., holding trophy in both hands. *B.M.C.* W393; *R.I.C.* 422   30

675 Bɪɪ, but ᴠᴄ for ᴀᴠɢ. Ꞧ. — Victory advancing l., holding wreath and palm over shoulder. *B.M.C.* W395 note; *R.I.C.* 424   30

675a Bɪɪ. Ꞧ. — As last. *B.M.C.* W395; *R.I.C.* 424   25

675b Bɪɪ, but A͡ᴠɢ. Ꞧ. — As last. *B.M.C.* W395 note; *R.I.C.* 424 note (*R. D. hoard*)   30

675c Bɪɪ. Ꞧ. — As last (*base or Æ*)   ..   ..

675d Bɪɪ. Ꞧ. — Victory advancing l., holding out wreath in both hands. *B.M.C.* W401; *R.I.C.* 426   35

677 Bɪɪ. Ꞧ. — Victory seated l., holding wreath and palm. *B.M.C.* p. 99, *; *R.I.C.* C427   35

680 ᴀ. Ꞧ. ᴠɪᴄ . ᴀᴠɢ . ᴛʀ . ᴘ . ᴄᴏꜱ., as last. *B.M.C.* p. 24; *R.I.C.* 21   ..

682 ᴀ (*Cohen has* ꜱᴇᴘᴛ. *in error*). Ꞧ. — Victory walking l., holding wreath and palm. *B.M.C.* W30-1; *R.I.C.* 22   25

682a As last, but Eastern fabric. *B.M.C.* p. 617 (*Ashmolean*)   30

682b Cɪɪ. Ꞧ. — As **682**. *B.M.C.* p. 616 (*Darfield Treasure Trove*)   30

688a Cɪɪ. Ꞧ. ᴠɪᴄᴛ . ᴀᴠɢ . ᴛʀ . ᴘ . ɪɪ . ᴄᴏꜱ . ɪɪ . ᴘ . ᴘ., as last. *B.M.C.* p. 30 (b); *R.I.C.* 29ᴀ   30

688b Cɪɪɪ. Ꞧ. — As last (*Vienna*)   30

690 Cɪɪɪ. Ꞧ. ᴠɪᴄᴛ . ᴀᴠɢ . ᴛʀ . ᴘ . ɪɪ . ᴄᴏꜱ . ɪɪ., Victory advancing (or running) r., holding wreath and palm. *B.M.C.* W72 note; *R.I.C.* 38   30

690a Cɪɪɪ. Ꞧ. ᴠɪᴄᴛ . ᴀᴠɢ . ᴛʀ . ᴘ . ɪɪ . ᴄᴏꜱ . ɪɪ . ᴘ . ᴘ., as last. *B.M.C.* W73 (cast?); *R.I.C.* 38ᴀ (*R. D. hoard*)   30

690b Cɪɪ. Ꞧ. — As last (*Rome*)   30

690c ꜱ . ʟ . ᴘᴇʀᴛᴇɴᴀɪᴄɪ ᴀᴠɢ . ᴄᴏꜱ. Ꞧ. — (*or as* **690**), Victory advancing r., holding trophy in both hands. *B.M.C.* W73 note; *R.I.C.* 38 note   ..

692 **Quinarius.** ʜ. Ꞧ. ᴠɪᴄᴛ . ᴀᴠɢɢ., Victory walking l., holding wreath and palm. *B.M.C.* 363; *R.I.C.* 294 (b)   110

692a ʜ. Laur. bust dr. r. Ꞧ. — As last. *B.M.C.* 364 (*base: ancient forgery?*); *R.I.C.* 294 (a) ..   ..

692   694

694 **Denarius.** Cx. Ꞧ. ᴠɪᴄᴛ . ᴀᴠɢɢ . ᴄᴏꜱ . ɪɪ . ᴘ . ᴘ., as last. *B.M.C.* W258-60; *R.I.C.* 120 (c)   25

694a ᴇ. Ꞧ. — As last. *B.M.C.* p. 178, † and p. 288, †; *R.I.C.* 141ᴀ (*R. D. hoard*) and 513ʙ (*Lawrence*)   30

695 Denarius. D. R. VICT. AVGG. COS. II. P. P., Victory walking l., holding wreath and palm. *B.M.C.* 634-5; *R.I.C.* 499 .. .. £25

695a H. R. VICTOR. ANTONINI AVG., Victory advancing r., holding wreath and palm (Hy.; *rev. of Elagabalus*). *B.M.C.* p. 229, 30; *R.I.C.* 328A.. ..

696 BII. R. VICTOR. AVG., Victory advancing r., holding trophy in both hands. *B.M.C.* W393 note; *R.I.C.* 423 30

696a BII. R. — Victory advancing r., holding trophy and wreath. *B.M.C.* W393 note; *R.I.C.* 423A (*R. D. hoard*) 30

695   697

697 BII. R. — Victory l., as **692**. *B.M.C.* W396-7; *R.I.C.* 425 25

698 L. SEV. PERCT. AVG. IMP. II. R. — As last. *B.M.C.* W434 note; *R.I.C.* 461 note .. ..

698a CII, but PERTE. R. — As last. *B.M.C.* W434-5; *R.I.C.* 461 (a) .. 25

698b CII, but PERET. R. — As last. *B.M.C.* W436; *R.I.C.* 461 (b) 25

698c CVII. R. — As last. *B.M.C.* W439; *R.I.C.* 471 25

699 CVIII. R. — As last. *B.M.C.* W450; *R.I.C.* 485 25

699a E. R. — As last. *B.M.C.* p. 288, † note; *R.I.C.* 514A (*R. D. hoard*) 35

700 BII. R. — Victory, naked to waist, stg. r., foot on globe, inscribing oval shield set on column. *B.M.C.* W394; *R.I.C.* 421 35

700a CII. R. — As last (*G. R. Arnold; mint of Laodicea ad Mare*) .. 40

700b BII. R. VICTO. . . . ., Victory stg. l., holding palm and inscribing AVG on shield set on column. *B.M.C.* p. 98, † note; *R.I.C.* 420 note (*R. D. hoard*) 45

700c H. R. VICTOR. AVG., Victory stg. r., foot on helmet, inscribing VIC. B. on shield (Hy.?). *B.M.C.* p. 229, 29; *R.I.C.* 298 note (*R. D. hoard*) ..

702 C. R. VICTORIA, Victory stg. l., inscribing AVG. on shield set on trunk of tree *B.M.C.* p. 89, *; *R.I.C.* 363 45

703 BI. R. — As last. *B.M.C.* p. 90, (1); *R.I.C.* p. 139, 9 45

703a BI or II. R. — Victory stg. half-left, inscribing AV / VG on shield set on column and holding palm. *B.M.C.* W402; *R.I.C.* 430 40

704 CVIII. R. VICTORIA AVG., Victory stg., l. foot on globe, holding shield in both hands. *B.M.C.* p. 113, †; *R.I.C.* 486 .. ..

704a A. R. VICTORIA AVGG., Victory running l., holding wreath and palm. *B.M.C.* W324; *R.I.C.* 350H 40

704b H. R. — Victory seated l., holding shield on knee and palm (Hy.; *plated*). *B.M.C.* p. 229, 31; *R.I.C.* 298 note (*Lawrence*) .. .. ..

705   717

704c Tetradrachm. IMP . C . L . SEP . SEVERVS P . AV. R . VICTORIA AVGVST., Victory flying l., holding open wreath in both hands over round shield set on base. *B.M.C.* 759 note; *R.I.C.* 532 ..   ..   £650

705 As last, but AVGVSTI on *rev.* (*Cohen gives* AVG. *on obv. in error*). *B.M.C.* 759; *R.I.C.* 532A. *Illustrated at bottom of last page*   650

706 IMP . C . L . SEPTI . SEVERVS P . P . AVG. R . VICTORIA AVGVSTI, Victory walking l., holding wreath and palm. *B.M.C.* 759 note; *R.I.C.* 532B (a)   650

706a IMP . CAES . L . SEP . SEVERVS PERT . AVG. R . — As last. *B.M.C.* 759 note; *R.I.C.* 532B (b)   650

707 Denarius. H. R . — Victory r., as **700c**. *B.M.C.* p. 223, *; *R.I.C.* 298

709 Tetradrachm. As **704c**. R . VICTORIAE AVG., as **704c**. *B.M.C.* 759 note; *R.I.C.* 533   650

709a Denarius. E. R . — As **706**, but Victory r. *B.M.C.* p. 178, ‡ note; *R.I.C.* 143 (a) note   ..   ..

711 E. R . VICTORIAE AVGG., as **706**. *B.M.C.* p. 178, ‡; *R.I.C.* 143 (a) ..

713 H. R . VICTORIAE above, AVGG. in ex., Victory, holding whip, in biga galloping r. *B.M.C.* 370; *R.I.C.* 299   55

713a As last, but Victory holds wreath and palm. *Seaby's Bull. Jan.* 1964, B41, pl. 3   60

713b As **713**, but quadriga instead of biga. (*G. R. Arnold*)   65

717 H. R . VICTORIAE AVGG., Septimius seated facing, holding small Victory in r. hand; at side on r., small kneeling figure holding shield on his head (or Atlas holding globe); on r., Victory flying l. crowning the emperor. *B.M.C.* 371-2; *R.I.C.* 301. *Illustrated at bottom of last page*   ..   350

719 E. R . VICTORIAE AVGG . FEL., as **706**, but Victory possibly flying, as there is no ground line. *B.M.C.* 139-40 and 678-9; *R.I.C.* 144 (b) and 516   ..   25

719a As last (Æ). *Seaby's Bull. Apr.* 52, B399 ..   ..

722 I. R . VICT . BRIT . P . M . TR . P . XIX . COS . III . P . P., Victory walking r. holding wreath and palm. *B.M.C.* p. 376, †; *R.I.C.* 247. (*Clay coll.*) ..   100

726a H. R . VICTORIAE BRIT., Victory running r., dragging captive and holding trophy. *B.M.C.* p. 224, * and p. 229, 32 (*specimen in* B.M., *cast from N*?); *R.I.C.* 302; *C.R.B.* 38 ..   ..

726b H. R . — Victory advancing l., holding wreath and palm. *B.M.C.* p. 618 (*Oldroyd*)   85

        727   731

727 I. R . — As last, but Victory r. *B.M.C.* G51-5; *R.I.C.* 332; *C.R.B.* 40   60

727a H. R . — As last. *C.R.B.* 40 note (*Walters and Messenger*) ·   85

728 I. R . — As last, but Victory, half-naked, stg. front, hd. l. *B.M.C.* G59; *R.I.C.* 333; *C.R.B.* 41   70

729 I. R . — Victory, half-naked, stg. front, hd. r., holding palm in r. hand, l. hand at her side; before, round shield on palm-tree. *B.M.C.* G58; *R.I.C.* 337; *C.R.B.* 45   70

729a H. R . — As last. *B.M.C.* p. 229, 33; *R.I.C.* 302A (*R. D. hoard*); *C.R.B.* 39   85

730 I. R . — As before, but Victory attaching the shield to the palm. *B.M.C.* G57; *R.I.C.* 336; *C.R.B.* 44   70

730a H. R . — As last (*Naples*)   85

731 **Denarius.** I. ℞. VICTORIAE BRIT.,Victory, half-naked, seated l. on shield or shields, holding shield on her knee and palm. *B.M.C.* G61-2; *R.I.C.* 335; *C.R.B.* 43 ·· ·· ·· ·· ·· ·· ·· £65

731a H. ℞. — As last. *B.M.C.* G61 note 85

738 A. ℞. VICTOR . IVST . AVG., Victory walking l., holding wreath and palm. *B.M.C.* W338; *R.I.C.* 362 ·· ·· ·· ·· ·· ·· ·· 55

739-40 BII (*Cohen omits* SEP. *in error*). ℞. — As last. *B.M.C.* W398; *R.I.C.* 427A ·· ·· ·· ·· ·· ·· ·· ·· ·· 55

740a A. ℞. VICTOR . IVST . AVG . II . COS. *B.M.C.* W338 note; *R.I.C.* 362A (*Third Dura hoard*) ·· ·· ·· ·· ·· ·· ·· 60

741 E. ℞. VICT . PARTHICAE, Victory walking l., holding wreath and trophy; at her feet, captive seated l., hands tied behind back. *B.M.C.* 137 and 672-5; *R.I.C.* 142 (a) and 514 ·· ·· ·· ·· ·· 25

742 Cx. ℞. — As last. *B.M.C.* W261-2; *R.I.C.* 121 ·· ·· ·· 25

742a Cx, but PER. ℞. — As last. *B.M.C.* W261 note; *R.I.C.* 121 note ·· 30

742b Cx, but SEP. ℞. VICT . P . . . IICAE. *B.M.C.* W261 note 30

744 H. ℞. VICT . PART . MAX., Victory running l., holding wreath and palm. *B.M.C.* 365-8; *R.I.C.* 295 ·· ·· ·· ·· ·· ·· 25

745 H. ℞. — As last (*base or* Æ). *B.M.C.* 365 note; *R.I.C.* 295 note ··

746 H. ℞. VICTORIA PARTH . MAX., as last. *B.M.C.* 365 note; *R.I.C.* 296 ·· 30

747a H. ℞. VICTORIA PARTHICA MAXIMA, as last. *B.M.C.* 365 note; *R.I.C.* 297 (*Tinchant cat.*) ·· ·· ·· ·· ·· ·· ·· ··

747b F. ℞. VICTORIAE PARTIC., Victory walking r., holding wreath and palm. *B.M.C.* G141 (*base*) ·· ·· ·· ·· ·· ·· ··

748 BI. ℞. VICTOR . SEVER . AVG., as last, but Victory l. *B.M.C.* p. 90, (k); *R.I.C.* p. 139, (8) ·· ·· ·· ·· ·· ·· ··

749 BII. ℞. — As last. *B.M.C.* W399-400; *R.I.C.* 428 ·· ·· ·· 35

749a BII. ℞. VICTOR . SEVER . AG., as last. *B.M.C.* W399 note; *R.I.C.* 428 note R. D. hoard) ·· ·· ·· ·· ·· ·· ·· ·· 40

750 BII. ℞. VICTOR . SEVER . C . AVG., as last. *B.M.C.* W399 note; *R.I.C.* 429 40

752 A. ℞. VIRT . AVG . TR . P . COS., Virtus (*Cohen*, Roma) stg. half-left. holding Victory and spear reversed. *B.M.C.* W33-4; *R.I.C.* 24 ·· 25

752a BI. ℞. — As last. *B.M.C.* p. 90, (m); *R.I.C.* p. 139, (10) ·· ·· 30

752b ⲦⲤ . SEPT . SEV . PER . AVG . V . IMP . III. ℞. — As last, but spear not reversed (Hy.; *ancient forgery?*). *B.M.C.* p. 30; *R.I.C.* 39 note ··

755 CIII. ℞. VIRT . AVG . TR . P . II . COS . II . P . P., as **752**. *B.M.C.* p. 32, †; *R.I.C.* 39 ·· ·· ·· ·· ·· ·· ·· ·· 30

755a BI or II. ℞. — As last. *B.M.C.* W404; *R.I.C.* 430A (*Fourth Dura hoard*) 35

761   763

761 F. ℞. VIRT . AVGG., as **752b**, but shield on ground also held in l. hand. *B.M.C.* 211-3; *R.I.C.* 171 (a) ·· ·· ·· ·· ·· ·· 25

762 E. ℞. — As last. *B.M.C.* 141; *R.I.C.* 145 (a) ·· ·· ·· ·· 25

762a H. ℞. — As last (Hy.; *plated*). *B.M.C.* p. 229, 34; *R.I.C.* 303 (*Lawrence*)

763 E. ℞. VIRTVS AVG., Septimius on horse prancing r., brandishing javelin at prostrate foe r. *B.M.C.* 143; *R.I.C.* 146 (a) ·· ·· ·· ·· 50

763a A. ℞. VIRTVS AVG . COS . II.,Roma seated l. on shield, holding Victory and spear. *B.M.C.* p. 85, †; *R.I.C.* 350I ·· ·· ·· ·· 40

763b A. ℞. — Virtus stg. l., holding Victory and spear. *B.M.C.* p. 85, ‡;
R.I.C. 350J £40

764 H. ℞. VIRTVS AVGG., Septimius (?) stg. l., holding globe and spear. *B.M.C.*
p. 229, 35; *R.I.C.* 303A 30

765 E. ℞. VIRTVS AVGVST., soldier stg. r., holding spear and club (?).
B.M.C. p. 180 (g); *R.I C* 147 (*doubtful*) .. ..

765a BI, but ends PERTI . AVG . IIII. ℞. VIRTVS AVGVSTI, Mars advancing r.,
holding spear and trophy. *B.M.C.* p. 101 (*bottom*); *R.I.C.* 436A (*Budapest*) 45

766 H. ℞. VIRTVS AVGVSTOR., Virtus or Roma seated l., resting l. elbow on
shield, holding Victory and parazonium. *B.M.C.* 373; *R.I.C.* 304 .. 25

766a H. ℞. — As last, but the shield behind Roma. *B.M.C.* 373 note; *R.I.C.*
304 note (*R. D. hoard*) 30

771 BII. ℞. VIRTVTE AVG., Virtus stg. half-right, holding reversed spear and
parazonium. *B.M.C.* W403; *R.I.C.* 431 30

771a BII. ℞. — Virtus stg. half-left, holding Victory and reversed spear.
B.M.C. W404; *R.I.C.* 431A (*Emperor* (?)—*R. D. hoard*) 35

777 CVIII. ℞. VOTA PVBLICA, Septimius, veiled, stg. half-left, sacrificing out of
patera over lighted tripod and holding roll. *B.M.C.* W178; *R.I.C.*
96 (a) 25

779a F. ℞. — As last (Hy?). *B.M.C.* p. 195, *; *R.I.C.* 172 .. ..

780 F, but PERT. for PART. ℞. — As last (Hy.). *B.M.C.* p. 195, * note;
R.I.C. 172 note .. ..

781 H. ℞. — As last (Hy.). *B.M.C.* p. 229, 36; *R.I.C.* 306 (*doubtful*) ..

785 H. ℞. VOTA SOLVT . DEC . COS . III., three figures sacrificing over tripod,
bull at side (Hy., *plated; rev. of Caracalla*). *B.M.C.* p. 230, 37; *R.I.C.* 307

786 H. ℞. VOT . SVSC . DEC . P . M . TR . P . X . COS . III . P . P., Septimius,
veiled, stg. half-left, sacrificing out of patera over lighted tripod, holding
roll. *B.M.C.* 388; *R.I.C.* 186 35

790 H. ℞. VOTA SVSCEPTA X., as last (Hy.; *rev. of Caracalla*). *B.M.C.* p. 230,
38; *R.I.C.* 329 40

791 H. ℞. VOTA SVSCEPTA XX., as last. *B.M.C.* 375; *R.I.C.* 308 25

794 H. ℞. — As last, but emperor r.; on r., attendant stg. l.; behind the
tripod, a flute-player stg. front. *B.M.C.* 377-8; *R.I.C.* 309 80

795a H. ℞. VOTA SVSCEPTA XX . COS . III . P . P., as last, but the figure on
the r. is about to sacrifice bull. *B.M.C.* p. 225, *; *R.I.C.* 310 90

796 E. ℞. VOTIS DECENNALIBVS, as **786.** *B.M.C.* 680; *R.I.C.* 519 .. 85

798 E. ℞. VOTIS / DECEN / NALI / BVS within laurel-wreath. *B.M.C.* 681;
R.I.C. 520 (a) 100

799 *Restitution by Trajan Decius.* **Antoninianus.** DIVO SEVERO, his radiate
hd. r. ℞. CONSECRATIO, eagle stg. r., looking back 70

800 — — ℞. — Lighted altar 70

SEPTIMIUS SEVERUS and JULIA DOMNA
Struck during the joint reign of Septimius and Caracalla
Obverses of Septimius Severus (see p. 18)

2 **Denarius.** F. ℞. Julia Domna *obv.* B. *B.M.C.* 193; *R.I.C.* 161 (a) .. 400

3 H. ℞. — As last. *B.M.C.* 342; *R.I.C.* 273 400

4a F. ℞. CONCORDIAE AETERNAE, jugate busts r. of Septimius, rad. and dr.,
and Julia, diad. and dr. on crescent. *B.M.C.* p. 298, ‡; *R.I.C.* 522 *Vienna*) 850

SEPTIMIUS SEVERUS, JULIA, CARACALLA and GETA
Struck during the joint reign of Septimius and Caracalla

3 Denarius. SEVERVS PIVS AVG . P . M . TR . P . X., his laur. hd. r.   R.
FELICITAS above, SAECVLI below dr. bust of Julia, facing, between laur. bust
of Caracalla dr. and cuir. r. and bare-headed bust of Geta dr. l. *B.M.C.*
379 note; *R.I.C.* 181 (a)   .. ..

6 SEVER . P . AVG . P . M . TR . P . X . COS . III., his laur. bust dr. and cuir. r.
R. — As last. *B.M.C.* 380 note; *R.I.C.* 181 (c)   .. .. ..
*It would seem that these two pieces are either originals from dies used for gold
or false copies of gold made in silver.*

SEPTIMIUS SEVERUS and CARACALLA
Struck during their joint reign
Obverses of Septimius Severus (see p. 18), except where given in full.

1 Denarius. H. R. AETERNIT . IMPERI., laur. and dr. (or dr. and cuir.)
busts of Septimius and Caracalla face to face. *B.M.C.* 307; *R.I.C.* 250 £450
1a As last, (*base*). *Seaby's Bull., June* 1938, 48904 .. ..
1b H. R. ANTONIN . PIVS AVG . PON . TR . P . V., laur. and dr. bust of
Caracalla r. *B.M.C.* p. 618 (*Oldroyd*) and p. 230, § note; *R.I.C.* 179 note;
Lucerne sale, 24/4/69, *lot* 299 400
2a F. R. ANTONINVS AVGVSTVS, laur. bust of Caracalla dr. and cuir. r.
B.M.C. 187-8; *R.I.C.* 157 400
2b F. R. — As before, but dr. only. *B.M.C.* 187 note; *R.I.C.* 157 .. 400
3 G. R. — As last. *B.M.C.* p. 202, * and p. 297, †; *R.I.C.* 151B and
521 (a) 400
4 G, but commences L . SEPT . SEVERVS (*Cohen has* TR . P . VIII *in error*).
R. ANTONINVS AVG . PON . TR . P . IIII., as 2a. *B.M.C.* p. 297, §; *R.I.C.*
521 (b) 400
5 H. R. As **1b**, but ANTONINVS. *B.M.C.* p. 230, §; *R.I.C.* 179 400
5a H. R. As **1b**, but laur. hd. r. *B.M.C.* p. 230, § note; *R.I.C.* 179 note 400
6 F. R. ANTONINVS PIVS AVG., laur. hd. of Caracalla. .. .. ..
6a E. R. As last. *Hunterian* (Hy.?; *thought to be genuine*). .. .. ..
7 SEVERVS PIVS AVG . P . M . TR . P . X. (*Cohen omits* PIVS *in error*?). R.
As last. *B.M.C.* p. 230, ‖ note; *R.I.C.* 180
7a Similar, but laur. bust of Caracalla dr. r. *B.M.C.* p. 230, ‖; *R.I.C.* 180A
(*Vienna*) 400
9 IMPP . INVICTI PII AVGG., jugate busts of Septimius and Caracalla r.,
both laur., dr. and cuir. R. VICTORIA PARTHICA MAXIMA, Victory advancing
l., holding wreath and palm. *B.M.C.* 265 note; *R.I.C.* 311 650

SEPTIMIUS SEVERUS, CARACALLA and GETA
Struck during the joint reign of Septimius and Caracalla
Obverses of Septimius Severus (see p. 18), except where given in full.

1a Denarius. F. R. AETERNIT . IMPERI., laur. bust of Caracalla, dr. and cuir.,
and bare-headed bust of Geta, dr., face to face. *B.M.C.* 184 note; *R.I.C.*
155 (b) note .. ..
3 SEVERVS PIVS AVG . P . M . TR . P . VIII. R. — As last. *B.M.C.* p. 189
(*doubtful*); *R.I.C.* p. 110, * and 174 note .. ..
3a As before, but TR . P . VIIII. *B.M.C.* 253 note; *R.I.C.* 174 550
3b As last, but Geta dr. and cuir. *B.M.C.* p. 619, A171A (*Oldroyd*); *R.I.C.*
174 .. ..

5a As **3a,** but TR . P . X. *B.M.C.* p. 230, ‡ note; *R.I.C.* 178A (a); *these two books quote C.5 as denarius, whereas Cohen gives* N   ..   ..   ..

6 H. R. — As **1a.** *B.M.C.* 308 note; *R.I.C.* 251 ..   ..   £500

6a H. R. — As **3b.** *B.M.C.* p. 618 (*Oldroyd*)   500

7 H. R. — Laur. hd. of Caracalla and bare hd. of Geta face to face. *B.M.C.* 308; *R.I.C.* 252   500

SEPTIMIUS SEVERUS and GETA
Struck during the joint reign of Septimius and Caracalla

Obverses of Septimius Severus.

2 Denarius. H. R. P. (and/or L.) SEPT . GETA CAES . PONT., bare-headed bust of Geta dr. r. *B.M.C.* p. 221, * note; *R.I.C.* 281   500

2a H. R. P . SEPTIMIVS GETA CAES., as last. *B.M.C.* p. 221, *; *R.I.C.* 281 (*DeQuelen; plated*)   ..   ..

3 F. R. P . SEPT . GETA CAES . PONT., as last. *B.M.C.* p. 193, *; *R.I.C.* 164

4 E. R. L . SEPTIMIVS GETA CAES., as before, but also cuir. *B.M.C.* p. 177, * and 662; *R.I.C.* 132 and 506   450

4a SEVERVS PIVS AVG. P.M.TR.P.X., his laur. and dr. bust r. R. As **3.** (*Leu auction, May* 1979, *lot* 297)   550

JULIA DOMNA

Julia Domna was the child of Julius Bassianus, a priest of Sol, and Soaemias, and born at Emesa in Syria. Although of humble family her horoscope was such that she firmly believed that sometime or other she would become the wife of a king, and as a young woman she came to Rome. Septimius, who was addicted to astrology, heard about her long before he had any hopes of becoming emperor, and, after the death of his first wife, married her about A.D. 173. It was not until 188 that she bore him his first son who was named Bassianus, afterwards changed to Antoninus, and nicknamed Caracalla. A year later another son, Geta, was born. Domna possessed beauty, wit, learning and eloquence; she had a brilliant intellect; Septimius often consulted her on state matters and was frequently guided by her counsels.

After the death of Septimius she was still treated with some degree of deference by Caracalla, but she was forced to witness the murder of Geta in her own arms. Afterwards, she succeeded in dissembling her grief, to secure the goodwill of her surviving son, who bestowed on her many honours. After Caracalla's murder she stayed on at Antioch until she was ordered to leave, when she committed suicide by refusing all nourishment.

Obverse legends.

Under Septimius Severus

A.   IVLIA DOMNA AVG. 193-196/7 A.D
B.   IVLIA AVGVSTA   196-211 A.D.

Under Caracalla

C.   IVLIA PIA FELIX AVG.

After her death

D.   DIVA IVLIA AVGVSTA

Obverse type.
Draped bust r., unless otherwise stated.

References.

In the case of *B.M.C.* numbers, prefix "W" indicates it comes under Wars of the Succession, "S" under the joint reign of Septimius and Caracalla, "G" under the pages of the joint reign of Septimius, Caracalla and Geta, and "C" under the sole reign of Caracalla. Those struck after her death come under Elagabalus and have the prefix "E".

In the *R.I.C.* coins are either prefixed "S" as a Septimius number or "C" for a Caracalla number.

Mints.

In the *B.M.C.* and *R.I.C.* all are attributed to Rome except:

Alexandria?: *B.M.C.* W329-34 (pp. 86-7); *R.I.C.* 607A-13 (p. 174)

Emesa and/or Laodicea ad Mare: *B.M.C.* W412-24 (pp. 102-5); *R.I.C.* 614-34A (pp. 175-7).

Laodicea ad Mare: *B.M.C.* S592-624 (pp. 276-80); *R.I.C.* 635-48.

In Pannonia: *R.I.C.* 648A (p. 179).

In Asia: *B.M.C.* p. 305; *R.I.C.* 649-50 (p. 179).

1   **Denarius.** A. Ŗ. AEQVITAS AVG., Aequitas stg. l. (or stg. front, hd. l.), holding scales and cornucopiae (Hy.?). *B.M.C.* p. 86, †; *R.I.C.* p. 174, *

2   B. Ŗ. — As last (Hy.?). *B.M.C.* G142 (*base, curious style*); *R.I.C.* S588

3   B. Ŗ. AEQVITAS AVGG., as last (Hy.). *R.I.C.* S589   ..   ..   ..

3a A. Ŗ. AEQVITAS II., as last (Hy.? *plated*). *B.M.C.* p. 86, †; *R.I.C.* S607A

4   **Silver medallion.** C, her diademed bust dr. l. Ŗ. AEQVITAS PVBLICA, the Three Monetae stg. l., each holding scales and cornucopiae; at feet of each, a pile of metal. *B.M.C.* p. 430, *; *R.I.C.* C395 ..   ..   *Very rare*

5a **Denarius.** B. Ŗ. AEQVITATI AVG., as **1** (Hy.). *R.I.C.* S590   ..   ..

7   B. Ŗ. AETERN . AVGG., Cybele in quadriga of lions. *B.M.C.* p. 170 (a); *R.I.C.* 166, * (*very doubtful*)   ..   ..

7a A. Ŗ. AETERNITAS, crescent and seven stars (Hy.?). *R.I.C.* Addenda (*Lawrence*)   ..   ..

8   A (*Cohen omits* AVG. *in error*). Ŗ. BONA SPES, Spes advancing l., holding flower and raising skirt. *B.M.C.* W412-3; *R.I.C.* S614 ..   ..   ..   £30

9   As last, but BONAE SPEI. *B.M.C.* W414; *R.I.C.* S615   30

10 As last. Ŗ. BONI EVENTVS, Bonus Eventus stg. l., holding plate of fruit and corn-ears. *B.M.C.* p. 86, ‡ and p. 102, *; *R.I.C.* S608 and S616 ..   35

10a A. Ŗ. — As last, but Bonus Eventus stg. r. (?). *B.M.C.* p. 102, * note; *R.I.C.* S616 note   ..   ..

11 A? Ŗ. CERER . AVG., Ceres stg., holding corn-ears and spear. *B.M.C.* p. 102, † note; *R.I.C.* S617 note   ..   ..

11a A. Ŗ. CERERE . AVG., Ceres stg. l., holding torch and corn-ears. *B.M.C.* p. 103, *; *R.I.C.* S617   35

12 A. Ŗ. CERERE . AVGVS., Ceres stg. l., holding corn-ears and torch. *B.M.C.* p. 102, † note; *R.I.C.* S618   35

13a A. Ŗ. CERER . FRVG., Ceres stg. l., holding two corn-ears and lighted torch. *B.M.C.* p. 102, †; *R.I.C.* S616A   35

14 (Rome mint)

14 B. Ŗ. CERERI FRVGIF., Ceres seated l., holding corn-ears and long torch (or sceptre). *B.M.C.* S10-13 and S592; *R.I.C.* S546 and S636. *Illustrated at bottom of last page.* £25

15 A. Ŗ. — As last (Hy.?). *B.M.C.* p. 103, †; *R.I.C.* S546 note (*doubtful*)

16 B (?) Ŗ. — As last (*base or Æ*). *B.M.C.* S10 note; *R.I.C.* S546 note ..

21 B. Ŗ. CONCORDIA, Concordia seated l., holding patera and double cornucopiae. *B.M.C.* S593-7; *R.I.C.* S637. 25

21a B. Ŗ. CONCORDIAE, as last. *B.M.C.* S593 note; *R.I.C.* S637 note ..

22 B. Ŗ. — As **21** (*base or Æ*). *B.M.C.* S693 note; *R.I.C.* S637 note ..

23 B. Ŗ. CONCORDIA FELIX, Septimius and Julia (or Caracalla and Plautilla) stg., clasping r. hands. *B.M.C.* p. 170, (c) (*possibly hybrid; rev. of Plautilla; ancient forgery?*); *R.I.C.* S547 .. ..

24   27 (Eastern mint)

24 D. Veiled and dr. bust r. Ŗ. CONSECRATIO, peacock, tail in splendour, stg. front, body and hd. inclined l. *B.M.C.* Elagabalus 9; *R.I.C.* C396 and Severus Alexander 715 350

27 B. Ŗ. DIANA LVCIFERA, Diana, crescent on shoulder, stg. half-left, holding long torch in both hands. *B.M.C.* S15-9; *R.I.C.* S548 and S638 25

27a As last, but without crescent on shoulder. *B.M.C.* S598-9; *R.I.C.* S638 30

32   35

32 C. Ŗ. — As before, without the crescent. *B.M.C.* C1-4; *R.I.C.* C373A 25

33 As last (*base or Æ*). *B.M.C.* C204; *R.I.C.* C373A note .. .. ..

35 B. Ŗ. FECVNDITAS, Fecunditas or Terra (the Earth), naked to waist, reclining l. under tree or vine, resting arm on basket of fruit (*Cohen says, wine-cup in l. hand*), and placing r. hand on semi-circle, or partly hidden globe, on which stars, and over which move four small figures—the four Seasons. *B.M.C.* S21; *R.I.C.* 549 55

39 B. Ŗ. — Fecunditas stg. l., holding child on l. arm, and with a child on either side of her. *B.M.C.* p. 159, *; *R.I.C.* S550 60

39a C. Ŗ. — As last. *B.M.C.* p. 435, (a) and p. 621 (*Oldroyd; base*); *R.I.C.* C374 .. ..

42 A. Ŗ. — Fecunditas seated r. on throne, holding child in arms, a second child stg. l. in front of her. *B.M.C.* W46; *R.I.C.* S534 40

42a B. Ŗ. — As last (Hy.?; *base*). *B.M.C.* p. 159, * note; *R.I.C.* S550 note (*Lawrence*) .. ..

47 B. Ŗ. FELICITAS, Felicitas stg. half-left, holding caduceus and long sceptre. *B.M.C.* S22-3; *R.I.C.* S551 25

49 Denarius. C. ℞. FELICITAS (*Cohen adds* s . c. *in error*), Felicitas stg. l., holding caduceus and cornucopiae. *B.M.C.* p. 435, (b); *R.I.C.* C375 ..

51 B. ℞. FELICITAS AVGG., as last (Hy.; *rev. of Septimius*). *B.M.C.* p. 170, (d) (*ancient forgery ?*); *R.I.C.* S591 .. ..

51a B. ℞. FELICITAS PVBLICA, as last (Hy., *plated; rev. of Septimius*). *R.I.C.* S592 .. ..

52 A. ℞. FELICIT . TEMPOR . ., vase-shaped basket, containing ears of corn, bunches of grapes, etc. *B.M.C.* W415-6; *R.I.C.* S619 .. .. .. £45

53 A. ℞. FELICITAS TEMPOR., as last. *B.M.C.* W415 note; *R.I.C.* S620 .. 50

54 A. ℞. — Corn-ear between two crossed cornuacopiae. *B.M.C.* p. 103, ‡; *R.I.C.* S621.. .. ..

55 B. ℞. FORTVNAE FELICI, Fortuna stg. almost front, hd. l., holding cornucopiae and resting l. arm on reversed rudder. *B.M.C.* S24-6; *R.I.C.* S552 25

55a B. ℞. — As before, but rudder on globe. *B.M.C.* S24 note; *R.I.C.* S552 note .. ..

55b B. ℞. — As **55**, but l. arm on sceptre (?). *B.M.C.* S24 note; *R.I.C.* S552 note .. ..

57 B. ℞. — Fortuna seated l. on throne, holding cornucopiae and resting l. hand on rudder on globe (*omitted in Cohen*); before her, small naked figure stg. r. *B.M.C.* S29; *R.I.C.* S554 25

58 B. ℞. — As last, but without small figure. *B.M.C.* S27-8; *R.I.C.* S553 25

59 As last (*base or Æ*). *B.M.C.* S28 note; *R.I.C.* S553 note .. ..

64 A. ℞. FORTVNAE REDVCI, Fortuna seated l., holding rudder and cornucopiae. *B.M.C.* p. 103, ‖ note; *R.I.C.* S626

65 A. ℞. FORTVN . REDVC., as last. *B.M.C.* p. 103, ‖; *R.I.C.* S624 .. 30

66 A. ℞. FORTVN . REDVCI, Fortuna or Ceres stg., holding corn-ears and cornucopiae. *B.M.C.* p. 103, ¶; *R.I.C.* S625 .. .. ..

67 A. ℞. FORTVN . REDVC. (*Cohen has* REDVX *in error*), Fortuna stg. half-left, holding a cornucopiae in each hand. *B.M.C.* W417; *R.I.C.* S623 .. 30

67a A. ℞. — Fortuna or Hilaritas seated l., holding long palm and cornucopiae. *B.M.C.* p. 104, *; *R.I.C.* S623A 35

68 A. ℞. FORT . R . AVG., Fortuna stg. l., holding rudder and cornucopiae. *B.M.C.* p. 103, §; *R.I.C.* S622 45

69 C. ℞. FORT . RED . TR . P . III . COS . II., as last (Hy.). *B.M.C.*, p. 436, (e); *R.I.C.* C393 .. .. ..

69a C. ℞. — As before, but Fortuna seated (Hy.; *rev. of Geta*). *B.M.C.* p. 436, (f); *R.I.C.* C393A .. ..

69b A. ℞. FORT . REDVCI COS., as **64**, but rudder on globe. *B.M.C.* p. 103, ‖ note; *R.I.C.* S624A (*R. D. hoard*) 45

70 B. ℞. FVNDATOR PACIS, Septimius stg. half-left, holding branch and roll (Hy.; *rev. of Septimius*). *B.M.C.* p. 170, (e) and G143 (*curious style*); *R.I.C.* S593 .. ..

Rome mint   Eastern mint

72 B. R. HILARITAS, Hilaritas stg. front, hd. l., holding long palm and cornucopiae. *B.M.C.* S31 and S600; *R.I.C.* S556 and S639 .. .. £25

76 B. R. — As before, but she holds long palm and sceptre. *B.M.C.* S32-3; *R.I.C.* S555 25

77 **Quinarius.** As last. *B.M.C.* S32 note; *R.I.C.* S555 180

78 **Denarius.** B. R. — Hilaritas stg. l., holding patera and long palm. *B.M.C.* p. 161, *; *R.I.C.* S558 .. ..

78a As last (*base*). *B.M.C.* p. 161, * note (*in B.M., probably ancient forgery*)

79 B. R. — Hilaritas stg. half-left between two naked boys; she holds long palm and cornucopiae. *B.M.C.* S34-6; *R.I.C.* S557 25

79a A. R. IESTPE SANCTAE, Vesta or Septimius stg. l., holding patera and sceptre (Hy.). *B.M.C.* p. 28 (*probably ancient forgery*); *R.I.C.* p. 165, * *R. D. hoard*) .. ..

80 B. R. INDVLGENTIA AVGG . IN CARTH., the Dea Caelestis riding r. on lion, holding drum (Hy.; *rev. of Septimius*). *R.I.C.* S594 .. .. ..

80a **Cistophoric tetradrachm** (=3 *denarii*). A. R. I . O . M. in field, TRI. in ex., temple of four columns; in centre, Jupiter seated; between columns, Juno and Minerva stg. *B.M.C.* p. 305, *; *R.I.C.* S649 1,200

82 **Denarius.** B. R. IVNO, Juno stg. half-left, holding patera and sceptre; in front, peacock stg. l., head turned back. *B.M.C.* S38-9; *R.I.C.* S559 25

83 **Quinarius.** As last. *B.M.C.* S40; *R.I.C.* S559 150

83a **Denarius.** As before, but peacock does not turn hd. back. *B.M.C.* S41 25

83b As **82,** but no peacock. *B.M.C.* S39 note; *R.I.C.* 559A 30

84 **Quinarius.** C. R. As **82.** *B.M.C.* C5; *R.I.C.* C376 150

86a **Denarius.** IVLIA PIA MATER CASTR. R. IVNO, Juno stg. r., holding patera and sceptre. *R.I.C.* S648A (*Budapest*) 100

87 **Quinarius.** C. R. IVNONEM, as **82.** *B.M.C.* C6; *R.I.C.* C378 .. 150

92 **Denarius.** C. R. IVNO CONSERVATRIX, as **82** or **83a.** *B.M.C.* p. 435, (c) (*uncertain*); *R.I.C.* C377 .. ..

97 B. R. IVNO REGINA, as **82.** *B.M.C.* S42-44 and S601; *R.I.C.* S560 and S640 25

97a As last, but reversed spear for sceptre. *B.M.C.* S602-3 25

101 B. R. LAETITIA, Laetitia stg. half-left, holding wreath and rudder. *B.M.C.* S45-46 and S604-10; *R.I.C.* S561 and S641 25

102a A. R. LEG . III . ITALI . TR . P . COS., legionary eagle between standards (Hy ?; *rev. of Septimius varied*). *B.M.C.* p. 86, §; *R.I.C.* S608A (*Budapest*)

103 A. R. LIBERAL . AVG., Liberalitas, modius on hd., stg. half-left, holding abacus and cornucopiae. *B.M.C.* W419; *R.I.C.* S627 30

103a As last, but Liberalitas stg. front, hd. l., without the modius. *B.M.C.* W418 30

103b A. R. — Liberalitas seated l., holding abacus and cornucopiae. *B.M.C.* p. 104, †; *R.I.C.* S627A (*R. D. hoard*) 40

103c B. R. LIBERALITAS AVG . II., Liberalitas stg. l., holding abacus and cornucopiae (Hy.; *rev. of Septimius*). *B.M.C.* p. 620, A175A (*Ashmolean*)

103d B. R. LIBERALITAS AVG . VI, as **103a** (Hy.; *rev. of Septimius*). *B.M.C.* G144 (*base*) .. ..

105 Denarius. C. R. LVNA LVCIFERA, Luna (*Cohen gives* Diana), with crescent on head and cloak floating round head, stg. in biga l., horses prancing. *B.M.C.* C10; *R.I.C.* C379 (c) £40

106 Antoninianus (=*double denarius*). C, her diad. bust dr., on crescent, r. R. — As last. *B.M.C.* C9; *R.I.C.* C379 (a)   85

106a   114

106a As last, but Luna without crescent. *B.M.C.* C8   85
107 As **106** (*base* or Æ). *B.M.C.* C8 note; *R.I.C.* C379 (a) note .. ..

111 Denarius. C. R. MAT . AVGG . MAT . SEN . M . PATR., Julia seated l., holding olive-branch and sceptre. *B.M.C.* C12-3; *R.I.C.* C381   35
114 C. R. — As before, but Julia stg. front, hd. l. (or stg. half-left). *B.M.C.* C11; *R.I.C.* C380   35
115 ? R. As last, but legend ends MAT . PAT. *B.M.C.* C11 note; *R.I.C.* C380 note (*doubtful*) .. ..
117 B. R. MATER AVGG., Cybele (or Julia as Cybele), towered, seated l. on throne in quadriga of lions; she holds branch. *B.M.C.* S48; *R.I.C.* S562   35
121a B. R. MATER CASTRORVM, Julia, veiled, stg. half-left, sacrificing out of patera over lighted altar and holding sceptre; before, three standards. *B.M.C.* S56 note; *R.I.C.* S563 (b) (*R. D. hoard*)   75
123 B. R. MATER DEVM, Cybele, towered, seated l. on throne between two lions, leaning on drum and holding branch and sceptre. *B.M.C.* S51 note; *R.I.C.* S564   30
126a B. R. As last, but no sceptre. *B.M.C.* S51-5; *R.I.C.* S565   30
These last two could be the same, the back of the throne being taken for sceptre.
128 B. R. — Cybele, towered, stg. front, hd. l., holding branch and drum; at her feet, lion stg. or seated l. *B.M.C.* S49; *R.I.C.* S566   35

117   137

130 Tetradrachm. B. R. MATRI CASTR., five corn-ears in bundle. *B.M.C.* p. 305, †; *R.I.C.* S650   900
131 Denarius. B. R. MATRI CASTRORVM, Julia, veiled, seated l. on throne, holding phoenix on globe and sceptre; before, two standards. *B.M.C.* S58-9; *R.I.C.* S568   65
132 As last, but three standards. *B.M.C.* S58 note; *R.I.C.* 569
134 B. R. — Julia, veiled, stg. half-left, sacrificing out of patera over lighted altar and holding box with open lid; before, two standards. *B.M.C.* S57; *R.I.C.* S567   65
137 C. R. MATRI DEVM, Cybele, towered, stg. half-left, leaning on column, legs crossed, holding drum and sceptre; before, lion seated l. *B.M.C.* C14-8; *R.I.C.* C382   30
138 As last, but without the lion. *B.M.C.* C14 note; *R.I.C.* C383   35

138a As **137,** but without sceptre. *B.M.C.* C14 note; *R.I.C.* C383A (*Tinchant cat.*) .. ..

139 B. Ŗ. As **137** (Hy. ?). *B.M.C.* p. 170, (f); *R.I.C.* S570 .. .. £40

142 B. Ŗ. MINER V . . . . . . Minerva stg. l., holding spear, trophy behind (Hy.; *rev. of Caracalla*). *R.I.C.* S595 .. ..

143 A. Ŗ. MONET . AVG., Moneta stg. half-left, holding scales and cornu-copiae. *B.M.C.* W329 note; *R.I.C.* S609 40

144 A. R. MONETA AVG., as last. *B.M.C.* W329; *R.I.C.* S610 40

144a A. Ŗ. — Moneta seated l., holding scales and cornucopiae. *B.M.C.* W420; *R.I.C.* S628 30

144b C. Ŗ. — Moneta stg. r., holding cornucopiae and scales. *B.M.C.* p. 436, (d); *R.I.C.* C383B .. ..

144c B. Ŗ. MONETA AVGG., as **144a** (*Eastern mint; G. R. Arnold*) 35

145 A. Ŗ. MONETAE AVG . II . COS., as **143** (Hy. ?; *rev. of Septimius ?*). *B.M.C.* W329 note; *R.I.C.* S611 .. ..

146 B. Ŗ. NOBILITAS, Nobilitas stg. front, hd. r., holding sceptre and palla-dium (Hy.; *rev. of Geta*). *B.M.C.* G145 (*odd style*); *R.I.C.* S596; *Seaby's Bull.*, Feb. 63, B1499 (*plated ?*) .. ..

146a B. Ŗ. PACI VAETERNAE, Pax seated l., holding branch and sceptre (Hy., base; *barbarous imitation of rev. of Septimius*). *R.I.C.* 601 (*Colchester*) ..

146b B. Ŗ. PART . MAX . P . M . TR . P . VIIII., two captives seated below trophy (Hy.; *rev. of Septimius*). *B.M.C.* G147 (*style slightly odd*) .. ..

146c A. Ŗ. PIETAS, Pietas seated l., resting l. arm on back of throne and holding palladium in r. hand. *B.M.C.* W330-1 45

146d A. Ŗ. — Pietas seated l. on throne, holding Victory and sceptre. *B.M.C.* W332; *R.I.C.* S612 45

146e As last, but no sceptre. *B.M.C.* W332 note; *R.I.C.* S612 note 45

146f A. Ŗ. PIETAS AVG., as **146c.** *R.I.C.* 612A (*R. D. hoard*) 45

150   168

150 B. Ŗ. PIETAS AVGG., Pietas, veiled, stg. half-left, dropping incense into lighted altar and holding box. *B.M.C.* S62-7; *R.I.C.* S572 25

151 **Quinarius.** As last. *B.M.C.* S68; *R.I.C.* S572 150

154 **Denarius.** B. Ŗ. — Pietas stg. by altar, raising both hands. *B.M.C.* S62 note (*a kind of hybrid; ancient forgery ?*); *R.I.C.* S573 .. ..

155 As last (*base or Æ*). *B.M.C.* S62 note; *R.I.C.* S573 note .. .. ..

155a B. Ŗ. — Pietas stg. half-right, holding sceptre and child to breast (Hy.; *rev. of Plautilla ?*), *B.M.C.* S611 .. ..

155b B. Ŗ. PIETAS PALICA, Pietas stg. front by altar, raising both hands (Hy.), *B.M.C.* p. 619, A175 (*very base; Oldroyd*) .. ..

156 Denarius. B. Ŗ. PIETAS PVBLICA, Pietas, veiled, stg. half-left before altar, raising both hands. *B.M.C.* S69-71 and S612; *R.I.C.* S574 and S643 .. .. £25

160 B. Ŗ. P . M . TR . P . VIII . COS . II . P . P., Aesculapius stg. (Hy.; *base, plated or Æ*). *R.I.C.* S597 .. ..

161 B. Ŗ. — Victory walking l., holding open wreath in both hands over shield on a base (Hy.; *rev. of Septimius*). *R.I.C.* S598 .. .. ..

161a B. Ŗ. P . M . TR . P . XII . COS . III . P . P., Genius stg. half-left, sacrificing out of patera over lighted altar and holding two corn-ears (Hy.; *rev. of Septimius*). *B.M.C.* G146 (*odd style*); *R.I.C.* S599 .. .. ..

162 B. Ŗ. P . M . TR . P . XVI . COS . III . P . P., Clementia (?) seated l., holding patera and sceptre (Hy.; *rev. of Septimius*). *R.I.C.* S600 .. ..

163 B. Ŗ. PROVID . AVGG., Providentia stg. l., touching with wand a globe at her feet and holding sceptre (Hy.; *rev. of Septimius*). *R.I.C.* S602 ..

164 B. Ŗ. PVDICITIA, Pudicitia (*Cohen says* Julia), veiled, seated l., hd. front, resting l. elbow on throne. *B.M.C.* S72 note; *R.I.C.* S576 note.. .. 30

165 C. Ŗ. — As last. *B.M.C.* C19 note; *R.I.C.* C386 30

168 B. Ŗ. — As before, but hd. l. and r. hand on breast. *B.M.C.* S72 note and S74 (*base*), also S614-6; *R.I.C.* S576 25

168a B. Ŗ. — As last, but seated on stool, with l. hand at side. *B.M.C.* S613; *R.I.C.* S644 30

169 B. Ŗ. — As **168**, but r. hand up to face. *B.M.C.* S72 note; *R.I.C.* S576 note 30

170 B. Ŗ. — As **164**, but hd. l., r. hand on breast and l. hand holds sceptre. *B.M.C.* S72-3; *R.I.C.* S575 25

171 Quinarius. As last. *B.M.C.* S72 note; *R.I.C.* S575 180

172 C. Ŗ. — As last. *B.M.C.* C19 note; *R.I.C.* C385 180

172a Denarius. As last. *B.M.C.* C19; *R.I.C.* C385 30

172b A. Ŗ. ROMAE AETERNAE, Roma seated l., holding Victory and sceptre, shield at side of chair. *B.M.C.* W334 (*ex Trau sale; crude style*) .. 75

173 A. Ŗ. SAECVL . FELICIT., seven stars above crescent. *B.M.C.* W421; *R.I.C.* S629 65

173a A. Ŗ. SAECVL . FELICITAS, as last. *B.M.C.* p. 617 (*Oldroyd*) .. 65

Rome mint   Eastern mint

174 B. Ŗ. SAECVLI FELICITAS, Isis, wearing polos on hd., stg. r., l. foot on prow, she holds Horus; behind, rudder which rests against altar (?). *B.M.C.* S75-82 and S618; *R.I.C.* S577 and S645 30

175 As last (*base or Æ*). *B.M.C.* S76 note; *R.I.C.* S577 note ..

175a B. Ŗ. — As before, but without rudder or altar. *B.M.C.* S76 note; *R.I.C.* S577 note (*R. D. hoard*) 35

181 A. Ŗ. SECVRITAS IMPERII, Securitas seated r., holding globe (Hy.; *rev. somewhat as Caracalla and Geta*). *B.M.C.* p. 105, (a); *R.I.C.* S634 ..

182 B. Ŗ. SEVERI TI . . . . . Septimius, in military dress, stg. l.; at his feet, mourning captive seated (*plated*). *B.M.C.* p. 170,(g) (*very doubtful*); *R.I.C.* S603 .. ..

185 B. Ŗ. VENERI GENETRICI, Venus stg. half-left, holding patera and sceptre. *B.M.C.* S84; *R.I.C.* S578 30

186   197 (Eastern)

186 **Antoninianus.** C, diad. bust dr. r. R. — As last, or with hand open
without patera. *B.M.C.* C20; *R.I.C.* C387 (*both these give obv. with bust
on crescent, but B.M. illustration shows it as catalogued here and in Cohen;
I believe it may occur with both obverses*) £100

187 **Denarius.** Probably as **185** .. ..

188a A. R. VENER . VICT., Venus, dr., stg. front, hd. l., holding apple and
sceptre. *B.M.C.* W422; *R.I.C.* S630   30

188b A. R. VENER . VICTOR., as last, but r. hand raised, no apple. *B.M.C.*
W422 note; *R.I.C.* S631A   35

189 A. R. — Venus, naked to waist, stg. r. with back to spectator and
resting l. elbow on column, holding apple and palm over l. shoulder.
B.M.C. W423; *R.I.C.* S633   30

191 A. R. VENERI VICT., as **188a**. *B.M.C.* W422 note; *R.I.C.* S631 ..   35

194 A. R. VENERI VICTR., as **189**. *B.M.C.* W49-54 and W424; *R.I.C.* S536
and S632   25

196a B. R. — As last (Hy.). *B.M.C.* G148 (*base*) .. ..

196b A. R. VENERI VICTRICI, as last. *B.M.C.* W424 note and p. 617 (*Oldroyd*);
R.I.C. S633A (*R. D. hoard*)   30

196c B. R. VENVS CAELESTIS, Venus stg. l., holding apple or globe and sceptre,
star in field to r. (Hy.; *rev. of Julia Soaemias*). *B.M.C.* G149; *R.I.C.* S605

196d As last, but patera for apple (Hy.). *R.I.C.* S604 ..

197 B. R. VENVS FELIX, Venus stg. half-left, holding apple and sceptre.
B.M.C. S85 note and S619-21; *R.I.C.* S580 note and S646 ..   25

198 B. R. — As before, but l. hand draws out fold of drapery. *B.M.C.* S85-9;
R.I.C. S580   25

201 **Quinarius.** B? R. — Venus stg. *B.M.C.* S85 note; *R.I.C.* S580 note

205 **Denarius.** C. R. VENVS GENETRIX, Venus seated l., holding apple and
sceptre; before her, Cupid stg. r., hand on her knee. *B.M.C.* C28; *R.I.C.*
C389 (b)   25

206   212

206 **Antoninianus** (*Cohen has MB in error*). C, diad. bust dr. r. on crescent
R. — As last. *B.M.C.* C27; *R.I.C.* C389 (a)   90

206a As last, but without Cupid. *B.M.C.* C27 note; *R.I.C.* C389 (a) note ..

211 As last, but without apple or Cupid. *B.M.C.* C22-3A; *R.I.C.* C388A ..   75

212 **Denarius.** C. R. — As last. *B.M.C.* C23B-26; *R.I.C.* C388C ..   25

214 As before (*base* or Æ). *B.M.C.* C23A note; *R.I.C.* C388A note .. ..

215   226

215 Denarius. B. R. VENVS VICTRIX, Venus, naked to waist, stg. half-
left, holding helmet and palm, resting l. elbow on column; at feet, l.,
shield. *B.M.C.* S90; *R.I.C.* S581 .. .. £25
216 As last (*base or Æ*). *B.M.C.* S90 note; *R.I.C.* S581 note .. ..
218 As **215**, but cuirass behind column, no shield. *B.M.C.* S90 note; *R.I.C.*
S581 note 30
218a B. R. — Venus stg. l., holding patera and palm; at feet, two Cupids.
B.M.C. S90 note; *R.I.C.* S581 note 45
221 A. R. VESTA, Vesta, veiled, seated l. on throne, holding palladium and
sceptre. *B.M.C.* W56-7; *R.I.C.* S538 30
223a B. R. — As last. *R.I.C.* S582 30
223b B. R. — As last, but without sceptre. *B.M.C.* S93-4; *R.I.C.* S582 note 30
223c B. R. — Vesta seated l., holding patera and short sceptre or torch
(*barbarous*). *B.M.C.* p. 170, (h); *R.I.C.* S582 note (*Lawrence*) .. ..
226 C. R. — Vesta, veiled, seated l. on stool, holding simpulum and sceptre.
B.M.C. C31-3; *R.I.C.* C391 25
227 As last (*base or Æ*). *B.M.C.* C31 note; *R.I.C.* C391 note .. ..
230 C. R. — Vesta, veiled, stg. half-left, holding palladium and sceptre.
B.M.C. C29-30; *R.I.C.* C390 25
231 As last (*base or Æ*). *B.M.C.* C29 note; *R.I.C.* C390 note .. ..
237 B. R. VESTA MATER, Julia or Vestal, veiled, stg. half-left before round
temple of Vesta, showing four columns; she sacrifices out of patera over
altar. *B.M.C.* S96; *R.I.C.* S584 250
238 B. R. — Two Vestals sacrificing over altar before similar temple; one
holds simpulum and the other, patera. *B.M.C.* S96 note and p. 618
(*Oldroyd*); *R.I.C.* S585 250
239a B. R. — Six Vestals sacrificing over altar before similar temple. *B.M.C.*
C97 note; *R.I.C.* 586 (*N only*) 300
240 Medallion. B, diad. and dr. half-length bust l., holding statuette of
Concordia and cornucopiae. R. — As last. *B.M.C.* S97 note; *R.I.C.*
S587A .. .. *Extremely rare*

245   246 (Eastern)

245 Denarius. B. R. — Vesta, veiled, seated l. on throne, holding palladium
and sceptre. *B.M.C.* S95; *R.I.C.* S583 25
246 B. R. VESTAE SANCTAE, Vesta, veiled, stg. half-left, holding patera and
sceptre. *B.M.C.* S99-101 and S622-4; *R.I.C.* S587 and S648 30
249 B. R. VICTORIA AVGG . FE., Victory advancing l., holding wreath in both
hands over shield on base (Hy.; *type of Septimius*). *R.I.C.* S606 ..

250 A. Ⓡ. VICTORIA IVST . AV., Victory seated l., holding wreath and palm (Hy.; *type of Niger or Septimius*). *B.M.C.* p. 105, (b); *R.I.C.* S634A ..

251 A. Ⓡ. VIRTVS AVG . COS. . . . Roma seated l. on shield, holding Victory and spear (Hy.). *B.M.C.* p. 28; *R.I.C.* S538A .. .. ..

251a C. Ⓡ. VOTA PVBLICA, Julia stg. l., dropping incense on lighted altar and holding open box (*Curtis L. Clay and Vienna*) £50

255 B. Ⓡ. VOTA SVSCEPTA XX., Septimius or priest sacrificing over tripod (Hy.; *rev. of Caracalla*). *R.I.C.* S607 .. ..

JULIA, SEPTIMIUS SEVERUS and CARACALLA

2 Denarius. IVLIA AVGVSTA, her bust dr. r. Ⓡ. AETERNIT . IMPERI., laur. hds. of Sep. Sev. and Caracalla face to face. *B.M.C.* S1 note; *R.I.C.* S539 (a) 550

2a — Ⓡ. — As before, but with cuirassed busts. *B.M.C.* S1 550

2b — Ⓡ. — As before, but with dr. and cuir. busts. *B.M.C.* S2; *R.I.C.* S539 (b) 550

3 IVLIA PIA FELIX AVG., otherwise as **2** (Hy?) .. ..

JULIA and CARACALLA

1 Denarius. IVLIA AVGVSTA, her bust dr. r. Ⓡ. ANTONINVS PIVS AVG., laur. and dr. boy's bust of Caracalla r. *B.M.C.* S7-8; *R.I.C.* S544 .. 500

1a — Ⓡ. — laur. hd. of Caracalla r. *B.M.C.* p. 618 500

2 — Ⓡ. ANTONINVS PIVS AVG . BRIT., laur. hd. of Caracalla, bearded, r. *B.M.C.* p. 158, * and p. 170, (b); *R.I.C.* S545 500

2a — Ⓡ. ANTONIN . PIVS AVG . PON . TR . P . V ., as **1**, *B.M.C.* S9; *R.I.C.* S542 500

2b — Ⓡ. ANTONINVS AVG . PON . TR . P . IIII., laur. bust of Caracalla dr. and cuir r. 550

JULIA, CARACALLA and GETA

2 Denarius. — Ⓡ. AETERNIT . IMPERI., laur. bust of Caracalla facing bare-headed bust of Geta, both young and dr. *B.M.C.* S5; *R.I.C.* S540 .. 550

2a — Ⓡ. — As last, but both busts cuir. *B.M.C.* S4 550

2b   2

3 — Ⓡ. — As last, but their heads only, no drapery. *B.M.C.* S6; *R.I.C.* S541 550

JULIA and GETA

1 Denarius. — Ⓡ. P . SEPT . GETA CAES . PONT., bare-headed bust of young Geta dr. and cuir. r. *B.M.C.* S60; *R.I.C.* S571 450

1a — Ⓡ. — As last, but bust draped only. *B.M.C.* S61 450

1b IVLIA PIA FELIX AVG., her bust dr. r. Ⓡ. As **1** or **1a** (Hy.). *B.M.C.* p. 436, (g); *R.I.C.* C394 .. ..

CARACALLA

198-217 A.D.

This emperor was born at Lugdunum on April 6th, 188 A.D., the elder son of Septimius Severus and Julia Domna, and named Bassianus, after his maternal grandfather. In 196, at Viminacium, he was created Caesar and renamed Marcus Aurelius Antoninus. The surname "Caracalla", by which he is known, was only a nickname, derived from a kind of long tunic of Gaulish origin, which he adopted and brought into fashion. In 198, after his tenth birthday, he was declared Augustus by his father and the army, and so became joint-ruler with Septimius. In 202 he married Plautilla and adopted the title Pius. In 208 he accompanied his father and brother to Britain and led the campaign here in 210.

On the death of Septimius at York, he reigned jointly with his brother, Geta, although he wanted to be the sole ruler. In 212, the two emperors returned to Rome, and started negotiations to divide the empire between them, but the treacherous Caracalla murdered Geta in the very arms of their mother. He then had put to death many distinguished Romans whom he thought might have favoured his brother.

His reign was marked by very much extravagance and cruelty, and in his wars more was achieved by treachery than by force of arms. He was eventually assassinated on April 8th, 217 A.D., by a soldier of his bodyguard, at the instigation of Macrinus, the praetorian prefect, whilst travelling between Edessa and Carrhae. The only good action that can be attributed to Caracalla was the granting of Roman citizenship to all free inhabitants of the empire in 212 A.D..

Obverse legends.

As Caesar, 196-198 A.D.

A. M . AVR . ANTONINVS CAES.

B.   ,,   ,,   ANTON . CAES . PONTIF

As Augustus; with Sept. Sev., 198-209; with Sept. Sev. and Geta, 209-11; with Geta, 211-2; sole reign, 212-7.

C. ANTONINVS AVGVSTVS,   199-201

D.   ,,   PIVS AVG.,   201-10

E.   ,,   ,,   ,, BRIT., 210-3

F.   ,,   ,,   ,, GERM., 213-7

G.   ,,   FEL . AVG.,   213

H. IMP . C . M . AVR . ANTON . AVG . P . TR . P.,   198

I.   ,,   ,,   ,,   ANTONINVS AVG.,   198-202

J.   ,,   ,,   ,,   ,,   PONT . AVG., 198

K. IMP . CAE . M . AVR . ANT . AVG . P . TR . P.,   198

L.   ,,   ,,   ,,   ,,   ,,   ,,   ,,   ,, . II., 199

M. IMP . CAES . M . AVR . ANTON . AVG.,   198-9

N.B.—*Obverse legend ' G ' is the same as ' A ' of Elagabalus, and the coins can only be separated by the portraiture, type and style. Coins of Caracalla with this legend are all from the mint of Rome, whilst those of Elagalabus are of Eastern mintage.*

Obverse types.

a. Boy's bare-headed bust draped right.

b.   ,,   ,,   ,,   draped and cuirassed right.

c. Older boy's laureate bust draped right.

d.   ,,   ,,   ,,   draped and cuirassed right.

e. Youth's laureate head right

f.   ,,   ,,   bust draped right.

g.   ,,   ,,   ,, draped and cuirassed right.

h.   ,,   ,,   head, bearded, right.

Obverse types (*continued*)

i.   Man's laureate head, bearded, right.
j.   "   "   bust, bearded, draped right.
k.   "   "   "   "   cuirassed right.
l.   "   "   "   "   draped and cuirassed right.
m.   "   radiate bust, bearded,   draped right, seen from front.
n.   "   "   "   "   draped right, seen half from back.
o.   "   "   "   "   cuirassed right.
p.   "   "   "   "   draped and cuirassed right, seen from front.
q.   "   "   "   "   "   "   seen half from back.

References.

In the *B.M.C.* this reign comes into five sections, each with numbers starting again from 1, we have therefore had to prefix the catalogue numbers for four sections.

Wars of the Succession, prefixed with W (pp. 50-115).
Joint reign of Septimius and Caracalla, prefixed with S (pp. 171-306).
Joint reign of Septimius, Caracalla and Geta, prefixed with SG (pp. 358-386).
Joint reign of Caracalla and Geta, prefixed with G (pp. 419- 421).
Sole reign of Caracalla, no prefix (pp. 430-468).

Mints.

B.M.C. and *R.I.C.* attribute all to Rome except:
Eastern mint, probably Laodicea ad Mare: *B.M.C.* W458-62 (p. 115), SC646-9 (pp. 283-4), SC691-711, SC716-8 (pp. 291-5), SC727-30 (pp. 298-300), SC761-2 (pp. 305-6); *R.I.C.* 329-358A (pp. 263-8).

3   8

3 **Denarius.** Dc. ℞. ADVENT . AVGG., galley l. with rowers (number varies) and three passengers. *B.M.C.* S267; *R.I.C.* 120 ..   ..   £50

5 E, but PL., i. ℞. ADVENTVI (*Cohen has* ADVENTVS *in error*) AVG., Caracalla galloping l. over fallen enemy (Hy. ?). *B.M.C.* p. 375, (a); *R.I.C.* 212 note

7 Ei. ℞. ADVENTVS AVGVSTI, Caracalla on horseback l., holding spear. *B.M.C.* p. 370, *; *R.I.C.* 212   55

8 Dc. ℞. ADVENTVS above, AVGVSTOR in ex., as **3.** *B.M.C.* S268-69; *R.I.C.* 121   50

8a As last, but unusual style (Eastern ?). *B.M.C.* S268 note; *R.I.C.* 121 note (*Lawrence*)   50

8b Dd. ℞. — As **8.** *B.M.C.* S270   50

9 Cc. ℞. AEQVITAS AVGG., Caracalla seated l. on curule chair, holding sceptre; before him, Aequitas stg., holding scales and cornucopiae (Hy.; *plated, ancient forgery*). *B.M.C.* p. 185, *; *R.I.C.* 31   ..   ..

9a Ei. ℞. — As last (Hy.) (*G. R. Arnold*) ..   ..

10 Medallion. IMP . M . AVR . ANTONINVS PIVS AVG . P . M . TR . P . XIII., laur.
mature bust, bearded, with light drapery on shoulder, r.   R.   AEQVITATI
PVBLICAE, the Three Monetae stg. l., each holding scales and cornucopiae;
heaps of money at their feet. *B.M.C.* p. 362, *; *R.I.C.* 114   *Extremely rare*

12a Quinarius. De.   R.   ANNONA AVG., Annona stg. l., holding corn-ears
over modius and cornucopiae. *B.M.C.* p. 255, ‡; *R.I.C.* 151A £200
13   Ei. R. As *obv.* (*not in B.M. as Cohen says*)   ..   ..   ..

14 Denarius. D ? R.   ARCVS AVGG., the Arch of Severus (*very doubtful*) ..

18a Cistophoric tetradrachm (=3 denarii). M, but ANTONINVS, e. R.
AVGVSTORVM across field, Roman eagle between two ensigns (*Tinchant cat.*)   900

19 Denarius. Cd. R.   BONVS EVENTVS, Bonus Eventus (*Cohen gives* Genius),
naked, stg. front, hd. l., holding patera over lighted altar and two corn-
ears. *B.M.C.* S159-60; *R.I.C.* 33   30
20   De. R.   CERERI FRVGIS, Ceres seated l., holding corn-ears and torch.
B.M.C. p. 300, *; *R.I.C.* 355   45
20a Dc or f. R. CONCORDIA, Concordia stg. l., holding caduceus and cornucopiae; star in field to r. (Hy. ?). *B.M.C.* p. 620, A176 (*Oldroyd*) ..   ..
20b Fi.   R. — Concordia stg. front, hd. l., sacrificing out of patera over
lighted altar and holding double cornucopiae, star in field to l. (Hy.;
rev. of time of Elagabalus). *B.M.C.* 203; *R.I.C.* 318   ..   ..   ..

23   32

23   Dc. R.   CONCORDIA FELIX, Caracalla stg. l., holding roll, and Plautilla
stg. r., clasping r. hands. *B.M.C.* S272-3; *R.I.C.* 124 (a)   40
23a Dd. R. — As last. *B.M.C.* S274; *R.I.C.* 124 (b)   40
25   Gi. R.   CONCORDIA MILIT., two standards between two legionary eagles.
B.M.C. p. 442, (a); *R.I.C.* 232 (*probably a coin of Elagabalus*) ..   ..
25a Gj. R. — Legionary eagle between standards (*barbarous style*). *B.M.C.*
p. 442, (b); *R.I.C.* 233 (*probably a coin of Elagabalus*)   ..   ..   ..
25b E, but PI . AVGV., i. R.   CONCORDIAE, Concordia seated l., holding patera
and double cornucopiae (Hy. ?). *B.M.C.* p. 375, (b); *R.I.C.* p. 243, *
(*R. D. hoard*) ..   ..
26a Dc. R.   CONCORDIAE AETERNAE, Caracalla and Plautilla stg. facing each
other, clasping r. hands (Hy. ?). (*New York*)   ..   ..
32   DIVO ANTONINO MAGNO, his bare hd., bearded, r. R. CONSECRATIO, eagle
stg. half-left on globe, hd. turned back. *B.M.C.* Elagabalus 7-8; *R.I.C.*
Severus Alexander 717   350

36 Quinarius. De. R.   COS . II., Victory advancing l., holding wreath and
palm. *B.M.C.* p. 252, *; *R.I.C.* 86   150
36a Df. R. — As last (*Vatican*)   150

38 Denarius. De. R.   COS . II. in ex., Caracalla, holding eagle-tipped sceptre,
in quadriga of horses pacing r. *B.M.C.* S488; *R.I.C.* 87 (a)   65
38a Df. R. — As last. *B.M.C.* p. 618 (*Ashmolean*)   65
39a De. R. — Triumphal arch. *B.M.C.* p. 252, †; *R.I.C.* 87A (*Ashmolean,*
East of England hoard)   500

39c   45a

39c **Cistophoric tetradrachm** (=3 denarii). I. Youthful laur. hd. l. ℞. cos.
II . across field, legionary eagle between two standards. *B.M.C.* S761;
R.I.C. 356 .. .. £800

40 **Denarius.** De. ℞. cos . III., Salus stg. l. *B.M.C.* p. 273; *R.I.C.* 201 ..

42 **Quinarius.** Ei. ℞. cos . III . P . P., Victory advancing l., holding wreath
and palm. *B.M.C.* SG108 note; *R.I.C.* 202b 150

43 Di (or e). ℞. — As last (Hy. ?). *R.I.C.* 202a .. ..

45 F (*Cohen has* E *in error*) i. ℞. cos . IIII . P . P., as last. *B.M.C.* C67;
R.I.C. 317 (b) or (d) 150

45a Fl. ℞. — As last. *B.M.C.* C66; *R.I.C.* 317 (a) or (c) 150

47 Dl (or g). ℞. — As last. *B.M.C.* C66 note; *R.I.C.* 317 (a) note (*error
or hybrid ?*) .. ..

50 **Denarius.** Dc. ℞. cos . LVDOS SAECVL . FEC., Bacchus or Liber and
Hercules stg. facing each other; the former, naked except for leopard-skin
and holding cup and thyrsus; at feet, leopard catching drips from cup;
the latter holds club and lion's skin. *B.M.C.* C75A and B; *R.I.C.* 74 (a) 200

53 Ba and/or b. ℞. DESTINATO IMPERAT., lituus, apex, bucranium and
simpulum. *B.M.C.* W193-6; *R.I.C.* 6 45

54 Ba ? ℞. DESTINATO IMPERATORE, similar. *B.M.C.* W193 note; *R.I.C.*
6 note (*very doubtful*) .. ..

58 Df. ℞. FELICIA above, TEMPORA in ex., the Four Seasons as boys at play.
B.M.C. p. 207, *; *R.I.C.* 126 350

59 De. ℞. — As last. *B.M.C.* S505; *R.I.C.* 153 .. ..

61 Cd (or c). ℞. FELICITAS AVGG., Felicitas stg. half-left, holding short
caduceus and cornucopiae. *B.M.C.* S61 note; *R.I.C.* 34 25

61a Cc. ℞. — Felicitas stg. front, hd. l., holding long caduceus and cornucopiae. *B.M.C.* S61 (*base; perhaps ancient forgery*) and S699; *R.I.C.* 35 .. 30

62 Lc. ℞. — As last. *B.M.C.* S691-2; *R.I.C.* 339 (a) 30

62a Ld. ℞. — As last. *B.M.C.* S693-5; *R.I.C.* 339 (b) 30

63 Mc. ℞. — As last. *B.M.C.* p. 173, *; *R.I.C.* 18 30

64 Dc and/or f. ℞. — As **61.** *B.M.C.* S276-8: *R.I.C.* 127.. 25

65 As last (*base or* Æ). *B.M.C.* S276 note; *R.I.C.* 127 note .. ..

65a Dc or f. ℞. FELICITAS PVBLICA, as last (Hy ?). *B.M.C.* p. 620, A177
(*Oldroyd*); *R.I.C.* p. 261, (a) (*Lawrence*) 35

66 ? ℞. — Felicitas seated, holding caduceus and cornucopiae. .. ..

70 ? ℞. FELICITAS TEMPOR., Felicitas, holding caduceus, and the emperor,
holding cornucopiae, stg. hand in hand .. ..

70a Gl. ℞. — As **61** or **61a.** *B.M.C.* p. 442, (c) (*quite doubtful*); *R.I.C.* 233A

71 A coin of Elagabalus (*see C.*282) .. ..

72 ? ℞. FELICITATEM ITALICAM, as **61** or **61a** .. ..

73 **Denarius.** Ab. ℞. FELICITATEM PVBLICAM, Felicitas stg. half-left, holding short caduceus and sceptre. *B.M.C.* p. 50, *; *R.I.C.* 1 .. .. £50
74 Bb (*Cohen* ANT. *in error*). ℞. — As last. *B.M.C.* W197-8; *R.I.C.* 7 .. 45
74a Ba. ℞. — As last (*Tinchant cat.*) 50
75 ? ℞. FIDEI AVG., Fides stg., holding two standards .. .. ..

76 Ei. ℞. FIDEI EXERCITVS, Fides stg. half-left, holding standard and legionary eagle; to r., another standard. *B.M.C.* SG71-2; *R.I.C.* 213. (*There are at least three variations of standard*) 25
77 A coin of Elagabalus (*see C.* 38) .. ..
78 Di. ℞. — Fides stg. facing, holding standard and phoenix on globe; behind, another standard. (*This piece is probably a misdescription of* 76 *or a hybrid*) .. ..
79 A coin of Elagabalus (*see C.* 28) .. ..
80 A coin of Elagabalus (*see C.* 38) .. ..
81 A coin of Elagabalus (*see C.* 44) .. ..
82 Kc. ℞. FIDES PVBLICA, Fides stg. front, head r., holding two corn-ears and plate of fruit. *B.M.C.* S102-4 and S636; *R.I.C.* 24 (a) and 344 .. 25
82a Kd. ℞. — As last. *B.M.C.* S102 note; *R.I.C.* 24 (b) and 334 .. 30
82b Kc and/or d. ℞. — As last, but Fides stg. l. *B.M.C.* S102; *R.I.C.* 24A 35
82c Mc. ℞. — As last, but Fides stg. r. *B.M.C.* p. 173, † and p. 284, *; *R.I.C.* 19 and 330A 30

82a   83

83 Ba. ℞. — As 82 (Hy?). *B.M.C.* p. 54; *R.I.C.* 8; (*G. R. Arnold coll.*) 40
83a Ei. ℞. FID . EXERC . TR . P . XIII . COS . III . P . P., as 76 (Hy., *plated; ancient forgery*). *B.M.C.* p. 364, (b); *R.I.C.* p. 229, * .. ..
84 Ei. ℞. FORT . RED . P . M . TR . P . XIIII . COS . III . P . P., Fortuna stg. half-left, holding cornucopiae and leaning on reversed rudder (*Cohen says* column), wheel at feet. *B.M.C.* G1-2; *R.I.C.* 189 30
84a Ei. ℞. — As last, but no wheel. *B.M.C.* G1 note; *R.I.C.* 189 note; (*Mazzini cat.*) 35
88a Ei. ℞. — Fortuna seated l., holding rudder and cornucopiae, wheel below throne. *B.M.C.* G3; *R.I.C.* 190 (a) 35
89 Ei. ℞. FORT . RED . TR . P . XIIII . COS . III., as last. *R.I.C.* 190 (a) note (*confirmed by Charles Davis, also specimen from same rev. die now in B.M.*) 35
89a Di. ℞. FORTVNAE FELICI, Fortuna stg. facing, hd. l., holding cornucopiae and resting l. hand on rudder (Hy.; *curious style, rev. legend of J. Domna*). *B.M.C.* p. 261, (a); *R.I.C.* 154 .. ..

89b Di. R. — Fortuna stg. facing, hd. l., holding patera and cornucopiae (Hy.; *crude style obv.*). *B.M.C.* SG151 .. ..

89c C. R. FORTVNA REDVX, Fortuna stg. l., holding rudder and cornucopiae (Hy.; *plated; ancient forgery*). *B.M.C.* p. 188 (a); *R.I.C.* 37 .. ..

90 Dc. R. FVNDATOR PACIS, emperor stg. l., holding branch and sceptre (Hy.; *rev. of Septimius*). *B.M.C.* p. 212, (a); *R.I.C.* 129 .. .. ..

90a De. R. — Caracalla, togate, stg. l., holding branch (Hy.; *ancient forgery*). *B.M.C.* p. 261, (b); *R.I.C.* 154A (*R. D. hoard*) and 318A (*Lawrence*) ..

90b De. R. GAVDIA PVBLICA, four females supporting a large cornucopiae; the two on the l., stepping r. and the two on the r., stepping l. *Archeologia Classica*, 1952, p. 209 .. .. *Excessively rare, if not unique*

90c Gj. R. GENIO SENATVS, Genius of the Senate, togate, stg. l., holding branch. *B.M.C.* p. 442, (d); *R.I.C.* 234. (*Doubtful, or possibly a coin of Elagabalus*) .. ..

91 A coin of Elagabalus (*see C.* 54-6) .. ..

92a Tetradrachm. Ie. R. IMP . CAES . M . AVREL . ANTONINVS AVG. in laurel-wreath. *B.M.C.* p. 305, ‡; *R.I.C.* 357 (a) £750

92b As last, but rev. ends AVG . P . M. *B.M.C.* p. 305, ‡ note; *R.I.C.* 357 (b) 750

93 Denarius. Df. R. IMP . ET CAEASR AVG . FILI . COS., Caracalla and Geta seated front on curule chairs on platform, looking at each other; between them, behind, a facing half-length figure (Septimius ?). *B.M.C.* S278A; *R.I.C.* 75 250

94 Jd. R. IMPERII FELICITAS, Felicitas stg. l., holding caduceus downwards and child at breast on arm. *B.M.C.* p. 284, †; *R.I.C.* 331 30

94a Jd. R. — As last, but child does not show (*base*). *B.M.C.* SG152 ..

95 Ba. R. — As **94**. *B.M.C.* W199-201; *R.I.C.* 9 35

97   108

97 Dc. R. INDVLGENTIA AVGG. around, IN CARTH. in ex. (*Cohen* CART. *in error*), Dea Caelestis, holding thunderbolt and sceptre, seated facing, hd. r., on lion running r. over water gushing from rock. *B.M.C.* S280-2; *R.I.C.* 130 (a) 30

102 Dc R. INDVLGENTIA AVGG . IN ITALIAM, Italia, towered, seated l. on globe, holding cornucopiae and globe. *B.M.C.* p. 209, *; *R.I.C.* 132 .. 150

103 Fi. R. INDVLGENTIAE AVG., Indulgentia seated l., holding patera and sceptre. *B.M.C.* 68-9; *R.I.C.* 300 30

104 Ei. R. INDVLG . FECVNDAE, Indulgentia (Julia Domna ?), veiled and towered, seated l. on curule chair, extending the r. hand and holding sceptre. *B.M.C.* SG73-5; *R.I.C.* 214 40

105 De. R. INVICTA VIRTVS, Caracalla on horse galloping r., brandishing javelin at prostrate foe. *B.M.C.* S506; *R.I.C.* 155 55

107 Fi. R. IOVI CONSERVATORI, Jupiter stg., holding thunderbolt and sceptre, eagle at feet, two standards behind. *B.M.C.* p. 447, (a); *R.I.C.* 301 ..

107a De. R. — Bust of Jupiter, wreathed and with touch of drapery, r. (*Paris*) . 250

108 De. R. IOVI in ex., SOSPITATORI around, Jupiter stg. front, holding thunderbolt and sceptre, in flat-roofed temple showing four columns. *B.M.C.* S507; *R.I.C.* 156 125

113   115a

113 Denarius. Hd. ℞. IVSTITIA, Justitia seated l., holding patera and sceptre.
B.M.C. S637-8; *R.I.C.* 335 .. .. £30
113a Jc. ℞. — As last. *B.M.C.* p. 284, ‡ note; *R.I.C.* 331A note .. 35
113b Jd. ℞. — As last (*crude style*). *Seaby's Bull.*, *Sept.* 1937, 42440 ..
114 IMP . CAE . AVR . ANTON . AVG . PIVS, c. ℞. — As last. *B.M.C.* p. 284,
‡ note; *R.I.C.* 331A note (*doubtful*) .. ..
114a De. ℞. — As last. *B.M.C.* p. 300, †; *R.I.C.* 355a (*R.D. hoard*) .. 35
114b Jd. ℞. IVSTITIA TR . P., as last. *B.M.C.* p. 284, ‡; *R.I.C.* 331A (*Lawrence*) 35
115 Mc. ℞. IVVENTA IMPERII, Caracalla, in military dress, stg. half-left, holding
Victory on globe and spear downwards; captive seated l. at his feet. *B.M.C.*
S115-6; *R.I.C.* 20 45
115a Kc. ℞. — As last. *B.M.C.* p. 171, *; *R.I.C.* 24B 50
118 De. ℞. LAETITIA above, TEMPORVM in ey., ship, with mast and sail, in
circus, four quadrigae above and to r.; below, ostrich, lion, stag, bull, etc.
B.M.C. S508; *R.I.C.* 157 225
121 Dc and/or d. ℞. LIBERALITAS AVGG., Liberalitas stg. half-left, holding
abacus (counting board) and cornucopiae. *B.M.C.* p. 212, (b); *R.I.C.*
134 (a, b) .. ..
121a De. ℞. LIBERALITAS AVG . III., as last (Hy ?). *B.M.C.* p. 261, (c); *R.I.C.*
158 note .. ..
122 Dd. ℞. IIII. LIBERALITAS AVG., as last (*probably an error for next*) ..

122a   128

122a Dc. ℞. IIII. LIBERALITAS AVGG., as last. *B.M.C.* S284-5; *R.I.C.* 135 .. 30
122b De. ℞. LIBERALITAS AVG . IIII., as last (Hy ?). *B.M.C.* p. 261, (d); *R.I.C.*
158 note .. ..
124 Df. ℞. LIBERALITAS AVGG . V., as last. *B.M.C.* S286-7; *R.I.C.* 136 (b) 30
125 Fi. ℞. LIBERALITAS AVG . V., as before, but double cornucopiae (Hy ? *or
false*). *B.M.C.* p. 447, (c); *R.I.C.* 302 note .. .. ..
125a Ei. ℞. — As **121** (*this could be a true hybrid, with Geta rev.; i.e., mule*).
B.M.C. SG76; *R.I.C.* 215A 40
128 De. ℞. LIBERALITAS AVG . VI., as last. *B.M.C.* S509-10; *R.I.C.* 158 .. 25
129 Ei. ℞. — As last. *B.M.C.* SG76A, 77; *R.I.C.* 216 30
129a As last, but with globe at feet of Liberalitas. *B.M.C.* SG78; *R.I.C.* 217 30
131 Ei. ℞. LIB . AVGG . VI. ET V., Caracalla and Geta seated l. on platform; to l.
of them stands Liberalitas; below, citizen sitting on foot on steps and
holding out fold of toga. *B.M.C.* p. 371, * note; *R.I.C.* 215 (b) ..
133 Ei. ℞. LIBERALITAS AVG . VII., as **121**. *B.M.C.* SG79 note; *R.I.C.* 218 45
134 Ei. ℞. LIBERALITAS AVG . VIII., as last. *B.M.C.* SG79; *R.I.C.* 219 .. 30
135 Fi. ℞. — As last (Hy ?). *B.M.C.* p. 448, (d); *R.I.C.* 305 .. ..

135a Denarius. Ei. Ŗ. — As before, but Liberalitas leans on column or sceptre (?), l. hand empty. *B.M.C.* SG79 note; *R.I.C.* 220 (*probably misdescription, and is as next*) .. ..

135b Ei. Ŗ. — Liberalitas stg. l., holding tessera and leans'on reversed rudder. *B.M.C.* SG80 (*misdescribed, see* pl. 55, 7) £40

139 Fi. Ŗ. LIBERAL . AVG . VIIII., as **121.** *B.M.C.* 70-1; *R.I.C.* 302 .. 25

140 Fi. Ŗ. LIBERALITAS AVG., as **125** (Hy?). *B.M.C.* p. 447, (b); *R.I.C.* 304

141 De. Ŗ. LIBERALITAS AVGVS., Liberalitas stg. l., holding caduceus and cornucopiae (Hy.; *ancient forgery? or misdescription of* **128**). *B.M.C.* S509 note; *R.I.C.* 160 .. ..

142 A, boy's bare hd. r. Ŗ. LIBERO PATRI, Liber (Bacchus) stg. l., holding cup and thyrsus, panther at feet (Hy.; *rev. of Septimius*). *B.M.C.* p. 51; *R.I.C.* p. 212, * .. ..

143 D (*Cohen omits* PIVS) e. Ŗ. LIBERTAS AVG., Libertas stg. l., holding pileus and rod. *B.M.C.* S511-2; *R.I.C.* 161 25

144 A coin of Elagabalus (*see C.* 90) .. ..

144a Ei. Ŗ. — Libertas stg. l., holding caduceus (?) and cornucopiae (Hy?). *B.M.C.* p. 375, (d); *R.I.C.* 221 .. ..

146 Probably a misdescribed piece of Elagabalus .. ..

147 Antoninianus (=*double denarius*). Fq. Ŗ. MARS VICTOR, Mars, naked but with cloak floating behind, advancing r., holding spear and trophy (*plated; ancient forgery*). *B.M.C.* p. 444, †; *R.I.C.* 306 .. .. ..

147a Denarius. M, but ANTONINVS, rad. bust r. Ŗ. — As last. *B.M.C.* p. 174 (*extremely doubtful*); *R.I.C.* p. 214, * .. ..

147b IMP . CAES . ANTONINVS AVG., laur. bust r. Ŗ. — As last. *B.M.C.* p. 174 (*extremely doubtful*); *R.I.C.* p. 214, * .. ..

148 Ba. Ŗ. MARS VLTOR, as last. *B.M.C.* W202 note; *R.I.C.* 10 .. ..

149 Ei. Ŗ. MARTI PACATORI, Mars, naked to waist, stg. front, hd. l., holding branch and spear and leaning on shield. *B.M.C.* SG81-6; *R.I.C.* 222 .. 25

149a Ei. Ŗ. MARTI PROPVGANATORI, as next (Hy.). *B.M.C.* SG88 note; *R.I.C.* 223A .. ..

150 Ei. Ŗ. MARTI PROPVGNATORI, Mars, in military dress, hurrying l., holding spear and trophy. *B.M.C.* SG87-8; *R.I.C.* 223 25

151 Gi. Ŗ. — As last. *B.M.C.* 60-1; *R.I.C.* 235 30

152 Fi. Ŗ. — As last. *B.M.C.* 72-3; *R.I.C.* 307 25

153 As last (*base or* Æ). *B.M.C.* 72 note; *R.I.C.* 307 note .. .. ..

154 Ba. Ŗ. MARTI VLTORI, Mars, naked except for cloak floating around waist, walking r., holding spear and trophy. *B.M.C.* W202; *R.I.C.* 11 .. 30

154a Bb. Ŗ. — As last (*New York*) 30

157a Ei. Ŗ. MATRI DEVM, Cybele, towered, stg. half-left, leaning on column, legs crossed, holding drum and sceptre; before, lion seated l. (Hy.; *rev. of Julia Domna; ancient forgery?*). *B.M.C.* p. 375, (e); *R.I.C.* p. 242, * (*R. D. hoard*) .. ..

149   159

159 Kc. Ŗ. MINER . VICTRIX, Minerva stg. half-left, holding Victory and spear, shield at feet, trophy behind. *B.M.C.* S107-13 and S640 note; *R.I.C.* 25 (b) and 336 (b) 25

159a Denarius. Kd. ℞. MINER . VICTRIX, Minerva stg. half-left, holding
Victory and spear, shield at feet, trophy behind. *B.M.C.* S107 note and
S640 (*misdescribed in text, see illustration*); *R.I.C.* 25 (b) and 336 (b) .. £30

159b Kc. ℞. — As last, but no shield. *B.M.C.* S107 note; *R.I.C.* 25 note
(*Tinchant; the books say* CAES *on obv., but his own catalogue gives* CAE) 35

161 Md. ℞. — As **159a.** *B.M.C.* S117; *R.I.C.* 21 30

162 Lc. ℞. — As last. *B.M.C.* p. 292, *; *R.I.C.* 340 30

163 As last (*base or* Æ). *B.M.C.* p. 292, * note; *R.I.C.* 340 note .. ..

165 Ei. ℞. MONETA AVG., Moneta stg. half-left, holding scales and cornucopiae. *B.M.C.* SG90-4; *R.I.C.* 224 25

166 Gi. ℞. — As last. *B.M.C.* 62-3; *R.I.C.* 236 25

167 Fi. ℞. — As last. *B.M.C.* 74-5; *R.I.C.* 308 25

167a Md. ℞. — As last (Hy ?). *B.M.C.* p. 618 (*Ashmolean*) .. ..

165   168e

168 K, laur. hd. with slight drapery on l. shoulder. ℞. MONETA AVGG.,
Moneta stg. front, hd. l., holding scales and cornucopiae. *B.M.C.* S641 note;
R.I.C. 337 (a) .. ..

168a Kd. ℞. — As last. *B.M.C.* S641 note; *R.I.C.* 337 (b) (*G. R. Arnold*)

168b H, laur. hd. with slight drapery on l. shoulder. ℞. — As last. *B.M.C.*
S645 (pl. 43, 17); *R.I.C.* 337 (c) 30

168c Hc. ℞. — As last. *B.M.C.* S641-2; *R.I.C.* 337 (d) 25

168d As last, but barbarous fabric. *B.M.C.* S641 note; *R.I.C.* 337 note (*R. D.
hoard*) .. ..

168e Hd. ℞. — As **168.** *B.M.C.* S642 (*ex Tinchant cat.*) 30

169 Quinarius. De. ℞. NOBILITAS, Nobilitas stg. r., holding sceptre and
palladium (Hy.; *rev. of Geta*). *B.M.C.* p. 261; *R.I.C.* 162. (*On the Paris
specimen, illustrated by Cohen, two letters of the legends have become filled in
on the die, or removed by tooling*) .. ..

171   175

171 Denarius. De. ℞. PACATOR ORBIS, rad. bust of young Sol dr. r. *B.M.C.*
S514; *R.I.C.* 163 90

172a Dc. ℞. PART . MAX . P . M . TR . P . IIII., two captives seated below
trophy (Hy., *base; rev. of Septimius*). *B.M.C.* SG160 .. .. ..

173 Dc. ℞. PART . MAX . P . M . TR . P . VIIII., as last (Hy.; *rev. of Septimius*).
B.M.C. p. 255 and SG161-2 (*one base*); *R.I.C.* p. 225, * .. ..

174 Dc. ℞. PART . MAX . P . M . TR . P . X., as last (Hy.; *rev. of Septimius*).
B.M.C. p. 267 and SG163; *R.I.C.* p. 226, * .. .. ..

175 Dc. ℞. PART . MAX . PONT . TR . P . III., as last. *B.M.C.* S262-3; *R.I.C.*
54 (b) 25

175a Dd. ℞. — As last. *B.M.C.* S264; *R.I.C.* 54 (a) 30

177 Cc. ℞. PART . MAX . PONT . TR . P . IIII . COS., as last. *B.M.C.* p. 204, *; *R.I.C.* 55 (*wrong obv. legend*) and 346 .. .. £30

177a Cd. ℞. — As last. *B.M.C.* S730; *R.I.C.* 55 note 30

178 Dc. ℞. PART . MAX . PONT . TR . P . V., as last. *B.M.C.* S391 (*see illustration*); *R.I.C.* 63 25

179 Dc. ℞. PART . MAX . PONT . TR . P . V . COS., as last. *B.M.C.* S392; *R.I.C.* 64 25

179a As last, but PON. *B.M.C.* S393 (*see illustration*) and p. 618 (*Oldroyd*); *R.I.C.* 65 25

179b M . AVR . ANT . CAES . PONTIF., b. ℞. — As last (Hy.; *plated*). *B.M.C.* S392 note; *R.I.C.* 65 note .. ..

180 B (*Cohen has* ANT *in error?*) a. ℞. PIETAS, Pietas stg. half-left, raising r. hand over altar and holding box of incense in l. *B.M.C.* W204-5; *R.I.C.* 12 35

181 Cd. ℞. P . MAX . TR . P . III., Roma seated l. on shield, holding Victory and spear or sceptre. *B.M.C.* S716 note; *R.I.C.* 342 (b) 35

181a Cc. ℞. — As last. *B.M.C.* S716-7; *R.I.C.* 342 (a) 30

183 Cd. ℞. P . MAX . TR . P. IIII . COS., Caracalla, veiled, stg. half-left, sacrificing out of patera over lighted tripod and holding roll. *B.M.C.* S727 note; *R.I.C.* 344 (b) 30

183a Cc. ℞. — As last. *B.M.C.* S727-8; *R.I.C.* 344 (a) 30

N.B. *In many cases it is difficult to decide whether a bust is* draped *or* draped and cuirassed. *Sometimes both do not exist even if given, it is just different authorities deciding on different descriptions.*

184 Dd. ℞. — As last. *B.M.C.* S727 note; *R.I.C.* 344 note (*Lawrence*) .. 40

184a De. ℞. P . M . TR . P . II . COS . II . P . P., figure leaning on column, holding cornucopiae, globe at feet. *B.M.C.* p 184; *R.I.C.* p. 216, * (*very doubtful*) .. ..

184b Ei. ℞. P . M . TR . P . IIII . COS . V . P . P., Victory advancing l., holding in both hands open wreath over shield set on base (Hy.). *B.M.C.* SG154; *R.I.C.* 319 .. ..

184c Ci. ℞. P . M . TR . P . VIII . COS . II . P . P., as last (Hy.; *rev. of Septimius*). *B.M.C.* p. 467, 1; *R.I.C.* 319 (a) .. ..

184d Ba. ℞. P . M . TR . P . XI . COS . III . P . P., Fortuna seated l., holding rudder and cornucopiae (Hy.; *rev. of Septimius*). *B.M.C.* SG155 (*base*) ..

185 Ee. ℞. P . M . TR . P . XIII(?) . COS . III . P . P., Caracalla, in military dress, stg. front, holding roll and reversed spear. *B.M.C.* p. 364, (a); *R.I.C.* p. 229, * (*doubtful*) .. ..

185a Ei. ℞. P . M . TR . P . XIIII . COS . III . P . P., Liber (Bacchus) seated on barrel, three-quarter front, hd. l., holding wine-cup and sceptre. *B.M.C.* p. 419, *; *R.I.C.* 182 .. .. .. *Extremely rare, if existence confirmed*

186 Ei. ℞. — Virtus stg. half-right, foot on helmet, holding spear and parazonium. *B.M.C.* p. 420, *; *R.I.C.* 187 25

187 De. ℞. — Annona stg. l., holding corn-ears over modius and cornucopiae (Hy., *plated; rev. of Septimius; ancient forgery*). *B.M.C.* p. 420, (a); *R.I.C.* p. 237, * .. ..

187a As last, but perhaps not plated (Hy.). *B.M.C.* p. 620 (*Oldroyd*); *R.I.C.* p. 261, (a) (*Lawrence*) .. ..

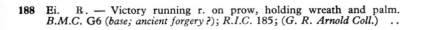

181a 188

188 Ei. ℞. — Victory running r. on prow, holding wreath and palm. *B.M.C.* G6 (*base; ancient forgery?*); *R.I.C.* 185; (*G. R. Arnold Coll.*) .. 35

188a Denarius. ANTONINVS AVGVSTV., e? Ɽ . P . M . TR . P . XIIII . COS . III . P . P., Victory, towered, seated r. on shield, holding palm and globe (Hy.). *B.M.C.* p. 421, (c); *R.I.C.* 185 note

189 Quinarius. Ei. Ɽ. — Victory advancing l., holding wreath and palm. *B.M.C.* G7; *R.I.C.* 186 .. .. £150

190 Denarius. Ei. Ɽ. — Pax running l., holding branch and sceptre. *B.M.C.* G4-5; *R.I.C.* 184 25

191 Di. Ɽ. — Figure running l., raising r. hand and holding bunch of corn-ears. *B.M.C.* p. 421, (b); *R.I.C.* 184 note (*perhaps only a faulty description or hybrid of last piece*) .. ..

192 Ei. Ɽ. — Concordia seated l., holding patera and double cornucopiae. *B.M.C.* p. 419, †; *R.I.C.* 183 40

192a Ei. Ɽ. — As last, but single cornucopiae (*Mazzini cat.*) 40

194 De. Ɽ. — Emperor (Caracalla or Septimius) on horse galloping r., holding spear at rest (Hy.). *B.M.C.* SG156; *R.I.C.* 320 (XVIII *in error*). *The B.M.C. and R.I.C. list* C194 *under* p. 421, (d) *and* 188 *respectively and say not in B.M., forgetting they have it under "hybrids"*

195 Ei. Ɽ. P . M . TR . P . XV . COS . III . P . P., Serapis, wearing modius, stg. front, hd. l., raising r. hand and holding transverse sceptre (*Cohen*, spear). *B.M.C.* 39-41; *R.I.C.* 194 (*misdescribed*) 25

195a As last, but the hd. of Serapis is facing. *B.M.C.* 42; *R.I.C.* 193 (?) .. 25

189   196

196 Ei. Ɽ. — Hercules, naked, stg. half-left, holding branch and club with lion's skin. *B.M.C.* 35-8; *R.I.C.* 192 25

197 Quinarius. As last. *B.M.C.* 36 note; *R.I.C.* 192 (*doubtful*) .. ..

203 Denarius. Ei. Ɽ. — Virtus stg. r., holding spear and parazonium. *B.M.C.* p. 438 (*confirmation needed*) .. ..

204 Quinarius. De. Ɽ. — Victory advancing l., as **189**. (*This piece was illustrated by an engraving in R. Belge Num., 1854 and Mr. Clay says "the piece seems to be a genuine hybrid of 207 A.D., the reverse being from a Severus die"*). *B.M.C.* p. 438, *; *R.I.C.* 197 150

205 Denarius. Ei. Ɽ. — Annona seated l., holding corn-ears over modius and cornucopiae. *B.M.C.* 44; *R.I.C.* 195 25

205a As last, but Annona on throne instead of stool. *B.M.C.* 43 25

206   208

206 Ei. Ɽ. — Salus seated l., feeding, out of patera, snake coiled around altar and holding cornucopiae. *B.M.C.* 45-6; *R.I.C.* 196.. 25

208 Ei. Ɽ. — Elephant walking r. *B.M.C.* 47; *R.I.C.* 199 55

211 Ei. Ɽ. P . M . TR . P . XVI . COS . IIII . P . P., Serapis, as **195**. *B.M.C.* 50-2; *R.I.C.* 208 (a) 25

212 Gi. Ɽ. — As last. *B.M.C.* 56; *R.I.C.* 208 (b) 30

213 Fi. Ɽ. — As last. *B.M.C.* 59; *R.I.C.* 208 (c) 25

216 Ei. ℞. — Mars stg.; behind, two standards. *B.M.C.* p. 441, (a); *R.I.C.* 207 .. ..

220 Ei. ℞. — Hercules, as **196**. *B.M.C.* 48-9; *R.I.C.* 206 (a) £25

221   244

221 Gi. ℞. — As last. *B.M.C.* p. 440, *; *R.I.C.* 206 (b) 30

222 Fi. ℞. — As last. *B.M.C.* 58; *R.I.C.* 206 (c) 25

224 Ei. ℞. — Libertas stg. front, hd. l., holding pileus and rod. *B.M.C.* 53-4; *R.I.C.* 209 (a) 25

226 Gi or l. ℞. — As last. *B.M.C.* 57 note; *R.I.C.* 209 (b) 30

226a De or i. ℞. — As last (Hy.?). *B.M.C.* p. 441, (b); *R.I.C.* 209 (d) ..

229a Fi. ℞. — Caracalla seated l., sacrificing out of patera over tripod, and holding sceptre (Hy.; *base or* Æ). *B.M.C.* p. 441, (c); *R.I.C.* 211 ..

230 Ei. ℞. — Elephant walking r. *B.M.C.* p. 439, *; *R.I.C.* 211A.. .. 60

238 Ei. ℞. P . M . TR . P . XVII . COS . III . P . P., Neptune stg. l., foot on rock, holding dolphin (?) and trident (Hy.; *rev. of Septimius*). *B.M.C.* p. 451, (b); *R.I.C.* p. 246, * .. ..

238a Fi. ℞. — As last (Hy.). *B.M.C.* p. 467, 2; *R.I.C.* 319B .. ..

238b Fi. ℞. — Jupiter stg. l. between two small figures, holding thunderbolt and sceptre (Hy.; *rev. of Septimius*). *B.M.C.* p. 450, (a); *R.I.C.* p. 246, *

238c Ei. ℞. P . M . TR . P . XVII . COS . IIII . P . P., as **238** (Hy. ?) (*Cohen note, Copenhagen*) .. ..

239 Fi. ℞. — Jupiter, naked, but for cloak on shoulder (*C. and R.I.C.*, half-naked), stg. half-left, holding thunderbolt and long sceptre, eagle at feet. *B.M.C.* 94; *R.I.C.* 240 25

239a As last, but no cloak. *B.M.C.* 95 25

241 Fi. ℞. — Serapis, modius on hd., stg. half-left, raising r. hand and holding sceptre. *B.M.C.* 97-8; *R.I.C.* 244 .. .. ..

242 Fi. ℞. — Apollo, naked to waist, seated l., holding branch and leaning on lyre set on tripod. *B.M.C.* 91-2; *R.I.C.* 238A 25

242a Ei. ℞. — As last (Hy.). *B.M.C.* p. 451, (c); *R.I.C.* 238A note (*R. D. hoard*) 40

243 **Antoninianus. Fp.** ℞. — Sol, radiate, stg. l., raising hand and holding globe. *B.M.C.* p. 451; *R.I.C.* 245. *This is a coin of 214 A.D., if it is a true reading, so must be one of the earliest antoniniani, as the main issue does not start until the following year. It may very well be a misreading of* **287** ..

244 **Denarius. Fi** (*Cohen has wrong obv. type in error*). ℞. — Hercules, naked, stg. half-left, holding branch and club with lion's skin. *B.M.C.* 93; *R.I.C.* 239 25

246 Fj. ℞. — Roma stg. l., holding Victory and spear. *B.M.C.* p. 461, (d) (*confirmation required*); *R.I.C.* 243 ..

247 Fi. ℞. — Genius of the Senate (*Cohen* Caracalla *in error*) stg. half-left, holding branch and short sceptre or baton. *B.M.C.* 99; *R.I.C.* 246 .. 25

248 As last (*base or* Æ). *B.M.C.* 99 note; *R.I.C.* 246 note .. ..

251 Fl. ℞. — Four figures sacrificing in front of temple of Vesta. *B.M.C.* 101 note .. ..

251a Fi. ℞. — Elephant (Hy. ?). *B.M.C.* p. 451, (f); *R.I.C.* 250A .. ..

253a Fi. ℞. P . M . TR . P . XVII . IMP . III . COS . IIII . P . P., as **247**. *B.M.C.* 99 note; *R.I.C.* 247 35

277 Antoninianus. Fp. ℞. P . M . TR . P . XVIII . COS . IIII . P . P., Jupiter seated l., holding Victory and eagle, eagle at feet. *B.M.C.* 117; *R.I.C.* 260 (b) £65

277a Fq. ℞. — As last. *B.M.C.* 118 65

277b Fo. ℞. — As last (*B.M., ex Lawrence; Ashmolean; Paris*) 65

278 Fp. ℞. — Jupiter, naked except for cloak on shoulder, stg. half-left, holding thunderbolt and sceptre (*Cohen*, reversed spear). *B.M.C.* 111; *R.I.C.* 259 65

278a Fq. ℞. — As last (*Budapest; Vienna*) 65

279 Fp. ℞. — As last, but Jupiter stg. half-right. *B.M.C.* 110; *R.I.C.* 258 (a) 65

279a Fo. ℞. — As last. *B.M.C.* 112-3; *R.I.C.* 258 (b) 65

279b Denarius. Fi. ℞. — As last. *B.M.C.* 114-5; *R.I.C.* 258 (c) 30

280 Fi. ℞. — As **277** (*base or* Æ). *B.M.C.* 119 note; *R.I.C.* p. 249, † ..

281 Fi. ℞. — As **277**. *B.M.C.* 119; *R.I.C.* p. 249, † 30

282 288

282 Fi. ℞. — Apollo, naked except for cloak from shoulder, stg. front, hd. l., holding branch and leaning on lyre on low base or altar. *B.M.C.* 107-9; *R.I.C.* 254 25

283 Fi. ℞. — Apollo (?), laur., seated l., holding uncertain object and sceptre. *B.M.C.* 107 note; *R.I.C.* 252 note

284 Fi. ℞. — Apollo (?), laur. and in long dress, stg. l., holding branch and leaning on spear. *B.M.C.* 107 note; *R.I.C.* 255 (*Probably misdescription of* **314**) .. ..

287 Antoninianus. Fp. ℞. — Sol, rad., naked except for cloak over shoulder and arm, stg. front, hd. l., raising r. hand and holding globe in l. *B.M.C.* 135, 138; *R.I.C.* 264 (c) 65

287a Fq. ℞. — As last. *B.M.C.* 136-7 65

287b Fo. ℞. — As last. *B.M.C.* 135 note; *R.I.C.* 264 (b) 65

287c Fm. ℞. — As last. *B.M.C.* p. 621 (*Oldroyd*) 65

287d Fn. ℞. — As last. (*Frank Sternberg auction, Nov.* 1981, *lot* 693) .. 65

288 Denarius. Fi. ℞. — As last. *B.M.C.* 139-40; *R.I.C.* 264 (a).. .. 25

289 Antoninianus. Fp. ℞. — Sol, as before, mounting quadriga l., horses galloping. *B.M.C.* 141 note; *R.I.C.* 265 (c). (*The Paris coin Cohen quotes is obv. Fp not Fm*) 75

289a Fq. ℞. — As last. *B.M.C.* 141-2; *R.I.C.* 265 (e) 75

289b Fo. ℞. — As last. *R.I.C.* 265 (d) 75

289c Fn. ℞. — As last. *Mazzini* pl. 30 75

289b 294

292 Denarius. Fi. ℞. — Bacchus (?) stg. l., holding branch and thyrsus. *B.M.C.* p. 459; *R.I.C.* p. 249, * (*very doubtful*) (*Perhaps a misdescription of* **314**) ..   ..

294 Antoninianus. Fo. ℞. — Diana or Luna, crescent on hd. and fold of drapery in circle around hd., in biga of oxen prancing l. *B.M.C.* 121; *R.I.C.* 256 (b). *Illustrated at bottom of last page* £75

294a Fp. ℞. — As last. *B.M.C.* 120; *R.I.C.* 256 (c)   75

294b Fq. ℞. — As last. *B.M.C.* 120 note; *R.I.C.* 256 (c)   75

295 Fo. ℞. — Serapis, modius on hd., stg. front, hd. l., raising r. hand and holding long sceptre (*Cohen,* spear) in l. *B.M.C.* 128-9; *R.I.C.* 263 (d) .. 65

295a Fp. ℞. — As last. *B.M.C.* 120; *R.I.C.* 263 (e) 65

295b Fq. ℞. — As last. *B.M.C.* 126-7, 131; *R.I.C.* 263 (e) note   65

295c Fq, with aegis. ℞. — As last. (*Brussels*) 65

295d Fn. ℞. — As last. *B.M.C.* 126 note; *R.I.C.* 263 (c) (*Brussels*)..   .. 65

295   296

296 Denarius. Fi. ℞. — As last. *B.M.C.* 133; *R.I.C.* 263 (f)   30

297 Antoninianus. Fp. ℞. — Pluto or Minos, modius on hd., seated l., holding sceptre or grasping top of throne, and extending r. hand towards Minotaur stg. at his feet. *B.M.C.* 122; *R.I.C.* 262 (b)   90

297a Fm, or o or q. ℞. — As last. *B.M.C.* 122 note; *R.I.C.* 262 (a) 90

297b Denarius. Fi. ℞. — As last. *B.M.C.* 122 note; *R.I.C.* 262 (c) (*R. D. hoard*) 35

299 Fi. ℞. — Pluto, modius on hd., seated l. on stool, holding sceptre and extending r. hand towards Cerberus at his feet. *B.M.C.* 125; *R.I.C.* 261 (a) 30

299a Antoninianus. Fo. ℞. — As last. *B.M.C.* 124; *R.I.C.* 261 (c) (*draped in error*)..   75

299b Fp. ℞. — As last. *B.M.C.* 123; *R.I.C.* 261 (d) 75

299c Fq. ℞. — As last, but Pluto seated on throne. (*G. R. Arnold*) 75

299   302

302 Denarius. F (*Cohen omits* GERM *in error*) i. ℞. — Aesculapius stg. front, hd. l., holding serpent-entwined wand; globe on ground r. *B.M.C.* 103-4; *R.I.C.* 251   .. 30

302a Ei. ℞. — As last, but TR.I for TR.P. (Hy.). *B.M.C.* G157 (*slightly odd style; base*)   ..   ..

306 Fi. ℞. — As **302**, but no globe. *B.M.C.* 103 note; *R.I.C.* 252   ..

307 Fi. ℞. — As **302**, but Aesculapius with hd. facing and on l. stands small figure of Telesphorus. *B.M.C.* 105-6; *R.I.C.* 253   30

308 As last (*base or* Æ). *B.M.C.* 105 note; *R.I.C.* 253 note ..   ..   ..

313a Dc. ℞. — Concordia stg. front, hd. l., holding a standard in each hand (Hy.). *B.M.C.* G158 (*odd style*)   ..   ..

314 Denarius. Fi. ℞. P . M . TR . P . XVIII . COS . IIII . P . P., Pax stg. half-left, holding branch and sceptre. *B.M.C.* 147; *R.I.C.* 268 .. .. £25

315   337

315 Fi. ℞. — Fides Militum stg. front, hd. l., holding a standard in each hand. *B.M.C.* 143-5; *R.I.C.* 266 25
316 Fi. ℞. — As last, but an extra standard r. and l. *B.M.C.* 146; *R.I.C.* 267 25
321 Fi. ℞. — Lion, radiate, walking l., holding thunderbolt in its jaws. *B.M.C.* 151; *R.I.C.* 273 (e) 55
322 Antoninianus. Fp. ℞. — As last. *B.M.C.* 150; *R.I.C.* 273 (d) .. 90
322a Fm. ℞. — As last. *B.M.C.* 150 note; *R.I.C.* 273 (c) 90
322b Fo. ℞. — As last (*B.M. ex Lawrence, Paris, etc.*) 90
337 Denarius. Fi. ℞. P . M . TR . P . XVIIII . COS . IIII . P . P., Jupiter, naked except for cloak on shoulder, stg. half-right, looking back l., holding thunderbolt and long sceptre. *B.M.C.* 155-6; *R.I.C.* 275 (a) 25
338 Antoninianus. Fn. ℞. — As last. *B.M.C.* 152-3; *R.I.C.* 275 (b) .. 65
338a Fq. ℞. — As last. *B.M.C.* 154; *R.I.C.* 275 (c) 65
340 Denarius. Fi. ℞. — As **337,** but with eagle l. before Jupiter. *B.M.C.* 155 note; *R.I.C.* 276 30
342 Antoninianus. Fq. ℞. — Jupiter, half-naked, seated l., holding Victory and sceptre, eagle before. *B.M.C.* 158 note; *R.I.C.* 277 (a) .. 65

342a   358

342a Fn. ℞. — As last. *B.M.C.* 158; *R.I.C.* 277 (b) 65
343 Denarius. Fi. ℞. — As last. *B.M.C.* 159-60; *R.I.C.* 277 (c).. .. 25
346 Antoninianus. Fp or q. ℞. — Jupiter seated, holding sceptre and feeding eagle. *B.M.C.* 158 note; *R.I.C.* 278 .. ..
348 Denarius. Fi. ℞. — Serapis, modius on hd., stg. front, hd. l., raising r. hand and holding sceptre. *B.M.C.* 168; *R.I.C.* 280 (c) 25
349 Antoninianus. Fp. ℞. — As last. *B.M.C.* 167; *R.I.C.* 280 (e) .. 65
349a Fq. ℞. — As last (*B.M. ex Lawrence, Paris, etc.*) 65
349b Fn. ℞. — As last. *B.M.C.* 165-6; *R.I.C.* 280 (d) 65
352a Fn. ℞. — Pluto seated l., with Cerberus, as **299.** *B.M.C.* 163; *R.I.C.* 279 90
352b Denarius. Fi. ℞. — Pluto or Minos seated l., with Minotaur, as **297.** *B.M.C.* p. 460, *; *R.I.C.* 279A 40
355 Fi. ℞. — Sol mounting quadriga l., as **289.** *B.M.C.* 176; *R.I.C.* 282 (f) 40
356 Antoninianus. Fn. ℞. — As last. *B.M.C.* 175; *R.I.C.* 282 (e) .. 75
358 Fn. ℞. — Sol, radiate, stg. front, hd. l., raising r. hand and holding globe. *B.M.C.* 170-1; *R.I.C.* 281 (a) 65

358a Fq. ℞. P . M . TR . P . XVIIII . COS . IIII . P . P., as last *B.M.C.* 169
(*Dorchester hoard*) £65

358b As last (*base*). *B.M.C.* 169 note .. ..

359 Denarius. Fi. ℞. — As **358**. *B.M.C.* 172-3; *R.I.C.* 281 (b) 25

362 Fi. ℞. — Diana or Luna in biga of bulls l., as **294**. *B.M.C.* 162;
R.I.C. 274 (a) 45

362a As last (*base*). *B.M.C.* 162 note; *R.I.C.* 274 (a) note .. .. ..

363 Antoninianus. Fq (and p ?). ℞. — As **362**. *B.M.C.* 161 note and
p. 640 (*Oldroyd*); *R.I.C.* 274 (c) 75

363a Fn. ℞. — As last. *B.M.C.* 161; *R.I.C.* 274 (b) 75

367 Denarius. Fi. ℞. — Lion, radiate, walking l., holding thunderbolt in
jaws. *B.M.C.*178; *R.I.C.* 283 (c) 55

368   374a

368 Antoninianus. Fn. ℞. — As last. *B.M.C.* 177 note; *R.I.C.* 283 (b) 90

368a Fp. ℞. — As last. *B.M.C.* 177; *R.I.C.* 283 (b) 90

368b Fq. ℞. — As last (*Vienna*) 90

373 Denarius. Fi. ℞. P . M . TR . P . XX . COS . IIII . P . P., Jupiter, naked
except for cloak from shoulder, stg. half-left, holding thunderbolt and
sceptre. *B.M.C.* 181; *R.I.C.* 285 (a) 25

373a Fi. ℞. — As last, but Jupiter stg. front, inclined to r., hd. l., and holds
the thunderbolt down at his side. *B.M.C.* 180 25

374 Antoninianus. Fq. ℞. — As **373**. *B.M.C.* 179; *R.I.C.* 285 (d) .. 65

374a Fn. ℞. — As last. *B.M.C.* 179 note; *R.I.C.* 285 (c); (*Mazzini cat.*) .. 65

375 Fq. ℞. — As before, but reversed spear for sceptre. *B.M.C.* 179 note;
R.I.C. 285 (a) note 65

378 Denarius. Fi (*Cohen has obv. k, probably in error*). ℞. — Jupiter,
naked to waist, seated l. on throne, holding patera and sceptre. *B.M.C.*
183; *R.I.C.* 287a 30

380 Fi. ℞. — As last, but with eagle at feet. *B.M.C.* 183 note; *R.I.C.* 288 30

380a Antoninianus. Fq. ℞. — As **378** (*Vienna*) 90

382 Denarius. Fi. ℞. — Serapis, modius on hd., stg. front, hd. l., holding
wreath (?; *Cohen says* corn-ears) and sceptre. *B.M.C.* 188; *R.I.C.* 289 (c) 25

382a Fi. ℞. — As before, but Serapis raising r. hand and holding sceptre.
B.M.C. 188 note; *R.I.C.* 290 30

383 Antoninianus. Fp and/or q. ℞. — As **382**. *R.I.C.* 289 (f) (*B.M. ex
Lawrence, Paris, etc.*) 75

383a Fo. ℞. — As last. *B.M.C.* 187; *R.I.C.* 289 (e) 75

383b Fm or n. ℞. — As last. *R.I.C.* 289 (d) 75

385 Denarius. Fi. ℞. — Serapis seated l., holding uncertain object and
sceptre. *B.M.C.* 189; *R.I.C.* 291 (b) 30

386 Antoninianus. Fq. ℞. — As last. *B.M.C.* 189 note; *R.I.C.* 291 (c) 75

389 Denarius. Fi. ℞. P . M . TR . P . XX . COS . IIII . P . P., Sol, rad., stg.
half-left, raising r. hand and holding whip in l. *B.M.C.* 194; *R.I.C.* 293 (d)   £25

390 Antoninianus. Fn. ℞. — As last. *B.M.C.* 192-3; *R.I.C.* 293 (e) ..   65

390a Fq. ℞. — As last. *B.M.C.* 191; *R.I.C.* 293 (f)   65

390b Denarius. Fi. ℞. — As before, but Sol holds globe instead of whip.
B.M.C. p. 621 (*Ashmolean*)   30

390c Antoninianus. Fn. ℞. — As last (*Paris*)   75

390d Fq. ℞. — As last (*Rome*)   75

391a Denarius. Fi. ℞. — Sol, rad., mounting galloping quadriga l., raising
r. hand and holding whip. *B.M.C.* 195 note; *R.I.C.* 294 (c)   ..   ..

395 Fi (*Cohen has* Fl, *probably in error*). ℞. — Diana or Luna in biga of
bulls l., as **294.** *B.M.C.* 185; *R.I.C.* 284 (d)   45

396 Antoninianus. Fn. ℞. — As last. *B.M.C.* 184 note; *R.I.C.* 284 (a) ..   75

396a Fq. ℞. — As last. *B.M.C.* 184 (*This is probably the same as* **396** *differently
cataloged*)   75

400 *This denarius is probably* **650** *with* VIC . PART. *in ex. not showing*   ..

400a Fn (?) ℞. As **400** (*R. D. hoard*) (*This antoninianus could be* **648a**)   ..   140

402 Denarius. Fi. ℞. — Lion, rad., running l., holding thunderbolt in
jaws. *B.M.C.* 196 note; *R.I.C.* 296 (c)   55

402a Antoninianus. Fq. ℞. — As last (*Vienna*)   100

404a Denarius. Cc. ℞. PONTIFEX COS., Minerva stg. l., holding spear and
leaning on shield (Hy.; *rev. of Geta*). *B.M.C.* p. 620, A178A (*Ashmolean*)

390   406

406 Mc. ℞. PONTIFEX TR . P . II., Caracalla, in military dress with cloak
hanging from shoulder, stg. half-left, holding Victory on globe and reversed
spear captive seated l. before him. *B.M.C.* S153-5; *R.I.C.* 27 (a)   ..   30

406a K, but CAES., c. ℞. — As last (Hy., *good style*). *B.M.C.* p. 184   30

406b Mc. ℞. — Securitas seated r., resting r. arm on back of throne and
holding sceptre; before her, lighted altar. *B.M.C.* p. 183, *; *R.I.C.* 26A   35

408 Cd. ℞. PONTIFEX TR . P . III., as **406.** *B.M.C.* S718 note; *R.I.C.* 343 ..

413 Cd. ℞. PONTIF . TR . P . III., Caracalla, as Sol, stg. front, hd. l., holding
globe and spear. *B.M.C.* S179-83; *R.I.C.* 30 (a)   25

413a Cc. ℞. — As last. *B.M.C.* S179 note; *R.I.C.* 30 (b)   25

414 Fi. ℞. — As last (Hy.). *B.M.C.* p. 190; *R.I.C.* 30 note   ..   ..

415 Is a duplication of **413** and **413a**   ..   ..

415a Cc. ℞. PONTIF . TR . P . IIII., as last (Hy.). *B.M.C.* p. 204 (*in B.M.,
ancient forgery?*)   ..   ..

415b Dc. ℞. — As last *B.M.C.* p. 205; *R.I.C.* 55A (*R. D. hoard*)   35

416 Dc. ℞. PONTIF . TR . P . VI . COS., Roma, in military dress, stg. half-left,
holding Victory and reversed spear (Hy?). *B.M.C.* p. 241, *; *R.I.C.* 71

417 Cd. ℞. — As last (Hy.). *B.M.C.* p. 241; *R.I.C.* 71 note   ..   ..

420 Df. ℞. PONTIF . TR . P . VIII . COS . II., Mars, naked except for cloak from shoulder, stg. half-left, foot on helmet, holding branch and spear. *B.M.C.* S480; *R.I.C.* 80 (b) £25
420a Df. ℞. — As last, but spear reversed. *B.M.C.* S481 25
420b Dg. ℞. — As last. *B.M.C.* S478 25
420c Dg. ℞. — As last, but spear not reversed. *B.M.C.* S479 25
421 Df. ℞. — Mars, in military dress, stg. half-left, leaning on shield and holding spear reversed. *B.M.C.* S482-3; *R.I.C.* 81 25
422 Df. ℞. — Salus seated l., feeding, out of patera, snake coiling up from altar; her l. arm rests on side of throne. *B.M.C.* S484-6; *R.I.C.* 82 .. 25
423a Df. ℞. — Emperor stg. l., holding Victory and spear. *B.M.C.* p. 251; *R.I.C.* 82A .. ..
424 De, with and without side-whiskers. ℞. PONTIF . TR . P . VIIII . COS . II., Mars, as **421**. *B.M.C.* S498; *R.I.C.* 83 25
424a Df. ℞. — As last. *B.M.C.* S497; *R.I.C.* 83 25
424b De. ℞. — As before, but spear not reversed. *B.M.C.* S499-502; *R.I.C.* 83 25
425 As one of the last three (*base or Æ*). *B.M.C.* S497 note; *R.I.C.* 83 note
426a Df. ℞. — Liber stg. l., in car drawn by four leopards, holding cup and thyrsus (*Paris*) 150

420a   427

427 De. ℞. — Caracalla, in military dress, on horse galloping r., holding spear at rest. *B.M.C.* S503; *R.I.C.* 84 45
427a As before, but Caracalla helmeted. *B.M.C.* S504 (*curious style, ancient forgery?*) .. ..
429a De. ℞. — Galley l., with captain, steersman, etc. (*perhaps as* **443**). *B.M.C.* p. 255, †; *R.I.C.* 85A 65
431 De. ℞. PONTIF . TR . P . X . COS . II., Mars, naked except for cloak flying from waist, advancing r., holding spear and trophy over shoulder. *B.M.C.* S542-6; *R.I.C.* 88 25
432 De. ℞. — Mars stg. half-left, as **421**. *B.M.C.* S547-8; *R.I.C.* 89 .. 25
433 **Quinarius.** De. ℞. — Victory advancing l., holding wreath and palm. *R.I.C.* 94 150
433a As last, but with aegis or drapery on l. shoulder. *B.M.C.* 551 (*see illustration*) 150
434 **Denarius.** De. ℞. — Securitas seated l., on chair with legs and sides formed by crossed cornuacopiae, resting hd. on r. hand and holding sceptre; before her, lighted altar. *B.M.C.* S549-50; *R.I.C.* 92 .. 25
434a De. ℞. — As last, but no altar. *B.M.C.* S549 note; *R.I.C.* 93 .. 30
436 De. ℞. — Caracalla on horse galloping r., holding spear (as **427**). *B.M.C.* p. 267, *; *R.I.C.* 97 50
440 De. ℞. — Caracalla, in military dress, stg. half-right, r. foot on helmet, holding reversed spear and parazonium. *B.M.C.* S552-4; *R.I.C.* 95 .. 25
440a As last, but foot on globe. *B.M.C.* S552 note; *R.I.C.* 95 note (*probably a different interpretation of the previous coin*) 25

441 Denarius. De. ℞. PONTIF . TR . P . X . COS . II., Caracalla, in military dress, stg. front, hd. r., holding reversed spear and parazonium; at his feet, on l., river god reclining r. on urn; to r., two captives seated l., hands tied behind their backs. *B.M.C.* S555-6; *R.I.C.* 96 .. .. .. £50

442 As last, but only one captive on r. *B.M.C.* S555 note; *R.I.C.* 96 note .. 55

443 De. ℞. PONTIF . TR . P . X. around, COS . II. in ex., galley moving l., pilot or Caracalla seated under arched stern, with two rudders. *B.M.C.* S557; *R.I.C.* 98 100

445a De. ℞. PONTIF . TR . P . XI . COS . II., emperor on horseback r. *Seaby's Bull., Apr.* 1937, 39740 50

446-7   456a

446 and 447 De. ℞. PONTIF . TR . P . XI . COS . III., Mars, in military dress, with cloak floating behind, stg. front (or moving slowly l.), looking r., holding spear and shield. *B.M.C.* S569-70; *R.I.C.* 100 (*Cohen has* **446,** Mars stg. r.; **447,** Mars stg. r. in fighting attitude) 25

450 Quinarius. De. ℞. — Victory l., as **433.** *B.M.C.* 5571; *R.I.C.* 101 150

450a As last, but slight drapery on far shoulder (*Tinchant cat.*) 150

451 Denarius. De. ℞. — Caracalla in quadriga l. (*Vienna*). *B.M.C.* p. 271, † note; *R.I.C.* 104 100

453 De. ℞. — Caracalla, veiled, stg. l., sacrificing over tripod, between victimarius with bull and flute player. *B.M.C.* p. 271, ‡ note; *R.I.C.* 105 *Confirmation is required that this really exists*

456 De. ℞. — Caracalla and Geta seated on platform; between them, Severus stg. in priestly attire. *B.M.C.* p. 271, § note (*specimen now in B.M.*); *R.I.C.* 106 350

456a De. ℞. — Caracalla on horseback r., holding spear. *B.M.C.* p. 271, *; *R.I.C.* 102 (*G. R. Arnold*) 55

460 Dh. ℞. PONTIF . TR . P . XII . COS . III., Mars stg. r., holding spear and shield. *B.M.C.* p. 358, †; *R.I.C.* 110 .. ..

464   468

464 Dh. ℞. — Virtus, in military dress, stg. half-right, foot on helmet, holding reversed spear and parazonium. *B.M.C.* SG13; *R.I.C.* 112 .. 25

464a Ei. ℞. — As last (Hy., *base*). *B.M.C.* SG13 note; *R.I.C.* 112 note (*Lawrence*) .. ..

465 Dh. ℞. — Concordia seated l. on throne, holding patera and double cornucopiae. *B.M.C.* SG10-12; *R.I.C.* 111 25

466 As last (*base or Æ*). *B.M.C.* SG10 note; *R.I.C.* 111 note .. ..

468 Di. ℞. — Caracalla, in military dress, cloak floating behind, on horse galloping l., brandishing javelin at foeman on ground before him. *B.M.C.* SG14; *R.I.C.* 113 45

470 Ei. ℞. — As last (Hy.). *B.M.C.* SG14 note; *R.I.C.* 113 note ..

477 Di. ℞. PONTIF . TR . P . XIII . COS . III., Virtus stg. half-right, as **464**.
    B.M.C. SG32-3; *R.I.C.* 117 (a) £25
477a As last (*base*). *B.M.C.* SG164 .. ..
478 Ei. ℞. — As last. *B.M.C.* SG37-8; *R.I.C.* 117 (b) 25
483 Ei. ℞. — Concordia seated l., as **465**. *B.M.C.* SG34-6; *R.I.C.* 116 (b) 25
484 Di. ℞. — As last. *B.M.C.* SG 29-31; *R.I.C.* 116 (a) 25
485 Ei. ℞. — Concordia seated l. before altar, holding cornucopiae. *B.M.C.*
    SG29 note; *R.I.C.* 116 (b) note .. ..
486 Di. ℞. — Caracalla galloping l., as **468**. *B.M.C.* p. 363, ‡; *R.I.C.* 118 (a) 50
487 Ei. ℞. — As last. *B.M.C.* SG39; *R.I.C.* 118 (b) 45
493 Ei. ℞. PONTIF . TR . P . XIIII . COS . III. (*Cohen has* TR . P . XIII. *in error*),
    Concordia seated l., as **465**. *B.M.C.* SG113; *R.I.C.* 183 .: .. 25
494 Ei. ℞. — Virtus stg. half-right, as **464**. *B.M.C.* SG115; *R.I.C.* 191 .. 25
494a As last (*base*). *B.M.C.* SG114 (*slightly coarse style*) .. .. ..
498 Cd. ℞. PONT . TR . P . II., Securitas seated r. before a lighted altar, resting
    hd. on r. hand and holding sceptre. *B.M.C.* 157 (*possibly cast*); *R.I.C.* S29 25
498a Cc. ℞. — As last. *B.M.C.* S156 25
498b Mc. ℞. — As last (*Tinchant cat.*) 35
499 Dc. ℞. PONT . TR . P . VI . COS., Roma, in military dress, stg. half-left,
    holding Victory and reversed spear. *B.M.C.* S435-6; *R.I.C.* 69 .. 25
499a Dd. ℞. — As last. *B.M.C.* S434 25
499b Cc. ℞. — As last (Hy.). *B.M.C.* p. 241; *R.I.C.* 69 note (*R. D. hoard*)
500a D, boy's bust laur. r? ℞. PON . TR . P . VI . COS., as last (Hy?). *B.M.C.*
    p. 241, * note; *R.I.C.* 72 .. ..
501a De. ℞. PRIMI DECENALES in wreath (Æ ?, *forgery* ?) .. .. ..
502 Df. ℞. PRINC . IVVENT., prince stg. l., holding branch and reversed spear
    (Hy.; *rev. of Geta*). *B.M.C.* p. 212, (c); *R.I.C.* 140 .. ..
502a Cd. ℞. PRINC . IVVENTVTIS, prince stg. l., holding branch and sceptre;
    behind, shield against trophy (Hy.; *rev. of Geta*). *B.M.C.* p. 188; *R.I.C.*
    38A .. ..
503 Ei. ℞. — Caracalla stg. l., holding baton and sceptre; behind, sceptre
    (*barbarous fabric*). *B.M.C.* p. 375, (f); *R.I.C.* p. 244, * .. .. ..
503a Dc. ℞. — As **502a** (Hy.). *B.M.C.* p. 620, A179 (*Oldroyd*) .. ..
505 Bb. ℞. PRINCIPI IVVENTVTIS, Caracalla, in military dress with paluda-
    mentum over shoulder, holding baton and spear (*Cohen*, sceptre); to r.,
    trophy. *B.M.C.* W208 and W458; *R.I.C.* 13 (b) and 329 30
505a Ba. ℞. — As last. *B.M.C.* W209-13; *R.I.C.* 13 (a) 30

508   509a

508 Ei. ℞. PROFECTIO AVG., Caracalla, in military dress, stg. half-right,
    holding spear in both hands; behind him, two standards. *B.M.C.* SG97-8;
    R.I.C. 225 35
509 Ei. ℞. — As last, but behind, attendant holding standard. *B.M.C.*
    SG95-6; *R.I.C.* 226 40
509a As last, but soldier is closer to Caracalla and standard is held aloft.
    Seaby's Bull. Jan. 1942 (*G. R. Arnold*) 45

510 Denarius. De. ℞. PROF . in ex., PONTIF . TR . P . XI . COS . III. around, Caracalla, in military attire, on horse walking r., holding spear; before him, foeman kneeling r., raising r. hand. *B.M.C.* S574-5; *R.I.C.* 108.. .. £40

511 De. ℞. — As last, but without foeman. *B.M.C.* S572; *R.I.C.* 107 .. 45

512   542

512 De. ℞. — (*Cohen has* TR . P . VI. *in error*), as last, but soldier or Virtus walks in front, perhaps leading horse, and holding spear and shield. *B.M.C.* S573; *R.I.C.* 107 note 55

525 Is a coin of Elagabalus .. ..

525a Fi. ℞. PROVID . DEORVM, Providentia stg. half-left, holding wand over globe and sceptre (Hy.; *rev. of Geta*). (*Charles Davis*) .. .. ..

526 De. ℞. PROVIDENTIA, winged hd. of Medusa, facing. *B.M.C.* p. 258, †; *R.I.C.* 164 250

527 De. ℞. — Hd. of Medusa on aegis, facing. *B.M.C.* p. 258, ‡; *R.I.C.* 165 250

527a Ei. ℞. PROVIDENTIA DEORVM, as next, but cornucopiae for sceptre (Hy. ?) (*Brussels*) .. ..

529 Ei. ℞. PROVIDENTIAE DEORVM, Providentia stg. front, hd. l., holding wand over globe and sceptre. *B.M.C.* SG99-100; *R.I.C.* 227 25

542 Cd. ℞. RECTOR ORBIS, Caracalla as Sol, naked, but cloak falling over shoulder, stg. front, rad. hd. l., holding globe and reversed spear. *B.M.C.* S165; *R.I.C.* 39 (a) 25

542a Cc. ℞. — As last. *B.M.C.* S164; *R.I.C.* 39 (b) 25

545 Dc. ℞. — As last. *B.M.C.* S289-92; *R.I.C.* 141 (*Cohen has this as* 'MB', *but he probably has the denominations of* 546 *and* 545 *reversed*) 25

545a Dd. ℞. — As last. *B.M.C.* S293-4 25

545b Dc. ℞. — As last (*base*). *B.M.C.* SG165 .. ..

547 Cd. ℞. RECTORI ORBIS, as last. *B.M.C.* S166-8; *R.I.C.* 40 .. 30

549 De. ℞. RESTITVTOR VRBIS, Roma seated l., holding palladium (*Cohen*, Victory) and spear; at side of chair, round shield. *B.M.C.* S515-6; *R.I.C.* 166 30

549a Ic. ℞. — Roma seated l. on cuirass, holding Victory and spear; at side, shield on base (Hy. ?). *B.M.C.* p. 284; *R.I.C.* p. 264, † (*doubtful*) ..

551 Ei. ℞. — As 549 (Hy.; *ancient forgery*). *B.M.C.* p. 375, (g); *R.I.C.* 228

553 Cc. ℞. — Emperor, in military dress, stg. l., sacrificing out of patera over tripod and holding spear (Hy.; *rev. of Septimius*). *B.M.C.* p. 188, (c); *R.I.C.* 41 .. ..

553a Ei. ℞. — As last (Hy.). *B.M.C.* p. 620, A180 (*Oldroyd; very base*) ..

554a Dd. ℞. ROMA AETERNA, as 549. *B.M.C.* p. 210, †; *R.I.C.* 143 (*Lawrence*) 35

554b Dd. ℞. ROMAE AETERNAE, as last. *B.M.C.* p. 210, † note; *R.I.C.* 143 note *Lawrence; curious and inferior style*).. .. ..

554c Df. ℞. SACRA SAECVLARIA, Sept. Severus, Caracalla and Geta sacrificing over altar before a temple. (*Leu auction, May* 1981, *lot* 498) 500

557 Ba. ℞. SAECVLI FELICITAS, Felicitas stg. l., holding caduceus, l. hand at side. *B.M.C.* p. 54; *R.I.C.* 14 35

558 Cc. ℞. SAL . GEN . HVM., Salus stg. half-left, holding serpent-wreathed sceptre and extending r. hand to figure kneeling before her. *B.M.C.* S169 note; *R.I.C.* 42 (a) 50

558a   573a

558a Cd. ℞. — As last. *B.M.C.* S169-70 and S701-2; *R.I.C.* 42 (c) and 350 £45
558b As **558** (*plated*). *Seaby's Bull., Apr.* 1937, 39746 .. ..
559 Is a coin of Elagabalus .. ..
560 Fi. ℞. SALVS ANTONINI AVG., Salus stg., feeding snake (Hy.; *rev. of Elagabalus*). *B.M.C.* p. 468, 3; *R.I.C.* 324 .. ..
562 Ab. ℞. SECVRITAS PERPETVA, Minerva, with aegis on breast, stg. half-left, resting r. hand on oval shield and holding reversed spear (*Cohen*, sceptre). *B.M.C.* W181 note; *R.I.C.* 2.. 35
562a Aa. ℞. — As last. *B.M.C.*₁W181-2 35
566 Bb. ℞. — As last. *B.M.C.* W459-62; *R.I.C.* 330 35
566a Ba. ℞. — As last (*Mazzini cat.*) 35
567 As **566** (*base or* Æ). *B.M.C.* W459 note; *R.I.C.* 330 note 35
568 Jd. ℞. SECVRITAS PVBLICA, Securitas seated l., holding globe, l. arm resting on throne. *B.M.C.* S647-9; *R.I.C.* 332 30
569 De. ℞. SECVRITAS TEMPORVM, Securitas stg. *B.M.C.* p. 261, (e); *R.I.C.* 168 note .. ..
570 De? ℞. SECVRIT. IMPERI or IMPERII, Securitas seated r. on curule chair, with cornuacopiae as arms, propping hd. on r. hand and holding sceptre or spear; before, altar. *B.M.C.* S516A-17; *R.I.C.* 168 30
571 Md. ℞. SECVRIT . ORBIS, as last, but seated on throne. *B.M.C.* S118; *R.I.C.* 22 (b) 30
571a Md, but hd. *left*. ℞. — As last. (*G. R. Arnold*) 250
571b Mc. ℞. — As last. *B.M.C.* S119-20; *R.I.C.* 22 (a) 30
572 Cc. ℞. — As last. *B.M.C.* S171; *R.I.C.* 43 30
573a Cd. ℞. — As before, but Securitas seated l., and no altar. *B.M.C.* p. 187, * note and S703-9; *R.I.C.* 44 (b) and 351 (b) 30
574 Cc. ℞. — As last. *B.M.C.* p. 187, *; *R.I.C.* 44 (a) and 351 (a) .. 30

574a   590

574a Cc. ℞. — Securitas stg. l., leaning against column, holding sceptre (*Laodicea ad Mare; G. R. Arnold*) 40
587 Aa and/or b. ℞. SEVERI AVG . PII FIL., lituus, knife, jug, simpulum and sprinkler. *B.M.C.* W184-8; *R.I.C.* 4 40
588 Bb. ℞. — As last. *B.M.C.* p. 55 (Hy.?); *R.I.C.* 15 40
590 Cd. ℞. SEVERI PII AVG . FIL., Caracalla, in military dress, stg. front, hd. l., holding Victory on globe and spear reversed; at his feet, captive seated l. in attitude of sadness. *B.M.C.* S172-3; *R.I.C.* 45.. 30
594 Aa and/or b. ℞. SPEI PERPETVAE, Spes walking l., holding flower and raising skirt. *B.M.C.* W190-2; *R.I.C.* 5 30
597 Bb. ℞. — As last. *B.M.C.* p. 55 (Hy.?); *R.I.C.* 16 .. .. ..

599 Denarius. Kc. ℞. SPES PVBLICA, Spes walking l., holding flower and
raising skirt. *B.M.C.* S114 (*letterpress gives* CAES *on obv., but illustration
does not confirm this, it might be there is an* S *below first stroke of* M) *and*
p. 283, * note; *R.I.C.* 26 (a) and 338 (b) £25

600 Lc. ℞. — As last. *B.M.C.* p. 183, † and 697-8; *R.I.C.* 28 and 341 (a)   25
       — *ʌs* last. *B.M.C.* S696; *R.I.C.* 341 (b)   25
600b Md. ℞. — As last. *B.M.C.* p. 174, *; *R.I.C.* 22A   30
600c M, but AVG. for AVR, c. ℞. — As last. *B.M.C.* p. 284, §; *R.I.C.* 330B
       (*R. D. hoard*)   30

600   608

604 Antoninianus. Fq. ℞. VENERI VICTRICI, Venus stg. half-left, holding
Victory and sceptre and leaning on shield set on helmet. *B.M.C.* 77 note;
R.I.C. 310 (b)   70
604a Fo. ℞. — As last. *B.M.C.* 77; *R.I.C.* 310 (a)   70
   b Fm. ℞. — As last (*Ashmolean*)   70
604c Fp or q. ℞. — Venus stg. l., holding helmet and sceptre; at side,
       captive seated. *B.M.C.* 77 note; *R.I.C.* 310 (b) note (*R. D. hoard*)   ..   75
606 Denarius. Fi. ℞. VENVS VICTRIX, as **604**. *B.M.C.* 82-5; *R.I.C.* 311 (b) ..   25
606a Fi. ℞. — As last, but without helmet. *B.M.C.* 82 note; *R.I.C.* 311 (b)
       note   25

608c   612b

608 Antoninianus. Fp. ℞. — As **604**. *B.M.C.* 79; *R.I.C.* 311 (c)   ..   65
608a Fq. ℞. — As last. *B.M.C.* 78 (*obv. misdescribed; also Rome*)   65
608b Fm. ℞. — As last (*Ashmolean*)   65
608c Fn. ℞. — As last. *B.M.C.* 80-81; (*obv. m in error*) *R.I.C.* 311 (d)   ..   65
612 Fo. ℞. — Venus stg. half-left, holding helmet and sceptre, leaning on
       shield; captive seated on either side. *B.M.C.* 86 note; *R.I.C.* 312 (b) ..   65
612a Fm. ℞. — As last. *B.M.C.* 86 note; *R.I.C.* 312 (a)   65
612b Fq. ℞. — As last, but the shield is set on one of the captives. *B.M.C.* 86
       (*obv. p, in error; see pl.*); *R.I.C.* 312 (c)   65
613 Denarius. Fi. ℞. — As **612**. *B.M.C.* 87-8; *R.I.C.* 312 (d)   30
614 Cc. ℞. VICT . AETERN., Victory advancing or flying l., holding in both
       hands open wreath over shield on base. *B.M.C.* S174 note; *R.I.C.* 47 (b)   30
614a Cd. ℞. — As last. *B.M.C.* S174; *R.I.C.* 47 (a). *Illus. on next page*   30
614b De. ℞. — As last (Hy.). *R.I.C.* p. 261, (c) (*Lawrence*) ..   ..   ..
614c Cc. ℞. VICT . AETERNAE, as last. *B.M.C.* S174 note; *R.I.C.* 48   30
615 Mc. ℞. As **614** and/or last (Hy.?). *B.M.C.* p. 174, †; *R.I.C.* 23   ..   30

616 Quinarius. Cd. ℞. VICT . AVGG., Victory advancing l., holding wreath
and palm. £150
616a ANTONINVS CAES . AVG., c. ℞. — As last (Hy.). *B.M.C.* p. 212; *R.I.C.*
p. 233, * (*doubtful*) .. ..
616b Df. ℞. — As last (*B.M.*) 150

614a · 618

618 Tetradrachm. I, but IM. for IMP., e. ℞. VICTORIA AVGVSTI, as last.
B.M.C. S762; *R.I.C.* 358 (a).. 750
618a IMP . CAES . M . AVR. (or AVREL) ANTONINVS AVG., e. ℞. — As last. *B.M.C.*
S762 note; *R.I.C.* 358 (b) 750
618b As **618**, but Victory holds wreath in both hands over base. *B.M.C.* S762
note; *R.I.C.* 358A (*Vienna*) 750
618c IMP . CAES . M . AVR . ANTONINVS AVG., e. ℞. — Victory flying l., placing
wreath on cippus which is on altar (*Tinchant cat.*) 750
619 Denarius. Dc. ℞. VICTORIAE, two Victories flying, holding between them
shield inscribed AV . GG. and each holds palm; above, Caracalla stg.,
holding globe and sceptre; below, two captives seated back to back,
shield behind. *B.M.C.* p. 211, *; *R.I.C.* 146 350
620 Antoninianus? Fp (?, *Cohen has* hd. rad.). ℞. VICTORIA (or IAE) AVG.,
Victory in a quadriga, holding wreath and laurel-branch (or palm).
B.M.C. p. 448, (e); *R.I.C.* 313 (*doubtful*) .. ..
621 Tetradrachm. *Probably the same as* **618a** *incompletely described* ..

622 · 632

622 Denarius. De. ℞. VICTORIAE around, AVGG. in ex., Victory stg. in biga
of horses prancing r., holding whip and reins. *B.M.C.* S518; *R.I.C.* 170 55
622a As last, but Victory holds wreath and palm (*Tinchant cat.*) 60
626 De. ℞. VICTORIAE AVGVST., Victory seated r., l. hand on shield set on
altar. *B.M.C.* p. 261, (g); *R.I.C.* 171 .. ..
627 De. ℞. VICTORIA BRIT., Victory stg. r. *B.M.C.* p. 259, * note; *R.I.C.* 169;
C.R.B. 59 .. ..
629 Ei. ℞. VICTORIAE BRIT., Victory running r., holding trophy in both hands.
B.M.C. SG102-4; *R.I.C.* 231A; *C.R.B.* 70 65
630 As last (*base or Æ*). *B.M.C.* SG102 note; *R.I.C.* 231A note.. .. ..
630a De. ℞. — As last. *B.M.C.* p. 259, * note; *R.I.C.* 172A (*Fourth Dura
hoard*); *C.R.B.* 61 75
631 De. ℞. — Victory advancing l., holding wreath and palm. *B.M.C.*
p. 259, †; *R.I.C.* 173; *C.R.B.* 62 70
632 Ei. ℞. — As last. *B.M.C.* SG105-7; *R.I.C.* 231; *C.R.B.* 69 65

646 Denarius. Gl (or i ?). R. VICTORIA GERMANICA, Victory running r., holding wreath and trophy over shoulder. *B.M.C.* 64; *R.I.C.* 237 (*is the denarius genuine ?*) .. ..

648 Antoninianus. Fq. R. VIC . PART. in ex., P . M . TR . P . XX . COS . IIII . P . P. around, Victory seated r. on cuirass, inscribing VOT. (or VO.) XX. on shield held on knee; before, two captives seated below trophy. *B.M.C.* 199; *R.I.C.* 297 (d) £125

648a Fn. R. — As last. *B.M.C.* 198; *R.I.C.* 297 (c) 125

650 Denarius. Fi. R. — As **648**. *B.M.C.* 198 note and p. 621 (*Oldroyd*); *R.I.C.* 297 (e) 55

654 Antoninianus. Fq. R. VIC . PART . P . M . TR . P . TR . P . XX . COS . IIII . P . P., Caracalla, in military dress, stg. half-left, holding globe and spear, being crowned by Victory, who stands behind him and holds palm; before, captive seated l. *B.M.C.* 200 note (*B.M.*, *ex Lawrence*); *R.I.C.* 299 (d) 200

654a Fn. R. — As last (*Vienna*) 200

655 Denarius. Fi. R. — As last. *B.M.C.* 200 note; *R.I.C.* 299 (e) 85

656 Fi. R. VICT . PARTHICA, Victory seated r. on cuirass, inscribing VO. / XX. on shield held on knees, helmet at feet; in ex., javelin and hook. *B.M.C.* 89 note; *R.I.C.* 314 (a) note 65

656a Fi. R. — As last, but quiver and trumpet in ex. *B.M.C.* 89 note; *R.I.C.* 314 (a) (*Lawrence*) 65

656b Fi. R. — As last, but without helmet and nothing in ex. *B.M.C.* 89; *R.I.C.* 314 note 65

656c Antoninianus. Fq. R. — As before. *B.M.C.* 89 note and p. 620 (*Oldroyd*); *R.I.C.* 314 (b) 150

657 Denarius. Fi. R. — Caracalla, in military dress, stg. half-left, between two seated captives; he holds Victory and spear. *B.M.C.* 90 note; *R.I.C.* 315 (b) 60

657a Antoninianus. Fq. R. — As last. *B.M.C.* 90 note; *R.I.C.* 315 (a) (*Lawrence*) 150

657b Fn. R. — As last, but one captive kneeling. *B.M.C.* 90 150

658 Denarius. Dc. R. VICT . PART . MAX., Victory running l., holding wreath and palm. *B.M.C.* S296-7; *R.I.C.* 144 (b) 30

658a Dd. R. — As last. *B.M.C.* S296 note 30

659 Dc or d. R. — As last (*base or Æ*). *B.M.C.* S296 note; *R.I.C.* 144 (b) note .. ..

659a De. R. — As last. *B.M.C.* p. 261, (f); *R.I.C.* 168A (*R. D. hoard*) .. 30

661 Dc. R. VICTORIA PARTH . MAX., as last. *B.M.C.* S298-9; *R.I.C.* 145 .. 35

663 Cd. R. VIRT . AVGG., Virtus stg. l., holding spear and shield. *B.M.C.* p. 188, (e); *R.I.C.* 51 .. ..

664 Cd. R. — Virtus stg. r., holding Victory and spear. *B.M.C.* p. 188, (d); *R.I.C.* 50 .. ..

664a Cd. R. — Virtus stg. front, hd. l., holding Victory and reversed spear. *B.M.C.* S710-1; *R.I.C.* 354 30

664b C. Boy's laur. bust r., wearing cuirass ornamented with aegis. R. — As last. *Eastern mint* (*Lucerne sale, 25/4/69, lot 313*) 50

664c De. R. VIRTVS, Virtus stg. l., holding Victory and spear (*A.N.S.*) .. 40

665 Dc. R. VIRTVS AVGG., as **664**. *B.M.C.* S300 note; *R.I.C.* 147 30

665a 670

665a Dc. ℞. — As **664a,** but Virtus stg.|half-left. *B.M.C.* S300-1; *R.I.C.* 149 £30

666 Quinarius. Dc. ℞. — As last. *B.M.C.* S300 note; *R.I.C.* 148 .. 175

667 Denarius. Dd. ℞. — As last (*Cohen,* Mars). *B.M.C.* S300 note; *R.I.C.* 149 25

667a Dc. ℞. — Virtus stg. r., holding Victory and sceptre (*Brussels*) .. 30

670 De. ℞. — Caracalla, in military dress, stg. front, hd. r., holding spear and parazonium; at his feet l., river-god reclining r. on urn; on r., two captives seated l. *B.M.C.* S520-1; *R.I.C.* 175 45

670a M . ANTONINVS AVG (or AVGVSTVS), c. ℞. — Caracalla stg. l., sacrificing over altar and holding sceptre. *B.M.C.* p. 188, (f); *R.I.C.* p. 220, * (*very doubtful*) .. ..

672 De. ℞. VIRTVS AVGVSTOR., Virtus seated l., holding Victory and parazonium, resting l. elbow on oval shield; a round shield beside seat. *B.M.C.* S522-3; *R.I.C.* 176 25

680 De. ℞. VOTA PVBLICA, Caracalla stg., sacrificing out of patera over lighted tripod and holding roll (Hy. ?). *B.M.C.* S524 note; *R.I.C.* 178 ..

681 A ? a. ℞. ...... PVBLIC, as last. .. ..

681a Ei. ℞. — As next (*Vienna*).. .. ..

682 De. ℞. VOTA SOLVT . DEC . COS . III., as last, but with bull recumbent by tripod. *B.M.C.* S578; *R.I.C.* 204 40

684 De. ℞. VOTA SOLVT . DEC. around, COS . III. in ex., Caracalla, veiled, stg. r., sacrificing out of a patera over tripod; in front of him, victimarius raising axe to strike bull; behind, flute-player facing. *B.M.C.* S577; *R.I.C.* 205 100

686 693

686 Dc. ℞. VOT . SVSC . DEC . PON . TR . P . V . COS., Caracalla, veiled, stg. front, hd. l., sacrificing out of patera over tripod and holding roll. *B.M.C.* S396-7; *R.I.C.* 68 40

687 As last (*base or* Æ). *B.M.C.* S397 note; *R.I.C.* 68 note .. ..

688 Df. ℞. VOTA SVSCEPTA X., as **686.** *B.M.C.* S302-3; *R.I.C.* 150.. .. 25

689 De. ℞. — As last. *B.M.C.* S524-6; *R.I.C.* 179 25

690 Fi. ℞. — As last (Hy.). *B.M.C.* p. 468, 4; *R.I.C.* 325 .. .. ..

692 Df. ℞. VOTA SVSCEPTA XX., as last. *B.M.C.* S302 note; *R.I.C.* 151 ..

692a De. ℞. — As last. *B.M.C.* p. 260, †; *R.I.C.* 180 .. ..

693 De. ℞. — Caracalla stg. r., sacrificing out of patera over tripod; facing him, attendant holding staff (*Cohen gives* Sept. Sev. and Caracalla); behind tripod, flute-player facing. *B.M.C.* S527; *R.I.C.* 181 90

88

N.B.—*The obverses of the next five sections are all with portrait and legend of Caracalla and are lettered according to his obverses.*

CARACALLA and SEPTIMIUS SEVERUS

2 **Denarius.** Cd. R. AETERNIT . IMPERI., busts of Septimius and Caracalla face to face, both laur. dr. and cuir. *B.M.C.* S158 note; *R.I.C.* Caracalla 32 (b) £500
2a Cc. R. — As last. *B.M.C.* S158; *R.I.C.* 32 (a) 500
2b Dc. R. — As last, but busts not cuir. *B.M.C.* p. 206, *; *R.I.C.* 122 .. 500
2c Cd. R. — As last. (*G. R. Arnold*) 500
3 Cc. R. AETERNITAS IMPERII, as before, but perhaps Geta for Caracalla. *B.M.C.* S158 note; *R.I.C.* 32 note .. ..

CARACALLA and JULIA DOMNA

1 **Denarius.** De. R. IVLIA AVGVSTA, her bust dr. r. *B.M.C.* p. 618 (*Oldroyd; doubtful*) .. ..

CARACALLA, SEPTIMIUS and JULIA

5 **Denarius.** Dd. R. CONCORDIAE AETERNAE, jugate busts r., of Septimius, laur. dr. and cuir., and Julia, diad. and dr. with crescent. *B.M.C.* S275 note; *R.I.C.* Caracalla 125 (b) 900

5a Dc. R. — As last. *B.M.C.* S275; *R.I.C.* 125 (a) 900

CARACALLA and PLAUTILLA

3 **Denarius.** Dc. R. PLAVTILLA AVGVSTA, her bust dr. r. *B.M.C.* p. 2:0, * (*Pink considers it false*); *R.I.C.* 139 .. ..
3a De. R. — As last. *B.M.C.* p. 258, * note .. ..

CARACALLA and GETA

2 **Denarius.** Cd. R. P . SEPT . GETA . CAES . PONT., his bare-headed bust dr. and cuir. r. *R.I.C.* Caracalla 38 450
2a As last, but Geta's bust seen from the front. *B.M.C.* S162 450
3 Dd. R. — As 2, but perhaps only draped. *B.M.C.* S288; *R.I.C.* 137 .. 450
5 ANTONINVS AVG . PONT . TR . P . III., d. R. — As 2. *B.M.C.* p. 190, *; *R.I.C.* 29B 450
6a ANTONINVS AVG . PONT . TR . P . IIII., d. R. — As last. *B.M.C.* S729; *R.I.C.* 345 450
These last two are probably different readings of the same coin as the legend runs into the bust and Cohen quotes B.M. for **5.**
7 ANTONIN . PIVS AVG . PONT . TR . P., e. R. — As before, but only draped. *B.M.C.* p. 233, *; *R.I.C.* 62 450
10 **Small medallion** (3·81 gms.). IMP . ANTONIN . ET GETA CAES. around AVG . FIL. below laur. bust of Caracalla and bare-headed bust of Geta face to face, both dr. and cuir. R. VIRTVS AVGVSTOR., Virtus or Roma seated l. on throne, holding Victory and parazonium, resting l. elbow on shield
Extremely rare if genuine

89

PLAUTILLA

The daughter of the enormously rich and powerful praetorian prefect Plautianus, Fulvia Plautilla was married to Caracalla in 202 A.D., bringing with her a huge dowry. She was extremely haughty and was soon hated by her cruel husband. It was at his instigation, on the fall of her father in 205, that Septimius banished her to Lipari. She languished there miserably till after the death of Septimius, when she was assassinated on the orders of her husband.

Obverse legends.
A. PLAVTILLA AVG
B. PLAVTILLA AVGVSTA
C. PLAVTILLAE AVGVSTAE

Obverse types. Draped bust right, with:
a. Hair in horizontal waves and drawn into large bun at back
b. Hair in nearly vertical waves and drawn into large bun at back
c. Hair in horizontal waves and drawn into coiled plait on neck
d. Hair in nearly vertical waves and drawn into coiled plait on neck

References.
Reference numbers are under the joint reign of Septimius and Caracalla in the British Museum Catalogue and under Caracalla in Roman Imperial Coinage.

Mints.
All coins were struck at Rome except for the following attributed to Laodicea ad Mare: *B.M.C.* 734-40 (pp. 300-1); *R.I.C.* 370-2 (p. 271)

1(Bb)

7 Eastern mint

1 Denarius. Bb, d. ℞. CONCORDIA AVGG., Concordia, wearing diadem, stg. half-left, holding patera and sceptre. *B.M.C.* 411-5; *R.I.C.* 363 (a) and (b) ..	£45
2 Cb. ℞ — As last *B M.C.* 398-9; *R.I.C.* 359 ..	45
3 As last (*base or Æ*). *B.M.C.* 398 note; *R.I.C.* 359 note	
3a Quinarius. As last. *B.M.C.* 398 note; *R.I.C.* 359	350
7 Denarius. Cb. ℞. CONCORDIAE, Concordia seated l., holding patera and double cornucopiae. *B.M.C.* p. 235, * and 734-6; *R.I.C.* 360 and 370	55
8 Ab, d. ℞. — As last. *B.M.C.* 739-40; *R.I.C.* 372	55

10   12(Bd)

10 Denarius. Ca. ℞. CONCORDIAE AETERNAE, Caracalla and Plautilla stg. hand in hand, the former holds roll. *B.M.C.* 401-4; *R.I.C.* 361 .. .. £45

11 As last (*base or Æ*). *B.M.C.* 401 note; *R.I.C.* 361 note .. .. ..

12 Bb, c, d. ℞. CONCORDIA FELIX, as last. *B.M.C.* 418-9; *R.I.C.* 365 (a) and (b) 45

13 Bc. ℞. DIANA LVCIFERA, Diana, bow-case behind shoulders, stg. half-left, holding torch in both hands. *B.M.C.* 420-1; *R.I.C.* 366 65

14   25 (Bc)

14 Cb. ℞. HILARITAS, Hilaritas stg. half-left, holding long palm and cornucopiae. *B.M.C.* 737-8 (*note at top of page 239 would seem to be in error*); *R.I.C.* 371 60

14a B. ℞. MATRI DEVM, Cybele stg. l., leaning against column, holding large globe and sceptre (Hy.; *rev. imitated from Julia Domna*). *B.M.C.* p. 239; *R.I.C.* p. 269, *

16 Bc, d. ℞. PIETAS AVGG., Pietas (*Cohen*, Plautilla) stg. front, hd. r., holding sceptre and child on l. arm. *B.M.C.* 422-6; *R.I.C.* 367 45

21 Ca. ℞. PROPAGO IMPERI., Caracalla and Plautilla, as **10.** *B.M.C.* 406-10; *R.I.C.* 362 45

23 Quinarius. Bc. ℞. VENVS FELIX, Venus stg. l., holding apple and gathering up drapery on l. shoulder. *B.M.C.* p. 238, *; *R.I.C.* 368 .. 350

23a Denarius. B. ℞. VENVS GENETRIX,Venus seated l., holding globe and sceptre (Hy., *plated; rev. taken from Julia Domna*). *B.M.C.* p. 239; *R.I.C.* 368 note .. ..

23b B. ℞. — Venus seated l., holding apple and sceptre; before, Cupid holding helmet (Hy., *plated*). *B.M.C.* p. 239; *R.I.C.* 368 note ..

25 Bc, d. ℞. VENVS VICTRIX, Venus, naked to waist, stg. half-left, holding apple and palm; at side, shield; before, Cupid stg., holding helmet. *B.M.C.* 429; *R.I.C.* 369 .. ..

25a As last, but Cupid holds out both hands. *B.M.C.* 428 45

25b As last, but Cupid holds uncertain object; on the shield, she-wolf and Twins. *B.M.C.* 430; *R.I.C.* 369 note 50

26 As one of the last (*base or Æ*). *B.M.C.* 428 note; *R.I.C.* 369 note ..

29 C. ℞. VESTA, Vesta stg. l., holding palladium and sceptre (Hy. ?). *B.M.C.* p. 619 (*Ashmolean*) .. ..

GETA

209-212 A.D.

Lucius (then Publius) Septimius Julius Geta, the younger son of Septimius and Julia Domna, was born on 27th May, 189 A.D. He accompanied his father on the Parthian campaign, and when Caracalla was designated Augustus in 198, Geta was given the title of Caesar. He took part in the expedition to Britain in 208, and in the following year was made Augustus, it being his father's clear intention that the brothers should inherit the empire jointly. This they did when Septimius died at Eboracum (York) in 211. The savage and jealous nature of Caracalla would, however, admit of no such arrangement, and Geta was murdered in Feb. 212, after only twelve months of joint rule. Caracalla ordered that all statues of Geta should be destroyed, all inscriptions in his honour erased, and all coins bearing his effigy or titles melted down: his coins are thus somewhat scarcer than those of Caracalla. There followed a vigorous persecution of all the adherents of Geta in which, it is said, no less than 20,000 people met their deaths.

Obverse legends.

As Caesar

A. GETA CAES . PONT . COS., 203-8 A.D.
B. GETA CAES . PONTIF., *c.* 202 A.D.
C. L . SEPTIMIVS GETA . CAES., 198-200 A.D.
D. P . SEPT . GETA . CAES . PONT., 199-202 A.D.
E. P . SEPTIMIVS GETA CAES., 202-209 A.D.

As Augustus

F. IMP . CAES . P . SEPT . GETA PIVS AVG., 209-10
G. P . SEPT . GETA PIVS AVG . BRIT., 210-12 A.D.

Obverse types *(the bust seen partly from the back unless otherwise stated)*

a. Boy's bare-headed bust draped right
b.   ,,   ,,   ,,   ,, draped and cuirassed right
bf. ,,   ,,   ,,   ,,   ,,   ,,   ,, seen from the front
c. Older boy's or youth's bare-headed bust draped right
cl. ,,   ,,   ,,   ,,   ,,   ,,   ,,   ,, left
d. ,,   ,,   ,,   ,,   ,,   ,,   ,, draped and cuir. right
e. Youth's bare-headed bust right, draping on left shoulder
f.   ,, bare head right
g.   ,,   ,,   ,,   ,, bearded
h. Man's laureate head right, bearded

References.

In the British Museum Catalogue coins of Geta come into three of the sections with the numbering starting again from 1. We have therefore had to prefix the catalogue numbers for each section.

Joint reign of Septimius and Caracalla, prefixed with S (pp. 181-303). 198-209 A.D.
Joint reign of Septimius, Caracalla and Geta, prefixed with G (pp. 359-86). 209-11
Joint reign of Caracalla and Geta, prefixed with C (pp. 421-25).   211-12

Mints

B.M.C. and *R.I.C.* attribute all to Rome except:
Eastern mints—probably Laodicea ad Mare. *B.M.C.* S683-90 (pp. 290-1), S719-24 (pp. 296-7), S741-57 (pp. 301-3); *R.I.C.* 94-108 (pp. 328-9).

1 **Denarius.** P . SEPTIM . GETA CAESAR, laur. hd. R. ADVENTVS AVG., Geta
   on horseback. *B.M.C.* p. 247; *R.I.C.* p. 319, * (*very doubtful*) ..   ..

3 **Gh.** R. ADVENTVS AVGVSTI, Geta, in military dress with cloak flying, on
   horse walking r.; he raises r. hand and holds sceptre in l. *B.M.C.* G63;
   R.I.C. 84   ..   ..   £100

4 **Medallion (seven denarii).** Ee. R. AEQVITATI PVBLICAE, the three
   Monetae stg. l., each holding scales and cornucopiae; before each, a heap
   of metal. *B.M.C.* p. 244, †; *R.I.C.* 39   ..   ..   *Extremely rare*

10 **Denarius.** D, bare hd. R. BONVS EVENTVS, Genius, naked, stg. front,
   hd. l., sacrificing out of patera over altar and holding corn-ears (Hy. ?;
   coarse fabric, barbarous ?). *R.I.C.* p. 314, *..   ..   ..   ..

10a Ec. R. — As last. *B.M.C.* S741 note; *R.I.C.* 102 note (*R. D. hoard,
    large heavy flan*)   ..   ..

10b Ec. R. BORVS EVENTVS, as last. *B.M.C.* S741 (*very base*); *R.I.C.* 102
    (BONVS *in error*)   ..   ..

12   28

12 **Da.** R. CASTOR, Castor stg. half-left, beside horse l., holding sceptre.
   B.M.C. S216-7; *R.I.C.* 6   65

13 **Quinarius.** As last. *B.M.C.* S216 note and p. 618 (*Oldroyd; base silver*);
   R.I.C. 6   ..   ..

14 **Denarius.** As last (*plated, base or Æ*). *B.M.C.* S216 note; *R.I.C.* 6 note

17 **Gh** (*Cohen*, L . SEPT *in error*). R. CONCORDIA, Geta, togate, advancing r.
   and clasping r. hand of Concordia, veiled, stg. l. (*Cohen*, Caracalla and
   Plautilla ?) (Hy.). *B.M.C.* p. 369, (a) (*base, poor style*); *R.I.C.* 85 (*probably
   ancient forgery*)   ..   ..

17a Ec. R. — As last, or Caracalla and Geta. *B.M.C.* p. 245, *; *R.I.C.* 40   120

27   35

27 **Quinarius.** Ac. R. COS., Victory advancing l., holding wreath and palm.
   B.M.C. S437; *R.I.C.* 27   300

28 **Denarius.** Ec. R. — Geta, holding sceptre, in slow quadriga l.
   B.M.C. S443; *R.I.C.* 28   120

31 *Obv. ?* R. COS II., goddess stg., holding branch and cornucopiae. *R.I.C.*
   p. 329 (*too uncertain*) ..   ..

34 Ec. R. FELICIA TEMPORA, the Four Seasons as boys at play. *B.M.C.* p.
   245, †; *R.I.C.* 41   375

35 Ac. R. FELICITAS AVGG., Felicitas stg. half-left, holding caduceus and
   cornucopiae. *B.M.C.* S438-9; *R.I.C.* 29   40

36 **Da.** R. — As last. *B.M.C.* S218-9; *R.I.C.* 8   30

38 **Db.** R. FELICITAS PVBLICA, as last. *B.M.C.* 220 note; *R.I.C.* 9 (b)   ..   35

38a **Da.** R. — As last. *B.M.C.* S220-1; *R.I.C.* 9 (a)   30

39 **Da or b.** R. — As last (*base or Æ*). *B.M.C.* 220 note; *R.I.C.* 9 (b) note

44 (Rome mint)	44a (Eastern mint)

44 Ca. ℞. FELICITAS TEMPOR., Felicitas stg. half-left, holding caduceus and cornucopiae. *B.M.C.* S144-5 and S683-4; *R.I.C.* 2 and 95 .. .. £30

44a Cb. ℞. — As last. (*G. R. Arnold coll.*) 30

45 As **44** (*plated, base or Æ*). *B.M.C.* 144 note; *R.I.C.* 2 note .. ..

47 Da. ℞. — As last. *B.M.C.* p. 296, *; *R.I.C.* 97.. 40

49 Ca. ℞. — Felicitas stg. r., holding caduceus, clasping r. hands with Geta who stands front, hd. l., and holds cornucopiae. *B.M.C.* S146; *R.I.C.* 1 and 94 40

49a	62

49a Cb. ℞. — As last. *B.M.C.* S685-6; *R.I.C.* 94 note 40

50 Gh. ℞. FID . EXERC . TR . P . III . COS . II., Fides stg. l., holding standard; behind her, legionary eagle. *B.M.C.* G116 note; *R.I.C.* 74 (*perhaps a misdescription of the next*) .. ..

50a Gh. ℞. — Fides stg. almost front, hd. l., holding standard and legionary eagle; behind her, a second standard. *B.M.C.* G116-7; *R.I.C.* 74A .. 55

50b As last, but rev. legend ends COS . II . P . P. (*G. R. Arnold coll.*).. .. 60

51 Gh. ℞. FORT . RED . TR . P . III . COS . II., Fortuna seated l., holding rudder on globe and cornucopiae; under throne, wheel. *B.M.C.* G118; *R.I.C.* 75 50

51a As last, but no wheel. *B.M.C.* G118 note; *R.I.C.* 75 note (*Tinchant cat.*) 55

59 Gh. ℞. FORT . RED . TR . P . III . COS . II . P . P., as last. *B.M.C.* p. 421, *; *R.I.C.* 76 50

59a As last, but no globe under rudder (*A.N.S.*) 55

62 Gh. ℞. — Fortuna reclining r., elbow on wheel and holding cornucopiae. *B.M.C.* G10-1; *R.I.C.* 77 55

62a As last, but the COS . II . P . P. in ex. *B.M.C.* G8-9; *R.I.C.* 77 note .. 55

62b Gh. ℞. FORT . RED . TR . P . IIII . COS . II., Fortuna seated, as **51**. *B.M.C.* p. 425, *; *R.I.C.* 93A (*R. D. hoard—no* P.P. *on rev. ?*) .. .. ..

63 Ba. ℞. FVNDATOR PACIS, figure stg., holding olive-branch (Hy.; *rev. of Septimius*). *B.M.C.* p.201; *R.I.C.* p. 317, * .. ..

64 Ec. ℞. IMP . ET CAESAR AVG . FILI COS., Caracalla and Geta seated; in the background, between them, a facing figure (Septimius or Concordia?). *B.M.C.* p. 245, ‡; *R.I.C.* 42 250

65 Ec. ℞. IOVI in ex., SOSPITATORI around, Jupiter, wearing polos, stg. in rectangular shrine, holding sceptre; as Caracalla 108 (*Vienna*) 150

66a Da. ℞. LAETITIA PVBL., Laetitia stg. l., holding wreath and rudder on globe (Hy. ?). *B.M.C.* p. 201, (a); *R.I.C.* 10 .. ..

67   76a

67 Denarius. Ec. R. LAETITIA above, TEMPORVM in ex., ship in circus, four quadrigae above, various animals below. *B.M.C.* S452; *R.I.C.* 43   £250

67a As last, but only two quadrigae (*Tinchant cat.*)   250

67b Gh. R. LIBERALITAS AVG., Liberalitas stg. half-left, holding abacus and cornucopiae (Hy. ?). *B.M.C.* p. 620, A182 (*Oldroyd*)   ..   ..

68 Gh. R. LIBERALITAS AVG . V., as last. *B.M.C.* G65-67A; *R.I.C.* 88   ..   55

68a As last, but at the feet of Liberalitas, a globe. *B.M.C.* G65 note; *R.I.C.* 89   60

68b Dc. R. — As **68** (Hy.). *B.M.C.* p. 369 (b); *R.I.C.* 88 note (*R. D. hoard*)

69 Ec. R. LIBERALITAS AVG . VI., as last (Hy.; *rev. of Septimius*). *B.M.C.* p. 245, §; *R.I.C.* 44   ..

70a Da or c. R. LIBERALITAS AVGG . IIII., as last (Hy.; *base*). *B.M.C.* S222 note; *R.I.C.* 11 note ..

73 Dc. R. LIBERALITAS AVGVSTORVM, as last. *B.M.C.* S222; *R.I.C.* 11   ..   50

76 Ea. R. MARTI VICTORI, Mars, naked except for cloak flying out behind, advancing r., holding spear and trophy over shoulder. *B.M.C.* S742-8; *R.I.C.* 103   30

76a Eb. R. — As last. *B.M.C.* S742 note   35

77 Ec. R. MINERVA, Minerva stg. half-left, leaning on shield and holding spear. *B.M.C.* S454; *R.I.C.* 46   40

78 Ac. R. — As last. *B.M.C.* p. 242, *; *R.I.C.* 30..   45

79 Bc. R. — As last. *B.M.C.* p. 201; *R.I.C.* 25A   45

81 Ec. R. MINERVA PACIFERA around, COS. in ex., Minerva running r., hd. turned back, holding branch and spear and shield. *B.M.C.* S444-5; *R.I.C.* 31   50

83 Ec. R. MINERV . SANCT., as **77**. *B.M.C.* p. 245, ‖ and S750; *R.I.C.* 45 and 105 (a)   35

83a Ed. R. — As last. *B.M.C.* S751   35

83b (Eastern mint)   85

83b Ea. R. — As last (*G. R. Arnold coll.*)   35

84 Da. R. — As last. *B.M.C.* S719; *R.I.C.* 98   35

85 Ecl. R. — As last. *B.M.C.* S752-3; *R.I.C.* 105 (b)   90

86 Ec. R. MINERVAE VICTRICI, Minerva advancing l., brandishing javelin and holding shield; at her feet, a snake preceding her. *B.M.C.* S454 note; *R.I.C.* 47 (*Vienna*)   120

88 Ec. R. MINER . VICTRIX, Minerva stg. half-left, holding Victory and reversed spear; at feet l., shield; on r., trophy. *B.M.C.* S749; *R.I.C.* 104   40

88a D, but SEP., a or c. R. MONETA AVGG., Moneta seated l., holding scales and cornucopiae (Hy.; *ancient forgery?; rev. of Septimius*) (*Malcolm P. Hunt*)   ..   ..

90   97a

90	Da. ℞. NOBILITAS, Nobilitas stg. half-right (or front, hd. r.), holding sceptre and palladium. *B.M.C.* S223-7; *R.I.C.* 13 (a) £35

90a Db. ℞. — As last (*Malcolm P. Hunt*) 35
91 As one of the last (*base or* Æ). *B.M.C.* S223 note; *R.I.C.* 13 note ..
91a Quinarius. As **90.** *B.M.C.* S223 note; *R.I.C.* 13 (a) 350
92 Db. ℞. — As last. *B.M.C.* S223 note; *R.I.C.* 13 (b) 350
93 Ed. ℞. — As last. *B.M.C.* S455; *R.I.C.* 48 (a) 350
93a Ec. ℞. — As last. *B.M.C.* S455 note; *R.I.C.* 48 (a) note .. 350
93b Ac. ℞. — As last. *B.M.C.* p. 242, †; *R.I.C.* 32 350
93c Eg. ℞. — As before, but Nobilitas half-left. *B.M.C.* S456; *R.I.C.* 49 350

96 **Denarius** is imperfectly described, quoting B.M., and presumably should have been the last piece, a quinarius. *B.M.C.* S457 note; *R.I.C.* 49 note
97 Da. ℞. PIETAS, Pietas stg. half-left, raising r. hand over altar. *B.M.C.* S720-1; *R.I.C.* 99 35
97a Db. ℞. — As last, but also holding box of perfumes (*Brussels and G. R. Arnold*) 40
97b Da. ℞. PIETAS AVG., as last (Hy.; *ancient forgery?*). *B.M.C.* p. 201, (b); *R.I.C.* 13A .. ..
98 Da. ℞. PIETAS PVBLICA, Pietas stg. l. by altar, raising both hands (Hy.; *rev. of Julia Domna*). *B.M.C.* p. 201, (c); *R.I.C.* 14
99a Da. ℞. P.M.TR.P.III.COS.III.P.P., Providentia stg. l., holding baton over globe and cornucopiae, star in field (*cast; rev. of Elagabalus*). *C.R.B.* p. 21 (*Newcastle-upon-Tyne*) .. ..
100 Ec. ℞. PONTIFEX COS., helmeted hd. of Minerva r. *B.M.C.* S450; *R.I.C.* 35 250

101   114

101 Ec. ℞. — Minerva seated l., holding owl and sceptre or spear, and leaning on shield. *B.M.C.* p. 244, *; *R.I.C.* 36 50
101a Ec. ℞. — Aesculapius, naked, stg. facing in two columned temple; he holds serpent-wreathed staff, snakes rearing up either side of him (*Vienna*) 200
103a Ec. ℞. PONTIFEX COS. II., as **101.** *B.M.C.* p. 275, ‖; *R.I.C.* 66A (*R. D. hoard*) 55
103b Ec. ℞. — Geta stg. in triumphal quadriga r., holding eagle-tipped sceptre. *B.M.C.* S591 note and p. 618?; *R.I.C.* 66 200
104 Ed. ℞. PONTIF.COS., Minerva stg. front, hd. l., leaning on shield and holding reversed spear. *B.M.C.* S446 note; *R.I.C.* 34 (a) 30
104a Ec. ℞. — As last. *B.M.C.* S446-9; *R.I.C.* 34 (b) 30
104b Ec. ℞. — As **101.** (*G. R. Arnold*) 55
114 Eg. ℞. PONTIF.COS.II., Genius stg. facing, hd. l., holding patera over altar and two corn-ears. *B.M.C.* S579-83; *R.I.C.* 59 (b) 30
114a Ec. ℞. — As last. *B.M.C.* S584; *R.I.C.* 59 (a) 30

117 Denarius. Ec. R. PONTIF . COS . II., Geta stg. half-left, holding globe and parazonium (or short sceptre or roll). *B.M.C.* S586-7; *R.I.C.* 61 (b)   £35

117a   122a

117a Ed. R. — As last. *B.M.C.* S586 note; *R.I.C.* 61 (b)   35
119 Ec. R. — Geta, veiled, stg. half-left, sacrificing out of patera over tripod and holding short sceptre. *B.M.C.* S588-90; *R.I.C.* 62 (b)   ..   35
119a Ed. R. — As last. *R.I.C.* 62 (a)   35
122 Ed. R. — Geta in quadriga, as **103b**. *B.M.C.* S591 note; *R.I.C.* 63 ..   200
122a Ec. R. — As last (*G. R. Arnold coll.*)   200
123 Ef. R. — Geta on horseback galloping l. over fallen foe. *B.M.C.* p. 275, * note; *R.I.C.* 64 (b)   90

123a   137

123a Eg. R. — As last (*G. R. Arnold coll.*)   90
123b Ec. R. — As last. *B.M.C.* p. 275, *; *R.I.C.* 64 (a)   90
124 Fh. R. — As last. *R.I.C.* 64 note (*This could be a mistake for* 130)   ..
126 Ec. R. — Septimius seated facing on platform, between Caracalla and Geta seated facing each other. *B.M.C.* p. 275, † note; *R.I.C.* 65 (a)   ..   225
129 Fh. R. PONTIF . TR . P . COS . II., Genius, as **114**. *B.M.C.* G15-6; *R.I.C.* 67   55
130 Fh. R. — Geta on horseback galloping l., spearing fallen foe. *B.M.C.* G17; *R.I.C.* 68   85
137 Fh. R. PONTIF . TR . P . II . COS . II., Felicitas stg. half-left, holding cornucopiae and caduceus. *B.M.C.* G40-2; *R.I.C.* 69 (a)   50
138 Gh. R. — As last. *B.M.C.* G 47-8; *R.I.C.* 69 (b)   ..   50
139 Gh. R. — Genius, as **114**. *B.M.C.* G49; *R.I.C.* 70 (a)   ..   50
140 Fh. R. — As last. *B.M.C.* G43-5; *R.I.C.* 70 (b)   50
142 Fh. R. — Geta on horseback, as **130**. *B.M.C.* G46; *R.I.C.* 72   ..   85
149 Gh. R. PONTIF . TR . P . III . COS . II., Felicitas, as **137**. *B.M.C.* G119-20; *R.I.C.* 78 (a)   55
155 IMP . CAE . L . SEPT . GETA AVG . COS . II., h. R. PONTIF. TR . P . III . P . P., Sol stg. l., raising r. hand and holding whip. *B.M.C.* p. 303; *R.I.C.* 108. (*A curious piece, possibly false*)   ..   ..
155a Gh. R. PONTIF . TR . P . VI . COS . II., Felicitas, as **137**. *B.M.C.* G119 note; *R.I.C.* 78 (a) note (*R. D. hoard; probably meant for* **149**) ..   ..
157 Da. R. PRINC . IVVENT., Geta, in military dress, stg. half-left, holding baton (*C. and R.I.C.*, branch) and reversed spear or long sceptre; behind, trophy. *B.M.C.* S234 note; *R.I.C.* 16 (b)   45
157a Da. R. PRINC . IVVENTVT., as last. *B.M.C.* S234 note; *R.I.C.* 17   ..   45

157b   162a

157b Da. R. PRINC . IVVENTVTIS, as last. *B.M.C.* S234-9; *R.I.C.* 18 .. £30
158 Da. R. As **157** (*base or Æ*). *B.M.C.* S234 note; *R.I.C.* 16 (b) note ..
158a Db. R. As **157** (*Tinchant cat.*) 35
159 Da. R. PRINC . IVVENT., as before, but holding branch for baton and without trophy. *B.M.C.* S229-31; *R.I.C.* 15 (a) 35
159a Db. R. — As last. *B.M.C.* S232-3; *R.I.C.* 15 (b) 35
162 Ac. R. PRINC . IVVENT. around, COS. in ex., Severus, Caracalla and Geta (or more likely Geta and two knights) galloping r.; the leader turns his hd. back and throws out r. hand in gesture of encouragement. *B.M.C.* S440 note; *R.I.C.* 37 (a) 200
162a Ec. R. — As last. *B.M.C.* S451; *R.I.C.* 37 (b) (*has obv. legend A in error*) 200
162b Ecl. R. — As last (*Tinchant cat.*) 250
162c Ed. R. — As last (*Tinchant cat.*) 200
162d As last (*base or Æ*). *B.M.C.* S451 note; *R.I.C.* 37 note .. .. ..
169a Da. R. PROFECTIO AVG., Septimius (?), in military dress, on horse prancing r., holding spear (Hy.). *B.M.C.* G169 (*base; odd style; rev. of Septimius*) .. ..

170   183

170 Ec. R. PROVID . DEORVM, Providentia, diad., stg. half-left, holding wand and sceptre, globe at feet. *B.M.C.* S458-63; *R.I.C.* 51 30
170a Gh. R. — As last (Hy.; *local issue or ancient forgery, lettering crude*) (*Malcolm P. Hunt*) .. ..
171 Gh. R. PROVIDENTIA DEORVM, as last (Hy.). *B.M.C.* p. 369, (c); *R.I.C.* 90
171a L. SEPT . GETA CAES . PON., a. R. RECTOR ORBIS, Sol stg. front, hd. r., holding globe and sceptre (Hy.; *rev. of Caracalla*). *B.M.C.* p. 182; *R.I.C.* p. 314, *
172 Ec. R. RESTITVTOR VRBIS, Rome seated l. on low seat, holding Victory or palladium and sceptre or spear; at side, round shield. *B.M.C.* S464; *R.I.C.* 52 35
174 Ec. R. RESTITVTORI VRBIS, emperor or prince stg. l., sacrificing over lighted tripod and holding reversed spear (Hy.; *rev. of Septimius*). *B.M.C.* p. 247 (*ancient forgery*); *R.I.C.* 53 ..
175 Ba or c. R. — As last (Hy., *plated; rev. of Septimius*). *B.M.C.* p. 201 (*ancient forgery*); *R.I.C.* p. 317, * ..
176 Ec. R. ROMAE AETERNAE, Roma seated in hexastyle temple, statue at foot of each column; in pediment, Jupiter between reclining figures. *B.M.C.* p. 247, *; *R.I.C.* 54 250
176a Da or c. R. — Roma seated in hexastyle temple (Hy. ?). *B.M.C.* p. 201, (d); *R.I.C.* 19 ..

183   **Denarius.** Da. ℞. SECVRIT . IMPERII, Securitas seated l., holding globe and resting l. arm on side of throne. *B.M.C.* S240-3; *R.I.C.* 20 (a)   ..   £30

183a Db. ℞. — As last. *B.M.C.* S240 note; *R.I.C.* 20 (b)   30

184   **Quinarius.** Da. ℞. — As last. *B.M.C.* S240 note; *R.I.C.* 20 (a)   ..   350

184a Db. ℞. — As last. *B.M.C.* S240 note; *R.I.C.* 20 (b)   350

186   **Denarius.** Da. ℞. SECVRIT . ORBIS, Security seated r., head bent; at feet, modius (Hy.; *rev. somewhat as Caracalla*). *B.M.C.* p. 201, (e)   ..   ..

188   193a

188   Ca. ℞. SEVERI PII AVG . FIL., lituus, knife, jug, simpulum and sprinkler. *B.M.C.* S147-8; *R.I.C.* 3 (*Cohen gives* jug *before* knife)   40

189   Eb. ℞. — As last (knife *could be* axe). *B.M.C.* S754-7; *R.I.C.* 107 ..   40

189a Ea. ℞. — As last (*Mazzini cat.*)   40

192   Ca. ℞. SPEI PERPETVAE, Spes walking l., holding flower and raising skirt. *B.M.C.* S689-90; *R.I.C.* 96   35

192a Cb. ℞. As last. *B.M.C.* 688   35

193   Ca. ℞. SPES PVBLICA, as last. *B.M.C.* S149-50; *R.I.C.* 4   35

193a Cb. ℞. — As last (*G. R. Arnold coll.*)   35

195   196

195   L . SEPT . GETA CAES . PONT., a. ℞. — As last. *B.M.C.* S149 note; *R.I.C.* 4 note (*G. R. Arnold coll.*)   85

195a Da. ℞. — As last. *B.M.C.* p. 200, * note; *R.I.C.* 21A (*R. D. hoard*) ..   45

196   Da. ℞. TEM / POR . FELI / CITAS in three lines in laurel-wreath. *B.M.C.* S246; *R.I.C.* 22   125

196a Ca. ℞. TEMP / OR . FELI / CITAS, as last (*Curtis L. Clay; Vienna; Hanover*)   125

197   Gh. ℞. TR . P . III . COS . II . P . P., Janus stg. front, holding reversed spear and thunderbolt. *B.M.C.* C13-4; *R.I.C.* 79   60

197a   200

197a Gh. ℞. — As last, but sceptre for spear. *B.M.C.* C12; *R.I.C.* 79 ..   60

197b **Quinarius.** Gh. ℞. — Victory advancing l., holding wreath and palm (*Naples*)   325

198 **Denarius.** Gh. ℞. TR . P . III . COS . II . P . P., Felicitas stg. half-left, holding caduceus and cornucopiae. *B.M.C.* C15; *R.I.C.* 80 .. .. £50

200 Gh. ℞. — Goddess (variously described as Pax, Providentia? or Aeternitas?) stg. front, hd. l., holding lighted torch and globe. *B.M.C.* C16-7; *R.I.C.* 81 60

200a Gh. ℞. — As last, but hd. front. *B.M.C.* C16 note; *R.I.C.* 81 note (*R. D. hoard*) 60

200b Gh. ℞. — As last, but hd. r. *B.M.C.* C16 note; *R.I.C.* 81 note (*R. D. hoard*) 60

201 Gh. ℞. — As one of the last (*plated or Æ*). *B.M.C.* C16 note; *R.I.C.* 81 note .. ..

205 Da. ℞. VENVS GENETRIX, Venus seated l., offering apple to a child and holding spear (Hy., *plated; rev. of Julia Domna*). *B.M.C.* p. 201, (f) (*ancient forgery*); *R.I.C.* 23 note .. ..

206 219

206 Db. ℞. VICT . AETERN., Victory flying l., holding in both hands open wreath over round shield set on low base. *B.M.C.* S247-8 and S723; *R.I.C.* 23 and 101 30

206a Da. ℞. — As last. *B.M.C.* S724 30

207 Db. ℞. — As last (*plated or Æ*). *R.I.C.* 23 note .. .. ..

207a Ed. ℞. — As last (Hy.; *base*). *B.M.C.* p. 248; *R.I.C.* 55 note (*Lawrence*)

208 **Quinarius.** Da. ℞. VICT . AVGG., Victory advancing l., holding wreath and palm (*Vienna*) 300

219 **Denarius.** Gh. ℞. VICTORIAE BRIT., Victory, half-naked, stg. half-left, holding wreath and palm. *B.M.C.* G68-9; *R.I.C.* 92; *C.R.B.* 86 .. 75

220 Gh. ℞. — As last, but Victory advancing r. *B.M.C.* G67; *R.I.C.* 91; *C.R.B.* 85 85

220a Fh. ℞. — As last. *C.R.B.* 86a (*Seaby's Bull., July* 1950, B670 *and Aug.* 1952, RB31) 90

224a ? ℞. VIRT . AVG., Virtus stg. l., holding Victory and spear, shield at side (Hy.; *plated; rev. of Caracalla*). *Seaby's Bull., Dec.* 1967.. .. ..

224b SEP . GETA CAES., a. ℞. VIRTVS AVG., Virtus stg. l., holding globe (?) and spear (Hy.). *B.M.C.* G170 (*curious style*) .. ..

225 Ec. ℞. VIRTVS AVGVSTOR., Virtus seated l., leaning on shield, holding Victory and parazonium. *B.M.C.* p. 247, †; *R.I.C.* 56 50

227 Ec. ℞. VOTA PVBLICA, Geta, veiled, stg. half-left., sacrificing out of patera over lighted tripod, holding roll. *B.M.C.* S466; *R.I.C.* 57 35

228 Bc. ℞. — As last. *B.M.C.* S251; *R.I.C.* 26 35

230 Ac. ℞. — As last. *B.M.C.* S442; *R.I.C.* 38 (b) 35

231 Da. ℞. — As last. *B.M.C.* S250; *R.I.C.* 24 35

231a Gh. ℞. — As last, but sacrificial bull at base of tripod. *B.M.C.* G70 70

236 *Obv.?* ℞. — The three rulers sacrificing; near by, flute-player and another. *R.I.C.* p. 329 (*too uncertain*) .. ..

236a Gh. ℞. VOTA SVSCEPTA X., as **227** (Hy.?; *rev. of Caracalla*). *B.M.C.* p. 370, (d); *R.I.C.* 93 .. ..

GETA, SEPTIMIUS SEVERUS and CARACALLA

Obverses are of Geta (see page 91).

1 **Denarius.** Db. ℞. AETERNIT . IMPERI., laur. bust of Severus r., facing laur. bust of Caracalla l., both dr. and cuir. *B.M.C.* 214 note; *R.I.C.* Geta 5 ..   ..   £650

1a Da. ℞. — As last. *B.M.C.* 214   650

1b Da. ℞. — As last, but busts cuir. only. *B.M.C.* 215 ..   .ʌ   ..   650

MACRINUS
217-218 A.D.

Marcus Opelius Severus Macrinus was born in 164 A.D., of very humble parents, at Caesarea in Mauretania.   At first an advocate, he came to Rome and was favourably received by Septimius Severus.   After holding various appointments in the imperial household, Caracalla appointed him Prefect of the Praetorian Guards.   Hearing that the emperor intended to destroy him, he instigated the assassination of Caracalla whilst they were campaigning in Mesopotamia.   On April 11th, 217, he was saluted as Augustus by his troops, and his elevation was later confirmed by the Senate at Rome.   He almost immediately entered into a war with the Parthians, by whom he was defeated.   The ensuing peace was on terms so unfavourable to the Romans that it dimmed his popularity.   A conspiracy, fostered by Julia Maesa in favour of her grandson Bassianus (later the emperor Elagabalus), caused the Syrian army to break into open revolt.   In the ensuing struggle Macrinus was defeated and fled to Chalcedon, but was betrayed, captured and slain, together with his young son Diadumenian, after a reign of only fourteen months.   He was a man of good character, but with little skill in administration or military affairs.   However, his short reign was a period of sanity between the ferocious tyranny of Caracalla and the hideous criminality and extravagant folly of Elagabalus.

Obverse legend:

IMP . C . M . OPEL . SEV . MACRINVS AVG

Obverse types.

Rd.	Radiate bust right, draped.					
Rc.	,,	,,	,,	cuirassed.		
Rdc.	,,	,,	,,	draped and cuirassed.		
Rdc.hb.	,,	,,	,,	,,	,,	,,	seen half from the back.
Ld.	Laureate bust right, draped.					
Ld.hb.	,,	,,	,,	,,	seen half from the back.	
Lc.	,,	,,	,,	cuirassed.		
Ldc.	,,	,,	,,	draped and cuirassed.		
Ldc.hb.	,,	,,	,,	,,	,,	,,	seen half from the back.

(A) *Busts and Mints.*   There are two portraits: one stylized and with a short clipped beard; the other, a probably true portrait, with a longer beard and looking older.   The *B.M.C.* attributes the latter to the Antioch mint and the former to Rome.   We have added (A) to the obverse type for the long beard coins.

N.B.—*With some of the busts of Macrinus it is difficult to decide whether they are draped, cuirassed or draped and cuirassed.   It is probable that different cataloguers have described the same coin in different ways.*

2 **Denarius.** Ld.hb.(A).   ℞.   AEQVITAS AVG., Aequitas stg. half-left, holding scales and cornucopiae. *B.M.C.* 58 note; *R.I.C.* 53   ..   ..   £80

2a Lc.(A). ℞. — As last. *B.M.C.* 58 note; *R.I.C.* 53   80

2b Ldc.hb.(A). ℞. — As last. *B.M.C.* 58-9; *R.I.C.* 53   80

4 As 2 (*plated or* Æ). *B.M.C.* 58 note   ..   ..

8 Denarius. Lc. and/or dc. R. ANNONA AVG., Annona (*Cohen*, Abundantia) seated l. on throne, holding two corn-ears and cornucopiae; at her feet, modius filled with corn-ears. *B.M.C.* 6 and note; *R.I.C.* 55   ..   ..   £80
8a Lc.(A). R. — As last. *B.M.C.* 60; *R.I.C.* 56   80
8b Ldc.(A). R. — As last. *B.M.C.* 60 note ..   ..
15 Ldc.(A). R. FELICITAS TEMPORVM, Felicitas stg. half-left, holding long caduceus and cornucopiae. *B.M.C.* 63; *R.I.C.* 60   80
15a Lc. R. — As last. *B.M.C.* p. 496, † and pl. 78, 8 (*B.M.C.* 10 *misdescribed*)?; *R.I.C.* 59 (*Sydenham*)   80
15b Lc.(A). R. — As last. *B.M.C.* 62; *R.I.C.* 60   80
15c Ld.hb.(A). R. — As last (*A.N.S.*)   80
15d Ldc.hb.(A). R. — As last (*Tinchant cat.*)..   ..   ..   8)

8a   19a

19 Ld. R. — Felicitas stg. front, hd. l. (or stg. half-left), holding short caduceus and sceptre. *B.M.C.* 9 note; *R.I.C.* 62 (*This could be the next piece*) ..   ..
19a Lc. R. — As last. *B.M.C.* 9; *R.I.C.* 62   100
20 **Antoninianus** (=*double denarius*). Rd.hb. R. — As last. *B.M.C.* 7 note; *R.I.C.* 63   300
20a Rc. R. — As last. *B.M.C.* 7; *R.I.C.* 63   300
20b As last, but MCRINVS on *obv. B.M.C.* 7 note; *R.I.C.* 63 note (*Trau*) ..   300
20c Rcd.hb. R. — As before. *B.M.C.* 8; *R.I.C.* 63   300
20d Denarius. Lc.(A) R. — Felicitas stg. l., holding sceptre and cornucopiae. *B.M.C.* 62 note; *R.I.C.* 61 (*Lawrence*)   110
23 Ldc. R. FIDES MILITVM, Fides stg. front, hd. r., r. foot on helmet, holding standard in each hand. *B.M.C.* 12 (*perhaps more correctly described as next*)   80
23a Lc. R. — As last. *R.I.C.* 66 (*Lawrence*)   80
23b Ldc.(A). R. — As last. *B.M.C.* 65; *R.I.C.* 67   80
23c Lc.(A). R. — As last. *R.I.C.* 67 (*Brussels*)   80
23d Ld. R. — As last (*New York*)   80
23e Ld.hb.(A). R. — As last (*Tinchant cat.*)   80
23f Ldc.hb.(A). R. — As last (*Tinchant cat.*)   ..   ..
26 Lc. R. — Fides stg. front, hd. l., between two standards, and holding two more, one in each hand. *B.M.C.* 14; *R.I.C.* 68   100
26a Ldc.hb. R. — As last. *B.M.C.* 14 note; *R.I.C.* 68 (*Spink*)   100
27 **Antoninianus.** Rd.hb. R. — As last. *B.M.C.* 13; *R.I.C.* 69..   ..   300
27a Rc. R. — As last. *B.M.C.* 13 note; *R.I.C.* 69   300
27b Rdc. R. — As last. *R.I.C.* 69 (*B.M.*, *but not in cat.*, *possible meant for* 27)
N.B.—*Nos.* 30-33 *in Cohen have* SEV. *omitted on obv. in error.*
30 Denarius. Lc. R. FIDES MIL . P . M . TR . P., as last. *B.M.C.* p. 494, †; *R.I.C.* 1 (*Lawrence. Cohen says*, tête laurée, *which is obviously inadequate*)   110
31 Ld or c or dc. R. FIDES PVBLICA, as last. *B.M.C.* 15 (pl. 78, 12); *R.I.C.* 70   100
33 Lc or d or dc. R. IOVI CONSERVATORI, Jupiter, naked, stg. half-left, holding thunderbolt and sceptre. *B.M.C.* 17; *R.I.C.* 72   90

33a Lc.(A). ℞. — As last. *B.M.C.* 68; *R.I.C.* 73 .. .. £90
33b Ldc.(A). ℞. — As last. *B.M.C.* 66-7; *R.I.C.* 73 90

37   47a

37 Lc and/or d. ℞. — Jupiter, naked except for cloak over l. shoulder and
r. arm, stg. half-left, holding thunderbolt and sceptre; under his r. arm,
a small figure (Macrinus) stands. *B.M.C.* 20-3; *R.I.C.* 76 80
38 **Antoninianus.** Rd.hb. ℞. — As last. *B.M.C.* 18 note; *R.I.C.* 77
(*probably the same coin as* 38b) 300
38a Rc. ℞. — As last. *B.M.C.* 18; *R.I.C.* 77 300
38b Rdc.hb. ℞. — As last. *B.M.C.* 19 300
40a **Denarius.** Lc. ℞. IOVI STATORI, Jupiter stg. front, hd. r., holding
sceptre and thunderbolt. *B.M.C.* p. 621 (*Kamenica hoard*) 110
41 Ld and/or dc.hb.(A). ℞. LIBERALITAS AVG., Liberalitas stg. front, hd. l.,
holding abacus (counting board) and cornucopiae. *B.M.C.* 69-70;
R.I.C. 78 100
41a Lc. ℞. — As last. *R.I.C.* 78 (*Tinchant*) 100
45 *Obv.?* ℞. P . M . TR . P . COS . P . P., Jupiter stg. l., holding thunderbolt
and reversed spear. *B.M.C.* 31 note (*quite uncertain*); *R.I.C.* 14. .
47 Ldc.hb.(A). ℞. P . M . TR . P . II . COS . P . P., Annona (*Cohen*, Abundantia)
stg. front, hd. l., holding two corn-ears and cornucopiae; at her feet,
modius filled with corn-ears. *B.M.C.* 44; *R.I.C.* 26 80
47a Ld.hb.(A). ℞. — As last. *B.M.C.* 41-2; *R.I.C.* 26 80
47b Lc.(A). ℞. — As last. *B.M.C.* 43; *R.I.C.* 26 80
48 As **47a** (*plated or Æ*). *B.M.C.* 44 note .. ..
51 Ldc.(A). ℞. — Macrinus seated l. on curule chair, holding globe and
court (short) sceptre. *B.M.C.* 45-6; *R.I.C.* 27 90

51a   60

51a Ld.hb.(A). ℞. — As last. *B.M.C.* 47-8; *R.I.C.* 27 90
51b Lc.(A). ℞. — As last. *B.M.C.* 49-50; *R.I.C.* 27 90
54a Ldc.(A)? ℞. PONTIF . MAX . TR . P., Fides stg. front, hd. r., r. foot on
helmet, holding standard in each hand. *B.M.C.* p. 499, ‡ note; *R.I.C.* 3
note (*Vienna*) 100
55 Ldc.(A). ℞. PONTIF . MAX . TR . P . COS . P . P., Jupiter, naked (*Cohen
gives* cloak on l. shoulder *in error*), stg. half-left, holding thunderbolt and
long sceptre. *B.M.C.* 31 note; *R.I.C.* 17 80
55a Lc.(A). ℞. — As last. *B.M.C.* 31-2; *R.I.C.* 15 80
55b Lc. ℞. — As last (*Brussels*) 90

56 Denarius. Ldc and/or c.(A). ℞ . PONTIF . MAX . TR . P . COS . P . P.,
Annona (*Cohen*, Abundantia) seated l. on throne, holding two corn-ears
and cornucopiae; at her feet, modius filled with corn-ears. *B.M.C.* 33;
R.I.C. 19 .. .. £80

60 — ℞. — Fides stg., as **54a**. *B.M.C.* 38; *R.I.C.* 22A 80

60a Ld. ℞. — As last (*Brussels*) 80

60b Lc.(A). ℞. — Fides stg. facing, hd. r., foot on helmet, between three
standards (*Tinchant cat.*) 110

62 Ldc and/or c.(A). ℞. — Securitas stg. front, legs crossed, looking l.,
holding sceptre and resting l. arm on column. *B.M.C.* 40; *R.I.C.* 24 .. 80

65 — ℞. — Felicitas stg. front, hd. l., holding long caduceus and cornucopiae. *B.M.C.* 35-6; *R.I.C.* 21 80

67   108

67 — ℞. — Salus seated l., on throne with high back, feeding out of patera
snake rising up from altar around which it is coiled, and extending r. hand
to stroke it. *B.M.C.* 39; *R.I.C.* 23 80

70 — ℞. PONTIF . MAX . TR . P . P . P., Jupiter, naked, stg. front, hd. l.,
holding thunderbolt and sceptre. *B.M.C.* p. 499, †; *R.I.C.* 2 90

70a — ℞. — As last (*base or* Æ). *B.M.C.* pl. 80, 14 .. .. ..

76 — ℞. — Fides stg., as **54a**. *B.M.C.* p. 499, ‡; *R.I.C.* 3 90

79 — ℞. — Felicitas stg., as **65**. *B.M.C.* 29; *R.I.C.* 4 90

79a Ld. ℞. — As last (*Brussels*) 100

81a Lc.(A). ℞. PONTIF . MAX . TR . P . II . COS . P . P., Jupiter stg., as **70**.
B.M.C. 51 90

82 Lc.(A). ℞. — Felicitas stg., as **65**. *B.M.C.* 52; *R.I.C.* 32 80

82a Ld.(A). ℞. — As last. *B.M.C.* 52 note; *R.I.C.* 32 (*Tinchant cat.*) .. 80

82b Lcd.(A). ℞. — As last. *B.M.C.* 52 note; *R.I.C.* 32 (*Baldwin*).. .. 80

85 Ld and/or c.(A). ℞. — Annona (*Cohen*, Abundantia) stg., as **47**. *B.M.C.*
p. 502, *; *R.I.C.* 30 90

86 Ldc and/or d or c.(A). ℞. — Fides stg., as **54a**. *B.M.C.* 53; *R.I.C.* 34 80

87 Lc.(A). ℞. — Securitas stg., as **62**. *B.M.C.* 54; *R.I.C.* 35 90

88 Lc.(A). ℞. — Macrinus stg. in slow quadriga l., holding eagle-tipped
sceptre and being crowned by Victory stg. behind him. *B.M.C.* p. 503, *;
R.I.C. 36 350

88a As last, but sceptre without eagle (*Tinchant cat.*) 350

89 Lc.(A). ℞. PONTIF . MAX . TR . P . II . COS . II . P . P., Jupiter stg., as **55**.
B.M.C. p. 503, †; *R.I.C.* 37 90

93 Lc.(A). ℞. — Felicitas stg., as **65**. *B.M.C.* 56 note; *R.I.C.* 42 .. 90

96 Lc and/or dc.(A). ℞. — Fides stg., as **54a**. *R.I.C.* 43 90

98 — ℞. — Securitas stg., as **62**. *B.M.C.* p. 504, *; *R.I.C.* 46 100

102 Ldc and/or c or d.(A).   R. PONTIF . MAX . TR . P . II . COS . II . P . P.,
Annona (*Cohen*, Abundantia) seated l., as **56**. *B.M.C.* 55; *R.I.C.* 39   ..   £90
103a Ldc.(A) R. — Salus seated l., as **67**. *B.M.C.* p. 503, ‡; *R.I.C.* 44A
(*R. D. hoard*)   ..   ..
108 Ld.hb.(A).   R. PROVIDENTIA DEORVM, Providentia stg. front, hd. l.,
holding wand and cornucopiae; at feet, globe. *B.M.C.* 73; *R.I.C.* 80 ..   80
108a Lc.(A). R. — As last. *B.M.C.* 74; *R.I.C.* 80   80
108b Lcd.hb.(A). R. — As last. *B.M.C.* 72; *R.I.C.* 80 (*illustration*)   ..   80
112 Lc. R. RESTITVTOR VRBIS, emperor stg. l., sacrificing over tripod, l. hand
on sceptre (Hy.; *rev. of Sept. Sev.*). *B.M.C.* p. 508, 2; *R.I.C.* 81   ..
114 *Obv.?* R. SALVS PVBLICA, Salus seated l., as **67**. *B.M.C.* 24 note; *R.I.C.*
84 (*cuir.*)   ..   ..
114a Ld.hb.(A). R. — As last. *B.M.C.* 76; *R.I.C.* 85   80
114b Lc or dc.(A). R. — As last. *B.M.C.* 75; *R.I.C.* 85   80
115 **Antoninianus.** Rd.hb. R. — Salus seated l., as last, but l. hand holds
sceptre instead of touching snake. *B.M.C.* 25 note; *R.I.C.* 88   300

115a Rdc.hb. R. — As last. (*G. R. Arnold coll.*)   300
115b Rc. R. — As last. *B.M.C.* 25; *R.I.C.* 88   300
116 **Denarius.** Ldc.(A). R. — As last. *B.M.C.* p. 507, *; *R.I.C.* 87   ..   80

116a   128a

116a Lc. R. — As last. *B.M.C.* 26; *R.I.C.* 86   80
116b Lc. R. — As last, but low seat without back. *B.M.C.* 26 note; *R.I.C.* 89
(*Baldwin*)   80
122 Ldc.(A). R. SECVRITAS TEMPORVM, Securitas stg., as **62**. *B.M.C.* 79;
R.I.C. 92   80
122a Ld.hb.(A). R. — As last. *B.M.C.* 77; *R.I.C.* 92   80
122b Lc. R. — As last. *B.M.C.* 28 note; *R.I.C.* 91   80
122c Lc.(A). R. — As last. *B.M.C.* 78 and 80; *R.I.C.* 92   80
126 **Antoninianus.** Rc. R. — Securitas seated l. on throne, before lighted
altar, holding sceptre and resting l. arm on back of throne and supporting
hd. with hand. *B.M.C.* 27; *R.I.C.* 95   300
126a Rdc. R. — As last. *B.M.C.* 27 note; *R.I.C.* 95   300
126b Rdc.hb. R. — As last (*Lucerne sale, 25/4/69, lot 361*)   300
128 **Denarius.** Ldc. R. — As last. *B.M.C.* 28 note; *R.I.C.* 94   ..
128a Lc. R. — As last. *B.M.C.* 28; *R.I.C.* 94   80
128b **Quinarius.** Ld? R. — As last. *B.M.C.* 28 note; *R.I.C.* 94A (*Vienna*)
Extremely rare

134	**Denarius.** Ld. (A?). R. VICTORIA PARTHICA, Victory advancing r.: holding wreath and palm. *B.M.C.* 81 note; *R.I.C.* 96	£120
135	Lc. (A). R. — As last. *B.M.C.* 81; *R.I.C.* 97	120
137	Lc. (A). R. VICT . PART . P . M . TR . P . II . COS . II . P . P., as last. *B.M.C.* p. 504, ‡; *R.I.C.* 49	120
142	Ld. R. VOTA PVBL . P . M . TR . P., Jupiter, naked except for cloak on shoulders, stg. front, hd. l., holding thunderbolt and sceptre; before, small figure of Macrinus stg. *B.M.C.* 1 note; *R.I.C.* 5	110
142a	Lc. R. — As last. *B.M.C.* 1; *R.I.C.* 5	100
142b	Lc. R. — As before, but Macrinus stands on r. of Jupiter. *B.M.C.* 1 note; *R.I.C.* 5 note (*R. D. hoard*)	110
144	Ld and/or c. R. — Fides stg. front, hd. l., between two standards, and holding two more, one in each hand. *B.M.C.* 3 note; *R.I.C.* 8 ..	100
145	**Antoninianus.** Rc. R. — As last. *B.M.C.* 3 note; *R.I.C.* 9 (*Rdc*) ..	300
145a	Rd. R. — As last. *B.M.C.* 3	300
147	**Denarius.** Ld. R. — Felicitas stg. half-left, holding caduceus and sceptre. *B.M.C.* 2 note; *R.I.C.* 6	90
147a	Lc. R. — As last. *B.M.C.* 2; *R.I.C.* 6	90
147b	**Antoninianus.** Rd. R. — As last. *B.M.C.* 2 note; *R.I.C.* 7 ..	300
147c	Rc. R. — As last. *B.M.C.* 2 note; *R.I.C.* 7 (*Lawrence*)	300
147d	Rdc. hb. R. — As last. *B.M.C.* 2 note; *R.I.C.* 7 (*Ciani*)	300
149	Rc. R. — Salus seated l., feeding out of patera snake coiled around altar, and holding sceptre. *B.M.C.* 4 note; *R.I.C.* 11	300
150	**Denarius.** Lc. R. — As last. *B.M.C.* 4; *R.I.C.* 10	100
153	Ldc. R. — Securitas seated l., as **126** (*Cohen has* spear *for* sceptre *in error*). *B.M.C.* 5 note; *R.I.C.* 13	100

DIADUMENIAN

218 A.D.

Marcus Opelius Diadumenianus, the son of Macrinus and Nonia Celsa, was born in A.D. 208, *on the 19th Dec., the anniversary of the birth of Antoninus Pius. He was given the rank of Caesar on the elevation of Macrinus, who gave him the additional name of Antoninus. In the following year he was raised to the rank of Augustus, although only nine years old. He only enjoyed this title for a month or so, as after the revolt that overthrew Macrinus he tried to escape to Parthia, but was captured and executed.*

Obverse legends.

As Caesar

A. M . OPEL . DIADVMENIANVS CAES.

B. M . OPEL . ANT . DIADVMENIAN . CAES.

As Augustus

C. IMP . C . M . OPEL . ANT . DIADVMEN . AVG.

Obverse types.

bd.	Bare-headed bust right, draped
bd. hb.	,, ,, ,, ,, seen half from back
bdc.	,, ,, ,, draped and cuirassed
bdc. hb.	,, ,, ,, ,, ,, ,, seen half from back
rd.	Radiate bust right draped, seen half from back
rdc.	,, ,, ,, draped and cuirassed
ld.	Laureate bust right, draped (and cuirassed ?), seen half from back.

References.

Except for Cohen the references are Macrinus numbers

1 bis Denarius. Cld. ℞. FELICITAS TEMPORVM, Felicitas stg. half-left, holding cornucopiae and caduceus. *B.M.C.* 95; *R.I.C.* 118 ..

Excessively rare, if not unique

1 Abd. ℞. FIDES MILITVM, Fides stg. l. between two standards, and holding two more, one in each hand (Hy. ?; *rev. of Macrinus*). *B.M.C.* p. 511, †; *R.I.C.* 100 .. ..

1a Bbdc. ℞. LVNA LVCIFERA, Luna stg. in biga prancing l. (Hy., *base or plated; rev. of Julia Domna*). *B.M.C* 96; *R.I.C.* p. 14 note. .. ..

1b Bbdc. ℞. PIETAS AVG., priestly emblems. *B.M.C.* p. 511, ‡ (Hy.). *R.I.C.* p. 14 note (*false*) .. ..

N.B. *Some of the standards in the following are legionary eagles*

3 Bbd. ℞. PRINC . IVVENTVTIS, prince stg. front or slightly l., hd. r., holding standard and sceptre or parazonium; to r., two standards. *B.M.C.* 87-91; *R.I.C.* 102 .. .. £200

3a   3b

3a Bbd. hb. ℞. — As last (*Tinchant cat. and G. R. Arnold coll.*) 200
3b Bbdc. ℞. — As last. *B.M.C.* 84 note; *R.I.C.* 102; (*Mazzini cat.*) .. 200
3c Bbdc. hb. ℞. — As last (*Tinchant cat.*) .. ..
4 Bbd. ℞. — As last (*plated or Æ*) .. ..
6 Abd. hb. ℞. — As last. *B.M.C.* 84 note; *R.I.C.* 104 200
6a Bbdc (and bd?). ℞. — As last, but prince's hd. l. *B.M.C.* 84 note; *R.I.C.* 105 and 102 note 225

11   14b

11 Antoninianus. Ardc. ℞. — Prince stg. half-left, holding baton and sceptre (or spear); to r., two standards. *B.M.C.* 82 note; *R.I.C.* 106 .. 750
11a Ard. hb. ℞. — As last. *B.M.C.* 82 and p. 621; *R.I.C.* 106 750
12 Denarius. Abd. hb. ℞. — As last. *B.M.C.* 82 note; *R.I.C.* 107 .. 200
12a Abdc. ℞. — As last. *B.M.C.* 82 note and p. 621; *R.I.C.* 107 .. 200
14 Bbd. ℞. — As last. *B.M.C.* 82 note; *R.I.C.* 109 200
14a Bbdc. ℞. — As last. *B.M.C.* 85-6; *R.I.C.* 108 200
14b Bbd. hb. ℞. — As last (*Tinchant cat. and G. R. Arnold coll.*) 200

17   21

17 Quinarius. Bbdc (or bd or bc). ℞. — Prince stg. front, hd. r., holding
standard and sceptre, another standard on r. *B.M.C.* 83; *R.I.C.* 111 *Extr. rare*
18 Denarius. Abd. ℞. PRINCIPI IVVENTVTIS, prince stg., as **11.** *B.M.C.*
p. 510, * (*very doubtful*); *R.I.C.* 112   ..   ..
21 Bbd. hb (*Cohen* DIADVMENIANVS *in error*). ℞. SPES PVBLICA, Spes walking
l., holding flower and raising skirt. *B.M.C.* 94; *R.I.C.* 116   ..   .. £200
21a Bbdc. ℞. — As last. *B.M.C.* 92-3; *R.I.C.* 117 200
21b Bbdc. hb. ℞. — As last (*Tinchant and Mazzini cat.*) 200

THE SEVERAN DYNASTY

m. = married

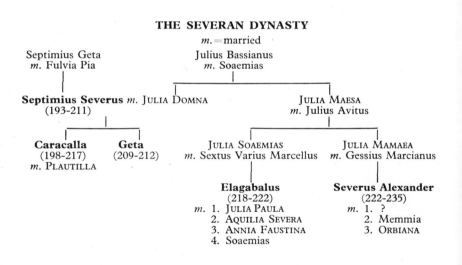

Septimius Geta   Julius Bassianus
m. Fulvia Pia   *m.* Soaemias

Septimius Severus *m.* JULIA DOMNA   JULIA MAESA
(193-211)   *m.* Julius Avitus

Caracalla   **Geta**   JULIA SOAEMIAS   JULIA MAMAEA
(198-217)   (209-212)   *m.* Sextus Varius Marcellus   *m.* Gessius Marcianus
m. PLAUTILLA

                              Elagabalus   **Severus Alexander**
                               (218-222)   (222-235)
                         m. 1. JULIA PAULA   *m.* 1. ?
                              2. AQUILIA SEVERA   2. Memmia
                              3. ANNIA FAUSTINA   3. ORBIANA
                              4. Soaemias

ELAGABALUS
218-222 A.D.

Varius Avitus Bassianus was the son of Sextus Varius Marcellus and Julia Soaemias, daughter of Julia Maesa, and niece of Julia Domna; he was therefore first cousin of Caracalla. He was born in 205 A.D. at Emesa in Syria. His connection with the imperial family and the wealth of his grandmother obtained for him the appointment of Priest of Elagabalus (or Heliogabalus), a deity much worshipped at Emesa. In 218, Maesa changed his name to Marcus Aurelius Antoninus and pretended he was not the son of his father but the result of intimacy between Soaemias and Caracalla. The troops at Emesa were won over by Maesa, and the youth, generally called Elagabalus, was proclaimed by them, as Macrinus had become unpopular. Following the defeat of the army of Macrinus, Elagabalus was accepted by the Senate and began a leisurely journey to Rome. On his arrival he gave some magnificent spectacles and had a temple built in honour of his Syrian god. Maesa, perceiving that he was displeasing the Romans, persuaded him to adopt his cousin Severus Alexander. His reign was notorious for religious fanaticism, for cruelty, bloodshed and excesses of every description. There was general satisfaction amongst the people when, in 222, the Praetorian guards mutinied and killed the emperor and his mother, their two bodies being dragged through the streets and thrown into the Tiber.

Obverse legends.

A. ANTONINVS PIVS FEL . AVG. 218-19 A.D. (Eastern mint only)
B. IMP . ANTONINVS AVG. 219 -20 A.D.
C. IMP . ANTONINVS PIVS AVG. 220-22 A.D.
D. IMP . CAES . ANTONINVS AVG. 219 A.D.
E. IMP . CAES . M . AVR ANTONINVS AVG. 218 A.D.

N.B.—*Obverse legend "A" is the same as "G" of Caracalla, and the coins can only be separated by the portraiture, type and style. Coins of Elagabalus with this legend are all from the Eastern mint, whilst those of Caracalla were struck at Rome.*

Obverse types.

Unless otherwise stated all are seen slightly from the back, and are to right.

l.   laureate head.
ld.   „   bust, draped
ldf.   „   „   „   seen from the front
ldfb.   „   „   „   „   „   „   „   bearded
ldfh.   „   „   „   with horn over forehead, seen from the front
ldfhb.   „   „   „   „   „   „   „   „   „   „   „   bearded
ldc.   „   „   draped and cuirassed
rd.   radiate bust, draped
rdc.   „   „   draped and cuirassed.

Mints.

The *British Museum Catalogue* attribute the ones marked with (A) after the obverse type to Antioch or some other eastern mint and the rest to Rome. *Roman Imperial Coinage* attribute to Antioch nos. 165-204 (pp. 40-4).

1 **Denarius.** Cl. ℞. ABVNDANTIA AVG., Abundantia stg. half-left, emptying cornucopiae held in both hands across body; star in field r. *B.M.C.* 192; *R.I.C.* 56 .. .. £30

1a   13

1a Cld. ℞. — As last. *B.M.C.* 189-91; *R.I.C.* 56 .., ... 30
1b Cld. ℞. — As last, but star in field l. *B.M.C.* 193-4; *R.I.C.* 56 .. 30
2 Bld(A). ℞. ADVENTVS AVG., emperor, in military dress, cloak floating behind, raising r. hand, on horse walking r. *B.M.C.* 309; *R.I.C.* 184 .. 65
5a Cldc. ℞. ADVENTVS AVGVSTI, as before, but horse l. and emperor holds spear in l. hand. *B.M.C.* 196 (*a fine cast from gold?*); *R.I.C.* 58 (*doubtful*)
11a A, but ends AG, ld(A). ℞. AEQVITATI AVGG., Aequitas stg. l., holding scales and cornucopiae (Hy.). *B.M.C.* p. 587, †; *R.I.C.* 163A (*R. D. hoard*)
12 Ald(A). ℞. AETERNITAS AVG., Aeternitas, diad., stg. l., holding patera over altar and sceptre. *B.M.C.* p. 573, *; *R.I.C.* 185 60
13 Bld. ℞. ANNONA AVGVSTI, Annona (*Cohen*, Abundantia) stg. half-left, holding corn-ears and resting l. arm on rudder set on globe; before her, modius filled with corn-ears. *B.M.C.* 126-7; *R.I.C.* 59 35
14 Bld(A). ℞. BONVS EVENTVS, Bonus Eventus, diad., stg. half-left, before lighted altar, holding patera and two corn-ears. *B.M.C.* 310 note; *R.I.C.* 186 35
14a Bldc(A). ℞. — As last. *B.M.C.* 310-1; *R.I.C.* 186 35

15   15d

15 Aldc(A). ℞. CONCORDIA around, MILIT. in ex., two standards between two legionary eagles (on *vexilla*). *B.M.C.* 275; *R.I.C.* 187 35
15a Al(A). ℞. — As last. *B.M.C.* 276; *R.I.C.* 187 35
15b Ald(A). ℞. — As last. *B.M.C.* 274; *R.I.C.* 60 (*irregular issue?*) .. 35
15c ANTONINVS FEL . AVG., l(A). ℞. — As last. *B.M.C.* 276 note (*regular issue?*); *R.I.C.* 187 note (*R. D. hoard*) 35
15d A, but FELIX AVG., ldc(A). ℞. — As last. (*G. R. Arnold*) 35
17 Clc, with only a touch of drapery, f. ℞. CONSERVATOR AVG., triumphal quadriga proceeding slowly l., and carrying the conical stone of Elagabalus of Emesa, in front of which is eagle with wings spread. *B.M.C.* 198 note; *R.I.C.* 62 .. .. *Extremely rare if genuine*
19 Cld. ℞. — Sol, rad., walking l., raising r. hand and holding whip; in field, star. *B.M.C.* 199-200; *R.I.C.* 63 35
20a Aldc(A). ℞. CONS . II . P . P., Roma seated l., holding Victory and spear (or sceptre); beside her, shield. *B.M.C.* p. 580, *; *R.I.C.* 165 45
20b ANTONINVS V . PIVS FEL . AVG., ld(A). ℞. — As last (*G. R. Arnold*). *Illustrated at top of next page* 45

20b   22

21 Aldc(A). ℞. CONSVL II., Aequitas stg. half-left, holding scales and
    cornucopiae. *B.M.C.* 307 note; *R.I.C.* 166   ..   ..   £35
22 Aldc(A). ℞. CONSVL II . P . P., as last. *B.M.C.* 307 note; *R.I.C.* 167 ..   35
23 Bld(A). ℞. — As last. *B.M.C.* 307 note; *R.I.C.* 168   35
23a Bldc(A). ℞. — As last. *B.M.C.* 307-8; *R.I.C.* 168   35
24 Aldc(A). ℞. — Roma seated, as **20a**. *B.M.C.* p. 580, *; note *R.I.C.* 169   45

26 Bld. ℞. COS . III . P . P., conical stone of Elagabalus of Emesa, adorned
    with stars, eagle with spread wings in front. *B.M.C.* p. 584; *R.I.C.* 176;
    (*G. R. Arnold*)   750
26a Aldc(A). ℞. FECVNDITAS, Fecunditas seated r., holding branch and
    sceptre, between two children (Hy.; *rev. somewhat as Julia Maesa*).
    B.M.C. p. 587, ‖; *R.I.C.* 164A   ..   ..
26b Ald(A). ℞. FELICITAS AVG., Felicitas stg. l., holding caduceus and
    cornucopiae. *B.M.C.* p. 573, †; *R.I.C.* 187A   ..   ..
26c **Antoninianus** (=*double denarius*). ANTONINVS PIVS AVG., rdc(A). ℞.
    FELICITAS AVGG., as last (Hy.). *B.M.C.* p. 621 (*Oldroyd*) ..   ..   ..
27 **Denarius.** Al(A). ℞. FELICITAS around, TEMP. in ex., galley with sail and
    seven or eight rowers proceeding r.; at stern, pilot, acrostolium and
    standard; at prow, furled sail or vexillum. *B.M.C.* 277 note; *R.I.C.* 188   65
27a Aldc(A). ℞. — As last. *B.M.C.* 277; *R.I.C.* 188   65
27b Alc(A). ℞. — As last. *B.M.C.* 277 note; *R.I.C.* 188   65
27c Al(A). ℞. — As last, but ten rowers. *B.M.C.* 278   65
27d Al(A). ℞. — As last, but five rowers (*Brussels*)   65

28 **Antoninianus.** Drdc. ℞. FIDES EXERCITVS, Fides seated l., holding eagle
    and standard, another standard before her. *B.M.C.* 106; *R.I.C.* 67 ..   70
28a Drd. ℞. — As last. *B.M.C.* 107; *R.I.C.* 67   70
30 **Denarius.** Dld. ℞. — As last. *B.M.C.* 109; *R.I.C.* 68   30

30a   32

30a **Denarius.** Dldc. ℞. FIDES EXERCITVS, Fides seated l., holding eagle
and standard, another standard before her. *B M.C.* 108; *R.I.C.* 68 .. £30
31 **Antoninianus.** Erdc. ℞. — As last. *B.M.C.* 11; *R.I.C.* 70 60
31a Erd. ℞. — As last. *B.M.C.* 12-14; *R.I.C.* 70 60
32 **Denarius.** Eldc. ℞. — As last. *B.M.C.* 15; *R.I.C.* 71 30
32a Eld. ℞. — As last. *B.M.C.* 15 note; *R.I.C.* 71 (*Lawrence*) 30
38 Bldc. ℞. FIDES MILITVM, Fides stg. facing, hd. r., holding vexillum
at side and standard across body. *B.M.C.* 137; *R.I.C.* 73 30

38a   39

38a Bld. ℞. — As last. *B.M.C.* 133-6; *R.I.C.* 73 30
39 **Antoninianus.** Brdc. ℞. — As last. *B.M.C.* 131-2; *R.I.C.* 72 .. 60
39a Brd. ℞. — As last. *B.M.C.* 128-30; *R.I.C.* 72 60
40 **Denarius.** Eld. ℞. — Fides stg., holding two standards, between
another two. *B.M.C.* p. 532, *; *R.I.C.* 74 40
41 Eldc (*Cohen*, ld *in error*). ℞. — Elagabalus, laur. and in military dress,
stg. (or advancing) half-right, between two soldiers, each carrying a
standard, the one in front also holding shield. *B.M.C.* 16; *R.I.C.* 75 200
43 Cld. ℞. — Legionary eagle between two standards. *B.M.C.* 202 note;
R.I.C. 77 35

44   47

44 Cld. ℞. — As last, but one or two shields at the base of each of them.
B.M.C. 201-2; *R.I.C.* 78 35
45 Eld. ℞. FIDES PVBLICA, Fides stg. r., holding corn-ears and basket of
fruit. *B.M.C.* p. 532, †; *R.I.C.* 79 .. ..
46 Cld(A ?). ℞. FORTVNA AVG., Fortuna stg. half-left, holding rudder on globe
and cornucopiae. *B.M.C.* 203 note; *R.I.C.* 80 40
47 Aldc(A). ℞. FORTVNA REDVX, Fortuna, wearing modius, seated l., holding
patera and cornucopiae; beside seat, wheel. *B.M.C.* 279 note; *R.I.C.* 81 35
47a Ald(A). ℞. — As last. *B.M.C.* 279; *R.I.C.* 189 35

47b Aldc. ℞. — As last, but rudder instead of patera. *R.I.C.* 81 note (*R. D. hoard*) £40
   Cohen has obv. legend commencing ANTONIVS *for* 47, *presumably in error, and this is dittoed for* 50 *and* 51.
48 Ald(A?). ℞. FORTVNAE AVG., Fortuna stg., as **46.** *B.M.C.* 279 note; *R.I.C.* 82A 40
48a Cld. ℞. — As last. *B.M.C.* 203 (no globe); *R.I.C.* 82 35
50 Ald(A?). ℞. FORTVNAE REDVCI, as last. *B.M.C.* 204 note; *R.I.C.* 83 .. 35
50a Cld. ℞. — As last. *B.M.C.* 205-8; *R.I.C.* 83A 30
50b Cld. ℞. — As last, but no globe. *B.M.C.* 204; *R.I.C.* 83A note .. 30
50c **Quinarius.** Cld. ℞. — As **50.** *B.M.C.* p. 621 (*poor silver; Oldroyd*) 300
51 Ald. ℞. — As last. *R.I.C.* 84 300

54 **Denarius.** Aldc(A). ℞. HILARITAS AVG., Hilaritas stg. front, looking l., holding patera or wreath and long palm, between two naked children who look up to her with outstretched hands. *B.M.C.* 282-3; *R.I.C.*190 .. 30
55 Al(A). ℞. — As last. *B M.C.* 280; *R.I.C.* 190 30
55a Ald(A). ℞. — As last. *B.M.C.* 281; *R.I.C.* 190 30
56 Bld(A?). ℞. — As last. *B.M.C.* p. 581, *; *R.I.C.* 85 35
57 As last (*bare or* Æ). *B.M.C.* p. 581, * note .. ..
58 Cldfh. ℞. INVICTVS SACERDOS AVG., Elagabalus stg. front, hd. l., holding patera over altar and branch; on ground, horn; star in field r. *B.M.C.* 209 note; *R.I.C.* 87 90
60 Cldfh. ℞. — As last, but without the horn, and the star like a comet. *B.M.C.* 209 note; *R.I.C.* 86 note 40

61   66

61 Cldfhb (some A). ℞. — As last, but Elagabalus holds patera and club, and recumbant bull behind altar; star or comet in field l. *B.M.C.* 212 and 330; *R.I.C.* 88 and 191 30
61a As last, but no star. *B.M.C.* 211 30
61b Cldfb. ℞. — As **61.** *B.M.C.* 209-10; *R.I.C.* 88 30
61c Cldfh. ℞. — As last, but Elagabalus wears pointed cap, and two stars in field, one l. and one r. *B.M.C.* 213 35
62 Cl. ℞. — As **61.** *B.M.C.* 209 note; *R.I.C.* 88 and 191 (a) 30
63 Cl? ℞. — As last (*base, plated or* Æ) .. ..
66 **Antoninianus.** Brdc. ℞. IOVI CONSERVATORI, Jupiter, naked except for cloak hanging from r. shoulder and l. arm, stg. front, hd. l., holding thunderbolt and sceptre; at feet l., eagle; on r., two standards. *B.M.C.* 139; *R.I.C.* 90 70
66b Brd. ℞. — As last. *B.M.C.* 138; *R.I.C.* 90 70
66b Drd. ℞. — As last (Hy.; *ancient forgery*) (*New York*) .. .. ..
67 **Denarius.** Bld. ℞. — As last. *B.M.C.* 140 note; *R.I.C.* 89 30
67a Bldc. ℞. — As last. *B.M.C.* 140; *R.I.C.* 89 30
68 Bldc. ℞. — As before, but only one standard. *B.M.C.* 141; *R.I.C.* 91 30
68a Bld. ℞. — As last. *B.M.C.* 142; *R.I.C.* 91 30

69 Denarius. *Obv.?* R. IOVI VICTORI, Elagabalus (probably Jupiter) stg., holding thunderbolt and spear; at feet, eagle; behind him, two standards. *B.M.C.* p. 566; *R.I.C.* 92 (*doubtful*) .. ..

70 Bldc. R. LAETITIA PVBL., Laetitia stg. half-left, holding wreath and rudder on globe. *B.M.C.* 147 note; *R.I.C.* 95 .. .. £30

70a Bld. R. — As last. *B.M.C.* 147; *R.I.C.* 95 30

71 Antoninianus. Brd. R. — As last. *B.M.C.* 143-4; *R.I.C.* 94 .. 60

72 Brdc. R. — As last. *B.M.C.* 145-6; *R.I.C.* 94 60

72a Erd. R. — As last, perhaps without globe. *B.M.C.* p. 532, ‡; *R.I.C.* 93

73 Denarius. Cldc. R. — As last (Hy.?, *plated*). *B.M.C.* p. 566; *R.I.C.* 96

73a Dl. R. — As last (Æ) (*Brussels*) .. ..

74a Cldc. R. LIB . AVG . II. in ex., P . M . TR P . II . COS . II . P . P. around, Elagabalus seated on platform, Liberalitas stg. and citizen mounting steps. *B.M.C.* p. 621 (*cast from N*); *R.I.C.* 9 note (*modern copy of N*) ..

78 *Obv.?* R LIBERALITAS AVG., Liberalitas stg. l., holding abacus and cornucopiae. *B.M.C.* p. 533, * and p. 568 (*doubtful*); *R.I.C.* 97.. ..

79   86

79 Bld. R. LIBERALITAS AVG . II., Liberalitas stg. front or slightly l., hd. l., holding abacus and cornucopiae set on base. *B.M.C.* 148-50 (*says,* on globe. *It is possible that the cornucopiae has a flat base and is then on globe*); *R.I.C.* 102 30

80 Bld. R. — As before, but no base or globe. *B.M.C.* 148 note; *R.I.C.* 99 35

80a Bl. R. — As last (*Gnecchi*)

81 Quinarius. Cld. R. — As last. *B.M.C.* 217A (*star in field?*); *R.I.C.* 101 300

81a Denarius. Cld. R. — As last. *B.M.C.* 214-5; *R.I.C.* 100 30

82 Eld. R. — As last. *R.I.C.* 98

86 Cld. R. LIBERALITAS AVG . III., as before, but star in field r. *B.M.C.* 216; *R.I.C.* 103 30

86a Cld(A). R. — As last, but star in field l. *B.M.C.* 311 35

86b Cld. R. — As last. *B.M.C.* 217 (*star in field r. as well?*); *R.I.C.* 103 30

87 As one of the last three (*base, plated or* Æ). *B.M.C.* 216 note .. ..

88 Cld. R. LIBERALITAS AVG . IIII., as **86.** *B.M.C.* 216 note; *R.I.C.* 104 (*Lawrence*) 50

90 Cld. R. LIBERTAS AVG., Libertas stg. half-left, holding cap (*pileus*) and sceptre or rod (*vindicta*). *B.M.C.* 220 note; *R.I.C.* 106 35

91 Quinarius. Cld. R. — As last. *R.I.C.* 109 250

91a Cld. R. — As before, but star in field r. *B.M.C.* 222A; *R.I.C.* 109 .. 250

92 Denarius. Cld. R. — As last. *B.M.C.* 221 (*and* 220, very large star); *R.I.C.* 107 30

92a Cld. R. — As before, but star in field l. *B.M.C.* 222; *R.I.C.* 107   ..   £30
92b Cldc. R. — As **91a**. *B.M.C.* 219; *R.I.C.* 107   30
93 Cldfb. R. — As last. *R.I.C.* 108   30
94 Quinarius. Cld to left. R. — As last. *B.M.C.* 222B; *R.I.C.* 110   ..   250
97 Denarius. Cldfb. R. — Libertas stg. l. (or half-left), holding cap and cornucopiae. *B.M.C.* 219 note; *R.I.C.* 111   30
98 Cldc. R. — As last, but with star in field. *B.M.C.* 219 note; *R.I.C.* 112   30
98a Cldf. R. — As last (*Brussels*)   30
100 Cldfb. R. — Libertas stg. l. (or half-left), holding cornucopiae and sceptre. *B.M.C.* 219 note; *R.I.C.* 113   35
101 Antoninianus. Brdc. R. LIBERTAS AVGVSTI, Libertas seated l., holding cap and sceptre or rod. *B.M.C.* 151 note; *R.I.C.* 114   90

101a   109

101a Denarius. Bld. R. — As last. *B.M.C.* 151-3; *R.I.C.* 115   30
101b Bld(A). R. — As last. *B.M.C.* 312   30
101c Eldc. R. — As last (*Brussels*)   35
102 Bld. R. — Libertas stg. l., holding cap and sceptre; star in field. *B.M.C.* 151 note; *R.I.C.* 116   35
102a Cld. R. — As last. *B.M.C.* 219 note; *R.I.C.* 117 (*Lawrence*)   35
102b Quinarius. Cld. R. — As last. *R.I.C.* 118   300
109 Dld. R. MARS VICTOR, Mars, naked except for cloak floating behind waist, advancing r., holding spear transversely and trophy over shoulder. *B.M.C.* 112-3; *R.I.C.* 121   30
110 Dldc. R. — As last. *B.M.C.* 112 note; *R.I.C.* 121   30
111 Antoninianus. Drd. R. — As last. *B.M.C.* 110; *R.I.C.* 120   ..   70
111a Drdc. R. — As last. *B.M.C.* 111; *R.I.C.* 120   70
112 Erd. R. — As last. *B.M.C.* 19-20; *R.I.C.* 122   60

113   120

113 Erdc. R. — As last. *B.M.C.* 17-18; *R.I.C.* 122   60
113a Denarius. Eldc. R. — As last. *B.M.C.* 21; *R.I.C.* 123   30
113b Eld. R. — As last. *B.M.C.* 22; *R.I.C.* 123   30
113c El. R. — As last. *B.M.C.* 21 note; *R.I.C.* 123   35
113d E, but AVG. for AVR., ld. R. — As last. *B.M.C.* 21 note; *R.I.C.* 121 note   35
119 Dld. R. NOBILITAS, woman stg., holding spear and a small Victory (Hy. ?). *R.I.C.* 124   ..   ..
120 Cld. R. PAX AVGVSTI, Pax running l., holding branch and sceptre. *B.M.C.* 223-4; *R.I.C.* 125   30

124 Antoninianus. Brdc. R. PIETAS AVG., Pietas stg. half-left, sacrificing over altar and holding box of perfume in l. hand. *B.M.C.* 154; *R.I.C.* 126   £90
R.I.C. 127 *gives a denarius of this type in error.*

125 Erd. R. P . M . TR . P . COS . P . P., Roma seated l. on throne, holding Victory and sceptre, shield at side. *B.M.C.* 4-5; *R.I.C.* 1 65

126 Erdc. R. — As last. *B.M.C.* 3; *R.I.C.* 1 65

126a Drd. R. — As last. *B.M.C.* 4 note; *R.I.C.* 2 (*Lawrence*) 75

127 Denarius. Eld. R. — As last. *B.M.C.* 6; *R.I.C.* 3 30

128 Eldc. R. — As last. *B.M.C.* 6 note; *R.I.C.* 3 30

133 IMP . ANTONI . . . . . VS ACI, ld. R. P . M . TR . . . . . COS . P., Apollo seated l., leaning elbow on lyre (Hy.; *plated or Æ; rev. of Caracalla*) ..

131a E, but without CAES. R. — Genius (?) stg. l., holding corn-ears (?) and sacrificing out of patera over altar (*barbarous, base; G. R. Arnold*) ..

134 Cld(A). R. P . M . TR . P . II . COS . II . P . P., Sol, naked except for cloak, stg. half-left, raising r. hand and holding whip in l. *B.M.C.* p. 546 (pl. 87, 2) and 304; *R.I.C.* 17 30

134a Bld. R. — As last. *B.M.C.* p. 544, *; *R.I.C.* 17 (*R. D. hoard*) .. 35

133 Eld. R. — Roma seated l., as **125.** *B.M.C.* 88; *R.I.C.* 13 30

138 Antoninianus. Erd. R. — As last. *B.M.C.* 84 note; *R.I.C.* 12 70

139 Erdc. R. — As last. *B.M.C.* 84-6; *R.I.C.* 12 70

139a Erd. R. — As last, but small globe in ex. *B.M.C.* 87; *R.I.C.* 12 note 70

140 Drdc. R. — As **125.** *B.M.C.* 89; *R.I.C.* 14 70

141   143

141 Drd. R. — As last. *B.M.C.* 89 note; *R.I.C.* 14 70

141a Denarius. Dld(A). R. — As last. *B.M.C.* 302; *R.I.C.* 15 and 171A 35

142 Bld. R. — As last. *B.M.C.* 93 (*and probably* 92); *R.I.C.* 16 .. 30

142a Bld(A). R. — As last. *B.M.C.* 303 35

143 Bld. R. — Pax running l., holding olive-branch and sceptre. *B.M.C.* 97-8; *R.I.C.* 21 30

144 Bld. R. — Providentia stg. front, with legs crossed, hd. l., leaning l. elbow on column and holding wand over globe at feet. *B.M.C.* 102-4; *R.I.C.* 23 30

144a Bldc. R. — As last (*New York*) 30

145 Antoninianus. Brdc. R. — As last. *B.M.C.* 99-100; *R.I.C.* 22 .. 70

146 Brd. R. — As last. *B.M.C.* 101; *R.I.C.* 22 70

147 Denarius. Cld. R. — Fortuna seated l., holding rudder on globe and cornucopiae; under throne, wheel. *B.M.C.* 305 note; *R.I.C.* 20 .. ..

148 Antoninianus. Brdc. R. — As last. *B.M.C.* 94; *R.I.C.* 18 70

148a Brd. R. — As last. *B.M.C.* 95; *R.I.C.* 18 70

149 Denarius. Bld. R. — As last. *B.M.C.* 96; *R.I.C.* 19 30

149a Bld or dc(A). R. — As last. *B.M.C.* 305 (*poorer style than last*) .. 35

150 Bld. R. — Elagabalus stg. l., sacrificing over altar; to l., horn; on r., star. *B.M.C.* p. 545 (*quite doubtful*); *R.I.C.* 24 .. .. ..

151 Bld. ℞. P . M . TR . P . III . COS . III . P . P., Jupiter, naked to waist, seated l. on throne, holding Victory and sceptre; at feet, eagle. *B.M.C.* 178; *R.I.C.* 27 .. .. £30

151a Bld(A). ℞. — As last. *B.M.C.* 326-8; *R.I.C.* p. 41, † 30

152 As the last two (*plated or Æ*) .. ..

153 Cldc. ℞. — Sol, as **134**, but advancing l.; in field, star. *B.M.C.* 180 note; *R.I.C.* 28 30

154 Cld. ℞. — As last. *B.M.C.* 179-80; *R.I.C.* 28 30

154a Cld(A). ℞. — As last. *B.M.C.* 329; *R.I.C.* p. 41, † 35

154b Cl. ℞. — As last. *B.M.C.* 180 note; *R.I.C.* 28 (*Baldwin*) 40

155 As **154** (*plated or base or Æ*). *B.M.C.* 180 note .. .. ..

161 *Obv.?* ℞. — Pax stg., holding branch and cornucopiae. *B.M.C.* p. 557, (c) (*doubtful*); *R.I.C.* 29 .. ..

163 Cld. ℞. — Providentia stg. l., globe at her feet; in field, star. *B.M.C.* p. 557, (b); *R.I.C.* 31 .. ..

164 *Obv.?* ℞. — Elagabalus stg., extending r. hand. *B.M.C.* p. 558, (d) (*doubtful*); *R.I.C.* 32 .. ..

180 Bld. ℞. — Elagabalus in slow quadriga, holding branch and eagle-tipped sceptre; behind him, Victory. *B.M.C.* p. 556, † (*confirmation required*); *R.I.C.* 36 .. ..

N.B.—*In nos.* 181-185 *Cohen omits the* P. *after* TR. *in error.*

182 Cldc and/or ld. ℞. P . M . TR . P . IIII . COS . III . P . P., Sol, rad., naked except for cloak over l. arm, stg. half-left, looking back r., raising r. hand and holding whip in l.; star in field l. *B.M.C.* 240 note and 245; *R.I.C.* 38 30

184 Cl. ℞. — Sol advancing l., partly dr. with flying cloak, otherwise as last. *B.M.C.* 242-3; *R.I.C.* 40 30

184a Cld. ℞. — As last. *B.M.C.* 244 (*large star*); *R.I.C.* 40 30

185 Eld. ℞. — As last (Hy.; *base, plated or Æ*). *B.M.C.* 244 note; *R.I.C.* 41

189 Cl. ℞. — Providentia stg. half-left, holding wand over globe at feet and cornucopiae; star in field r. *B.M.C.* 250; *R.I.C.* 42 30

189a Cld. ℞. — As last. *B.M.C.* 247-8; *R.I.C.* 42 30

189b Cld. ℞. — As last, but star in field l. *B.M.C.* 249; *R.I.C.* 42.. .. 30

189c Cld. ℞. — As last, but no star. *B.M.C.* 246; *R.I.C.* 42 30

190 Bld. ℞. — As one of the last (Hy.). *B.M.C.* 250 note; *R.I.C.* 190 ..

194 Cldc. ℞. — Victory advancing or flying l., holding open wreath, garland, or diadem in each hand, a small shield either side of her skirt; in field r., star. *B.M.C.* 253 note; *R.I.C.* 45 30

194a Cldc or ld. ℞. — As before, but star high l. *B.M.C.* 254; *R.I.C.* 45 .. 30

194b As last, but with horn over forehead. *B.M.C.* 255 30

195 Cld. ℞. — As **194**. *B.M.C.* 251-2; *R.I.C.* 45 30

195a Cl. ℞. — As last. *B.M.C.* 253; *R.I.C.* 45 30

196   205

196 Denarius. Cldfhb. ℞. — (*Cohen gives* COS . IIII. *in error*), Elagabalus
      stg. half-left, sacrificing out of patera over lighted altar, holding branch
      (cypress?) upwards in l. hand; in field, star. *B.M.C.* 256-8; *R.I.C.* 46 ..   £30
196a Cldfhb(A). ℞. — As last. *B.M.C.* 339; *R.I.C.* 177   30
      N.B.—*The object held by Elagabalus, branch or club (see* **208**), *is not easy
      to distinguish. The standards on* **204-7a** *are not normal standards and where
      there are two on the same side, the* B.M.C. *describes one as a spear; we have
      followed* R.I.C. *and Cohen.*
196b As last, but bust also cuir. *R.I.C.* 46 (*Baldwin*)   30
197 Quinarius. Cldf. ℞. — As last. *B.M.C.* 263; *R.I.C.* 47   300

197a Denarius. Cldfh. ℞. — As last, but with sacrificial bull in place of
      altar. (*G. R. Arnold*)   45
197b As last, but attributed to mint of Antioch. *B.M.C.* 338 (*misdescribed, but
      see pl.* 93, 4)   50
204 Cldfhb. ℞. — As **196,** but Elagabalus holds club and there is a standard
      on either side. *B.M.C.* 262; *R.I.C.* 51   35
204a Cldfhb(A). ℞. — As last. *B.M.C.* 340; *R.I.C.* 178   35
205 Cldfhb. ℞. — As before, but he holds branch (or club at side) and both
      standards are on r. *B.M.C.* 260; *R.I.C.* 49   35
206 Cldfhb. ℞. — As last, but standard on either side. *B.M.C.* 259 and
      p. 621 (*Oldroyd*); *R.I.C.* 48   35
207 Cldfhb. ℞. — As last, but only one standard. *B.M.C.* 259 note; *R.I.C.*
      50 ..   ..
207a Cldfhb(A). ℞. — As last. *R.I.C.* 179 ..   ..
208 Cldfhb. ℞. — As **196,** but holding club. *B.M.C.* 256-8   35
209 As last (*plated or* Æ) ..   ..
213 Cldfb. ℞. P . M . TR . P . V . COS . IIII . P . P., Elagabalus before altar, holding
      branch, as **196.** *B.M.C.* 268 note; *R.I.C.* 53 (*Lawrence*) 35
213a As last, but Elagabalus holds club and not branch. *B.M.C.* 268 and 270;
      R.I.C. 52   35
213b As last, but (A). *B.M.C.* 341; *R.I.C.* 181   35
213c Cldfhb. ℞. — As **213a,** but large star. *B.M.C.* 269   35
218 Cldfhb. ℞. — Elagabalus in slow quadriga l. *B.M.C.* p. 587, * note 271
      note (*very doubtful*); *R.I.C.* 55 and 183   ..   ..
222 E, but ends PIVS AVG., ld. ℞. PONTIF. MAX . TR . P., Roma seated l.,
      holding Victory and sceptre; at side, shield. *B.M.C.* 1 note; *R.I.C.* 6
      (*Perhaps this is a mistake of Cohen for the next; or a copy of a gold coin*)
222a Eldc. ℞. — As last. *B.M.C.* 1-2; *R.I.C.* 8   35
222b Eld. ℞. — As last. *B.M.C.* 1 note; *R.I.C.* 8 (*Tinchant cat.*)   35
224 Dld. ℞. — As last (Hy. ?). *B.M.C.* 1 note; *R.I.C.* 7   40

225 IMP . ANTONINVS PILS . AVG., ld.   R. — As last (*plated or* Æ)   .. ..

237 Aldc(A).   R. PONT . MAX . TR . P . II . COS . II., Mars hurrying l., holding laurel-branch and trophy.   *B.M.C.* p. 579, *; *R.I.C.* 172 ..   ..   .. £40

242 Bld.   R. PROVID . DEORVM, Providentia stg. half-left, holding globe on extended hand and cornucopiae.   *B.M.C.* 161; *R.I.C.* 128   30

242a Bl(A).   R. — As last (*G. R. Arnold coll.*)   35

243 **Antoninianus.** Brdc.   R. — Providentia stg. front, hd. l., leaning against column, legs crossed, holding wand over globe at her feet and cornucopiae.   *B.M.C.* 155-6; *R.I.C.* 129   65

243a Brd.   R. — As last.   *B.M.C.* 157 (*Dorchester hoard*); *R.I.C.* 129   .. 65

244   255

244 **Denarius.** Bld.   R. — As last, *B.M.C.* 158-60; *R.I.C.* 130   30

245 Bldc.   R. — As last.   *B.M.C.* 159 note; *R.I.C.* 130   30

245a Dl(A).   R. — As last (*G. R. Arnold coll.*)   40

246 Cldfhb.   R. SACRED . DEI SOLIS ELAGAB., Elagabalus (*Cohen*, sometimes horned) stg. r., sacrificing out of patera over lighted altar and holding club or rod upright; in field, star.   *B.M.C.* 225 note; *R.I.C.* 131   35

246a Cldf(b ?).   R. — As last.   *B.M.C.* 225 note; *R.I.C.* 131   35

246b Cldcf(b ?).   R. — As last, perhaps branch for club (*Tinchant cat.*)   .. 35

247 **Quinarius.** As Cohen gives the B.M. for the pedigree of this piece, his description is a mistake for the next. ..   ..

248 Cldb to left.   R. — As **246,** but without star.   *B.M.C.* 228; *R.I.C.* 133B 350

248a Cldb.   R. — As last.   *R.I.C.* 133A 300

249 **Denarius.** Cl(b ?).   R. — As before, but two stars.   *B.M.C.* 225 note; *R.I.C.* 134   40

249a Cldfhb.   R. — As last, with two stars, perhaps branch for club (*Tinchant cat.*)   40

250 Type as the last few (*base, plates or* Æ).   *B.M.C.* 225 note   ..   ..

250a Cldfhb.   R. — As **246,** but out of rod comes bust of Sun-god (?) *B.M.C.* 226   50

250b Cld(A).   R. — As **246,** but he holds transverse sceptre.   *B.M.C.* 332; *R.I.C.* 194 note (*reads* SACERP . PEI, *barbarous; this agrees with B.M. illustration*)

252 Cldfh.   R. — As **246,** but Elagabalus stg. half-left, and holds club upwards.   *B.M.C.* 227; *R.I.C.* 135 35

254 **Antoninianus.** Erd.   R. SALVS ANTONINI AVG., Salus stg. half-right, holding snake across body and feeding it with cake.   *B.M.C.* 26-7; *R.I.C.* 138   60

255 Erdc.   R. — As last.   *B.M.C.* 23-5; *R.I.C.* 138   60

256 **Denarius.** Eld.   R. — As last.   *B.M.C.* 28-9; *R.I.C.* 140   .. 30

258 Eldc.   R. — As last.   *B.M.C.* 28 note; *R.I.C.* 140   30

259 **Antoninianus.** Drd.   R. — As last.   *B.M.C.* 114-5; *R.I.C.* 137 65

260 Drdc.   R. — As last.   *B.M.C.* 116; *R.I.C.* 137   65

261 **Denarius.** Dld.   R. — As last.   *B.M.C.* 117-9; *R.I.C.* 139   .. 30

261a Dldc.   R. — As last.   *B.M.C.* 120; *R.I.C.* 139   30

264   271

264 Denarius. Bld. ℞. SALVS AVGVSTI, Salus stg. front, hd. l., feeding out of patera snake coiling up from around altar, and holding rudder on globe. *B.M.C.* 162-3; *R.I.C.* 141 .. .. £30
264a Eld. ℞. — As last, but SALV₂ (Hy. ?; *irregular*). *B.M.C.* p. 534, *; *R.I.C.* 142 (*Lawrence*) .. ..
266 Bld. ℞. SANCT . DEO SOLI around, ELAGABAL. in ex., slow quadriga r., bearing conical stone of Elagabalus of Emesa, on front of which, an eagle; about it, four parasols. *R.I.C.* 144. 175
267 ANTONINVS FEL . PIVS AVG. ldc(A). ℞. — As last. *B.M.C.* 287 note; *R.I.C.* 197 150

268 Aldc(A). ℞. — As last. *B.M.C.* 284-5; *R.I.C.* 195 150
268a Ald(A). ℞. — As last, but legend continuous and running into ex. *B.M.C.* 286; *R.I.C.* 195 150
269 ANTONINVS PIVS FELIX AVG., l(A). ℞. As **266.** *B.M.C.* 287; *R.I.C.* 196 (*who also gives obv. ldc as in B.M. in error*) 150
270 *Obv.* ? ℞. SECVRIT . IMPERI., Securitas seated, as next. *R.I.C.* 145 note (*a coin of Caracalla*) .. ..
271 Cld. ℞. SECVRITAS SAECVLI, Securitas seated r., supporting head on r. hand, arm resting on back of throne, holding sceptre in l. *B.M.C.* 229; *R.I.C.* 145 35
271a Cldc. ℞. — As last. *B.M.C.* 229 note; *R.I.C.* 145 (*Lawrence*) 35

273   276

273 Bldc(A). ℞. SPEI PERPETVAE, Spes walking l., holding up flower and raising skirt. *B.M.C.* 313-4; *R.I.C.* 199 30
273a Al(A). ℞. SPES BONA, as last. *B.M.C.* p. 575, *; *R.I.C.* 199A 35
274 Bldc(A). ℞. SPEI in ex., TRIB . P . II . COS . II . P . P. around, as last. *B.M.C.* p. 579, † ; *R.I.C.* 173 45
275 Is a coin of Caracalla .. ..
276 Cldfh. ℞. SVMMVS SACERDOS AVg., Elagabalus stg. half-left, sacrificing out of patera over tripod-altar, and holding branch; in field, star. *B.M.C.* 232-3; *R.I.C.* 146 30
276a Cldfh. ℞. — As last, but holding club. *B.M.C.* 231 30

276b Cldf. ℞. — As last. *B.M.C.* 230 .. .. £30
276c Cldfb(A). ℞. — As last. *B.M.C.* 333 35
276d Cldfh(A). ℞. — As last. *R.I.C.* 200 (*Baldwin*) 35
276e Cldfh. ℞. — As **276**, but with prostrate bull behind altar (*Tinchant cat.*) 40
276f Cldfh. ℞. — As **276**, but without star (*Tinchant cat.*) 35
277 Cldfh. ℞. — As **276**, but Elagabalus half-right. *B.M.C.* 232 note;
R.I.C. 147 35

278 289

278 Aldc(A). ℞. TEMPORVM FEL., Felicitas stg. front, hd. l, holding patera
and caduceus. *B.M.C.* 289-90; *R.I.C.* 201 30
279 Al(A). ℞. — As last. *B.M.C.* 289 note; *R.I.C.* 201 .. ..

280 **Antoninianus.** Brd. ℞. TEMPORVM FELICITAS, as before, but holding
caduceus and cornucopiae. *B.M.C.* 166; *R.I.C.* 149 65
281 Brdc. ℞. — As last. *B.M.C.* 164-5; *R.I.C.* 149 65
281a Erdc. ℞. — As last. *B.M.C.* p. 534, †; *R.I.C.* 148 70

282 **Denarius.** Bld. ℞. — As last. *B.M.C.* 168; *R.I.C.* 150 30
282a Bldc. ℞. — As last. *B.M.C.* 167; *R.I.C.* 150 30

285 289b

285 Ald or ldc(A). ℞. TR . P . II . P . P. around, COS . II. in ex.,
Elagabalus stg. in slow quadriga l., holding branch and eagle-tipped
sceptre. *B.M.C.* 306; *R.I.C.* 175 200
286 Bld. ℞. VENVS CAELESTIS, Venus stg. half-left, holding apple and sceptre,
star in field (Hy.; *base and/or plated; rev. of Julia Soaemias*). *B.M.C.*
p. 566 (*in B.M.*); *R.I.C.* 164 .. ..
287 Ald(A). ℞. VENVS VICTRIX, Venus stg. half-left, holding Victory and
palm, resting l. arm on column (Hy., *plated*). *B.M.C.* p. 576 (*in B.M.*);
R.I.C. 204 .. ..
289 Eldc. ℞. VICTOR . ANTONINI AVG., Victory running r., holding wreath
and palm over l. shoulder. *B.M.C.* 37; *R.I.C.* 156 30
289a Eld. ℞. — As last. *B.M.C.* 36; *R.I.C.* 156 30
289b Eldc or ld. ℞. — As before, but without palm. *B.M.C.* 37 note; *R.I.C.*
157A (*Ashmolean*) 40

290 **Quinarius.** Eld. ℞. — As **289**. *B.M.C.* 36 note; *R.I.C.* 157 .. 250

291 **Antoninianus.** Erdc. ℞. — As last. *B.M.C.* 32-4; *R.I.C.* 155 .. 60
291a Erd. ℞. — As last. *B.M.C.* 35; *R.I.C.* 155 60

293 **Denarius.** Dld. ℞. — As last. *B.M.C.* 124-5; *R.I.C.* 153 30

294 **Antoninianus.** Drd. ℞. — As last. *B.M.C.* 122-3; *R.I.C.* 152 .. 65

299 Denarius. Dld. R. VICTORIA AVG., Victory flying l., holding open wreath or diadem in both hands, a small shield either side of her skirt; in field, star. *B.M.C.* p. 548, *; *R.I.C.* 158 ..   ..

300 Cld. R. — As last. *B.M.C.* 235-6 (star r.), 237-9 (star l.); *R.I.C.* 161 ..   £30

300a Cldc. R. — As last. *B.M.C.* 234 (star r.); *R.I.C.* 161   30

300b Quinarius. Cld. R. — As last (*Tinchant cat.*)   300

301 Denarius. Bld. R. — As last. *B.M.C.* 169 note; *R.I.C.* 160..   ..

302 Eldc. R. — As last (Hy. ?). *B.M.C.* p. 535, *; *R.I.C.* 159   ..   ..

303 As last (*plated or Æ*). *B.M.C.* p. 535, * note   ..   ..

304 Bld. R. — Victory walking l., holding wreath and palm over l. shoulder. *B.M.C.* 169-70; *R.I.C.* 162   30

304a IMP . ANTONINVS PIVS FELIX AVG., ld. R. — As last. *B.M.C.* p. 566 (*anomalous*); *R.I.C.* 162 note (*R. D. hoard*)..   ..   ..

305 As **304,** but Victory walking r. *B.M.C.* 169 note; *R.I.C.* 163   35

305a Medallion. El. R. VICTORIA AVGVSTI, as **304.** *B.M.C.* p. 535, †; *R.I.C.* 162 note   ..   ..   *Extremely rare*

306 Denarius. Aldc(A). R. VOTA PVBLICA, Elagabalus stg. front, hd. l., sacrificing out of patera over lighted tripod and holding roll at side. *B.M.C.* 291 note; *R.I.C.* 202..   35

306a Ald(A). R. — As last. *B.M.C.* 291   35

306b Ald(A). R. — As last, but altar for tripod. *B.M.C.* 292   35

307 Type as one of the last three (*base, plated or Æ*). *B.M.C.* 291 note   ..

307a Bldc(A). R. — As **306.** *B.M.C.* 315; *R.I.C.* 202   35

ELAGABALUS and SOAEMIAS

1 Denarius. Cl. R. IVLIA SOAEMIAS AVG., her dr. bust r. *B.M.C.* p. 535, ‡; *R.I.C.* 207   ..   ..   *Extremely rare if genuine*

The obv. is not given by Cohen, but is taken from a poor metal cast in B.M. (B.M.C. p. 621).

ELAGABALUS and MAESA

1 Denarius. Cld. R. IVLIA MAESA AVG., her dr. bust r. *B.M.C.* p. 539, * (*doubtful*); *R.I.C.* 208   ..   ..

There is a Becker forgery with obv. B.

ELAGABALUS and CARACALLA

1 Denarius. Aldc(A ?). R. DIVI ANTONINI PII FIL., rad. bust of Caracalla cuir. r., hand raised (*irregular or hydrid*). *B.M.C.* p. 587, §; *R.I.C.* 163c

JULIA PAULA

Julia Cornelia Paula was the daughter of Julius Paulus, the Praetorian Prefect, and descended from an illustrious family. She became the first wife of Elagabalus in 219 A.D. The marriage was celebrated with unprecedented magnificence, but did not last long and she was repudiated after one year and stripped of her titles. She returned to private life and died in retirement.

Obverse legend:
ĪVLIA PAVLA AVG. unless otherwise stated.

Obverse type:
Bust, draped right, unless otherwise stated. The coins attributed to Rome have the hair fastened on the neck, whereas those given to the East have the hair in a flat bun at the back.

References.
Are to Elagabalus numbers.

(A)=Eastern mint attribution in *B.M.C.*

1 **Medallion.** IVLIA PAVLA AVGVSTA, her diad. bust dr. l. R. AEQVITAS PVBLICA, the three Monetae stg. l., each holding scales and cornucopiae; at the feet of each, a pile of metal. *Gnecchi* 22, 7 .. .. .. *Extremely rare*

6a

6 **Denarius.** R. CONCORDIA, Concordia seated l., holding patera; in field r., star. *B.M.C.* 171; *R.I.C.* 211 .. .. £85
6a As last, but star in field l. *B.M.C.* 172-4; *R.I.C.* 211 85
6b As the last type (*base*). *B.M.C.* 175.. .. ..
6c As 6a (A). *B.M.C.* 316-17 100
7 **Quinarius.** R. — As 6 or 6a. *B.M.C.* 176 note; *R.I.C.* 212 650

7a Diad. bust dr. r. R. — As last. *B.M.C.* 176; *R.I.C.* 213 650
12 **Denarius.** (A). R. CONCORDIA, Elagabalus and Julia Paula stg., hand in hand. *B.M.C.* 318-20; *R.I.C.* 214 100

12   16a

16 R. CONCORDIA AVGG., Concordia seated l., holding patera and double cornucopiae. *B.M.C.* p. 555, †; *R.I.C.* 216 100
16a (A). R. — As last, Concordia seated on curule chair. *B.M.C.* 321-2 .. 100

17 Denarius. (A). ℞. FELICIT . TEMPOR., Felicitas stg. l., holding caduceus
and cornucopiae. *B.M.C.* p. 582, *; *R.I.C.* 217 .. .. £120

17a (A). ℞. FORTVNA . . ., Fortuna seated l., holding rudder (or globe ?) and
cornucopiae (*barbarous*). *B.M.C.* p. 583, * note; *R.I.C.* 218 note (*Gnecchi*)

18 (A). ℞. FORTVNA FELIC., Fortuna seated l., holding globe and cornucopiae.
B.M.C. p. 583, *; *R.I.C.* 218..

19 ℞. IVNO CONSERVATRIX, Juno stg. l., holding patera and sceptre; at her
feet, peacock. *B.M.C.* p. 555, ‡; *R.I.C.* 219 120

20 (A). ℞. IVSTITIA, Justitia seated l., raising r. hand, l. rests on sceptre
(*barbarous*). *B.M.C.* p. 583, †; *R.I.C.* 220 .. ..

20a ℞. PIETAS, Pietas stg. l., raising r. hand and holding box of incense.
R.I.C. 221 .. ..

20b ℞. PIETAS AVG., Pietas raising both hands by lighted altar. *R.I.C.* 221
note .. ..

20c ℞. PVDICITIA, Pudicitia seated l., drawing veil over face and holding
sceptre. *B.M.C.* p. 555, §; *R.I.C.* 221A 120

20d ℞. PVDICITIA AVG., as last. *B.M.C.* p. 555, § note; *R.I.C.* 221B.. .. 120

21 ℞. VENVS GENETRIX, Venus seated l. on throne, holding apple (*Cohen*,
globe) and sceptre. *B.M.C.* 177 and 323-5(A); *R.I.C.* 222 100

22 ℞. VENVS VICTRIX, as last. *B.M.C.* 177 note; *R.I.C.* 223 .. ..

22a ℞. VESTA, Vesta stg. l., holding palladium and sceptre (*plated*). *B.M.C.*
p. 555, ‖; *R.I.C.* 224 .. ..

There is a Becker forgery with Vesta seated.

AQUILIA SEVERA

*Aquilia Severa was the daughter of Quintus Aquilius, who had twice been Consul
under Caracalla. She was taken by Elagabalus from the sacred community of the Vestals
and he made her his second wife in 220 A.D., to the great consternation of the priests and the
people of Rome. In a few days, she was divorced, but after Elagabalus had had other wives,
he again married Aquilia.*

Obverse legend and type:

IVLIA AQVILIA SEVERA AVG., her draped bust right.

References.

Are all to Elagabalus numbers.

(A)=Attributed to Antioch or other Eastern mint.

2a   6

2 Denarius. ℞. CONCORDIA, Concordia stg. half-left, sacrificing out of patera over lighted altar and holding double cornucopiae; star in field to r. *B.M.C.* 184 and 335(A); *R.I.C.* 226.. .. .. £160

2a As last, but star in field high l. *B.M.C.* 185-7 and 336(A); *R.I.C.* 225 .. 160

2b As before, but without star. *B.M.C.* 184 note and 335 note; *R.I.C.* 227 160

6 — Elagabalus and Aquilia stg. hand in hand; star in field between them. *B.M.C.* 337(A) and p. 558, † (*does it occur at Rome ?*); *R.I.C.* 228 .. 175

9a ℞. LAETITIA, Laetitia, veiled, stg. front, hd. l., holding wreath downward and rudder on globe. *B.M.C.* 188; *R.I.C.* 229 200

10 ℞. VENVS CAELESTIS, Venus stg. l., holding apple and sceptre, star in field (Hy., *plated or Æ; rev. of Soaemias*). *B.M.C.* p. 559 (*ancient forgery*) and p. 585 (*base*); *R.I.C.* 230 .. ..

12 ℞. VESTA, Vesta stg. l., holding branch and sceptre. *B.M.C.* p. 559, * and p. 585(A) (*doubtful*); *R.I.C.* 231.. 200

Becker made a forgery—VESTA, Vesta seated.

ANNIA FAUSTINA

Annia Faustina is believed to have been the daughter of Claudius Severus and Vibia Sabina (daughter of M. Aurelius and Faustina Junior). She married Pomponius Bassus, but when Elagabalus desired her he had her husband put to death. She was married to Elagabalus in 221 A.D., but very soon discarded and she retired to private life.

1 Denarius. ANNIA FAVSTINA AVG., her dr. bust r. ℞. CONCORDIA, Elagabalus and Annia Faustina hand in hand, star between them. *B.M.C.* p. 570, † and pl. 90, 16 (*Madrid*); *R.I.C.* Elagabalus 232.. 5,000

1a Medallion. As last, but AVGVSTA. *B.M.C.* p. 570, ‡; *R.I.C.* 233 (*Nordheim sale; doubtful*) .. ..

4 Denarius. As **1**, but bust on crescent. ℞. PIETAS AVG., Pietas stg. by altar, raising r. hand and holding box of perfume. *B.M.C.* p. 570 (*probably false; a Julia Maesa, tooled, perhaps*).. .. ..

JULIA SOAEMIAS

Julia Soaemias, mother of Elagabalus, was the daughter of Julius Avitus and Julia Maesa, sister of Julia Domna. She married Varius Marcellus, a senator, and gave birth to Elagabalus in 204 A.D. Becoming a widow she retired after the death of Caracalla to Emesa, where she and her mother persuaded the troops there to declare Elagabalus emperor. She returned to Rome and became a senator. She was to a great extent responsible for the excesses and cruelties of her son's reign, and fell a victim to the soldier's fury, who put her to death at the same time as they slew Elagabalus in 222 A.D.

Obverse legends and type.

A. IVLIA SOAEMIAS AVG.

B. IVLIA SOAEMIAS AVGVSTA

All coins show her draped bust right, except where stated.

References.

All are to Elagabalus numbers.

(A) denotes any piece attributed to Antioch or other Eastern mint by *B.M.C.*

1 Medallion. B, diad. bust dr. l. ℞. AEQVITAS PVBLICA, the three Monetae stg. l., each holding scales and cornucopiae; at feet of each, pile of metal. *B.M.C.* p. 538, * .. .. *Extremely rare*

2 Denarius. A (A?). R. ANNONA AVG., Annona or Abundantia stg. l., holding corn-ears and cornucopiae; on l. modius. *B.M.C.* p. 538, (a) (*hybrid?*); *R.I.C.* 234 .. ..

2a A (A?). R. IVNO, Juno stg. front, hd. l., holding patera and sceptre. *B.M.C.* 28 and p. 576, also pl. 91, 14 (*base, plated; ancient forgery?*); *R.I.C.* 235 .. ..

3 A. R. IVNO REGINA, Juno, veiled and diad., stg. half-right, holding sceptre and palladium. *B.M.C.* 41-3; *R.I.C.* 237 .. .. £85

3a As last (*base*). *B.M.C.* 40 .. ..

5a A. R. PIETAS AVG., Pietas sacrificing over altar and holding box of perfume (Hy., *base; rev. of Julia Domna*). *B.M.C.* p. 538, (b) (*ancient forgery*); *R.I.C.* 237A (*Gantz coll.*) .. ..

6 A. R. PVDICITIA, Pudicitia seated l., holding sceptre, r. hand raised to mouth (Hy.; *rev. of Julia Domna*). *B.M.C.* p. 538, (c) (*ancient forgery*); *R.I.C.* 238 .. ..

7 A. R. SAECVLI FELICITAS, Felicitas stg. l., sacrificing out of patera over lighted altar and holding caduceus (Hy.; *rev. of Julia Maesa*). *B.M.C.* p. 538, (d); *R.I.C.* 239 (*this could be a mint hybrid, as they were being made about the same time*) 100

8   14

8 A. R. VENVS CAELESTIS, Venus stg. half-left or front, hd. l., holding apple and sceptre; star in field to r. *B.M.C.* 45; *R.I.C.* 241 65

8a As last, but star low in field to l. *B.M.C.* 49-51; *R.I.C.* 241 65

8b As before, but star is large. *B.M.C.* 46-7; *R.I.C.* 241 65

8c Similar, but normal star, high l. *B.M.C.* 52-3; *R.I.C.* 241 65

8d As before, but no star. *B.M.C.* 44; *R.I.C.* 241 65

8e As 8 (*base*). *B.M.C.* 48 .. ..

10 Quinarius. A. R. — Type as before. *B.M.C.* 54 (*base; star does not show on illustration; Cohen quotes from this coin*); *R.I.C.* 242 (*say*, with star) 350

14 Denarius. A. R. — Venus seated l. on throne, holding apple and sceptre; in front, child stg. r., raising both hands. *B.M.C.* 55-60 (*describes some as holding* patera *instead of* apple); *R.I.C.* 243 65

15 Quinarius. As last. *B.M.C.* 56 note; *R.I.C.* 244 350

16 Denarius. As 14 (*base, plated or Æ*) .. ..

17 Antoninianus. A, bust dr. r. on crescent. R. As 14. *B.M.C.* 56 note; *R.I.C.* 245 .. .. Extremely rare

21 Denarius. B. R. VESTA, Vesta stg. l., holding palladium and spear. (Hy.; *rev. of Julia Maesa; see note after 7, but with this obv. it seems improbable*). *B.M.C.* p. 538, (e); *R.I.C.* 246 .. ..

22 A. R. — Vesta seated l., holding simpulum and sceptre (Hy., *plated or Æ; rev. of J. Domna*). *B.M.C.* p. 539, (f); *R.I.C.* 247 .. .. ..

22a B. R. — As last (Hy.). *B.M.C.* p. 539, (f) (*ancient forgery*); *R.I.C.* 248 (*Lang*) .. ..

JULIA MAESA

Julia Maesa, daughter of Julius Bassianus, priest of the Sun, was born at Emesa in Syria; she was the sister of Julia Domna. She married Julius Avitus by whom she had Julia Soaemias and Julia Mamaea, and was therefore grandmother of Elagabalus and Severus Alexander. She was a woman of great sagacity and courage and possessed great wealth. She retired to Emesa on Caracalla's death and succeeded in persuading the troops to proclaim Elagabalus emperor. She fought at the head of his troops against Macrinus. She then went to Rome and took a seat in the Senate, though contrary to the law. She died in 223 A.D., and was much missed for her wise counsels.

Obverse legends and types.

Under Elagabalus.

IVLIA MAESA AVG., her draped bust right, occasionally with diadem (stephane).

Memorial issue under Severus Alexander.

D = DIVA MAESA AVG., her draped bust right, occasionally veiled.

References and Mints.

All are Elagabalus numbers except for those prefixed D, which are numbers of Severus Alexander.

(A) Indicates that they are attributed to the Antioch or other Eastern mint.

1a Denarius. R. CONCORDIA AVGG., Concordia seated l., holding patera and double cornucopiae (Hy., *plated; rev. of Julia Paula*). *B.M.C.* p. 542, (a) (*ancient forgery ?; Lawrence*); *R.I.C.* 277 .. ..

2 D. R. CONSECRATIO, Maesa, holding sceptre, seated l. on an eagle bearing her upwards. *B.M.C.* 217 note; *R.I.C.* 377 .. .. .. £400

3 D. R. — As last, but peacock for eagle. *B.M.C.* 217; *R.I.C.* 378 .. 400

5 D. Her dr. bust veiled. R. — Funeral pyre of four stages. *B.M.C.* 218 note; *R.I.C.* 379 400

7 D(A ?). R. FECVNDITAS, Fecunditas seated l., holding flower and sceptre, between two children. *B.M.C.* Sev. Alex. p. 136 (*irregular copy of* **10**); *R.I.C.* 380 .. ..

7a R. — Fecunditas seated l., extending r. hand over child and holding sceptre, another child beside her. *B.M.C.* p. 540, * note; *R.I.C.* 249 note (*Ball sale*) 75

7b   8

7b (A). R. FECVNDITAS .., Fecunditas seated l., holding branch and sceptre; child stands in front, another behind (*G. R. Arnold coll.*) 75

8 R. FECVNDITAS AVG., Fecunditas stg. half-left, extending r. hand over child stg. before her, and holding cornucopiae. *B.M.C.* 61-5; *R.I.C.* 249 45

9 As last (*base, plated or Æ*). *B.M.C.* 61 note .. ..

10 Quinarius. R. — Fecunditas seated l., extending hand to a child stg. before her, and holding cornucopiae. *B.M.C.* p. 540, *; *R.I.C.* 250 .. 375

13 Denarius. R. FELICITAS PVBLICA, Felicitas stg. l., holding caduceus and
cornucopiae (Hy., *plated; rev. of Julia Mamaea*). *B.M.C.* p. 542, (b);
R.I.C. 251   ..   ..

13a (A). R. FIDES MILITVM, Fides, wearing a curious and unusual head-dress,
seated l., holding globe in r. hand and club (?) in l. *B.M.C.* 294 (*rev. of
Elagabalus*); *R.I.C.* 278 (*irregular or hybrid*). *There does not appear to be a
rev. of Elagabalus like this, so perhaps it was struck at the time Maesa was
fighting Macrinus* £75

14 (A?). R. FORTVNAE REDVCI, Fortuna or Fecunditas stg. l., holding
cornucopiae; on each side, a child stg. *B.M.C.* p. 577, *; *R.I.C.* 252   ..   60

16   20-21

16 R. IVNO, Juno, veiled, stg. half-left, holding patera and sceptre. *B.M.C.*
67-8; *R.I.C.* 254   45

20 and 21 Diad. bust (A). R. — As last, but with peacock at feet. *B.M.C.*
295; *R.I.C.* 256   50

20a As before, but without diadem. (A). *B.M.C.* 296   50

22 (A?). R. IVNO CONSERVATRIX, same type. *B.M.C.* 67 note and 297;
R.I.C. 257   60

23 As before, but diad. bust and without peacock. *B.M.C.* 67 note; *R.I.C.*
258   70

23a (A). R. IVNO REG., as before, but Juno holds ears of corn for patera.
B.M.C. 295 note; *R.I.C.* 259 note   70

24 Diad. bust (A). R. IVNO REGI., type as **20**. *B.M.C.* 295 note; *R.I.C.* 259   50

25 (A). As last, but IVNO REGINA. *B.M.C.* 295 note; *R.I.C.* 260   50

26 R. LAETITIA PVBL., Laetitia stg. front, hd. l., holding wreath and rudder on
globe. *B.M.C.* 69 and p. 577, † (A?); *R.I.C.* 261 (*probably Syrian*) ..   60

27 This piece, a quinarius, PAX AETERNA AVG., is probably Julia Mamaea 47,
as Cohen says ..

28 (A). R. PAX ETERNA (*sic*), Pax stg. l., holding olive-branch and sceptre
(*slightly barbarous*). *B.M.C.* p. 577, ‡; *R.I.C.* 262   70

29 R. PIETAS AVG., Pietas stg. half-left, extending r. hand, perhaps holding
patera, over altar before her, and holding incense box. *B.M.C.* 73-4;
R.I.C. 263   45

29a (A). As last, but larger hd. on obv. and of coarser style both sides.
B.M.C. 298-9   45

30 Antoninianus (=2 denarii). Diad. bust r. on crescent. R. — As **29**.
B.M.C. 70-2; *R.I.C.* 264   120

34 Denarius. Diad. bust r. R. — Pietas stg. l., raising both hands in prayer, altar at feet. *B.M.C.* 75 note (*who reads this as an* Ant.); *R.I.C.* 265 ... £60

34a As last, but bust not diad. *B.M.C.* 75; *R.I.C.* 266 (*Ashmolean*) 50

34b (A). As last, but larger hd. on obv. and of coarser style both sides (*G. R. Arnold coll.*) 60

35 As **34** (*base, plated or* Æ). *B.M.C.* 75 note .. ..

34b 36

36 R. PVDICITIA, Pudicitia seated l., raising veil and holding sceptre. *B.M.C.* 76-8; *R.I.C.* 268 45

39 Diad. bust r. R. — As last (*plated or* Æ) .. ..

43 Quinarius. R. — Pudicitia seated l., raising r. hand and holding sceptre. *B.M.C.* 76 note; *R.I.C.* 269 375

45 Denarius. R. SAECVLI FELICITAS, Felicitas stg. front, hd. l., sacrificing out of patera over lighted altar and holding long caduceus; in the field, star r. *B.M.C.* 79-80; *R.I.C.* 271 45

45a (A). As last, large star r. *B.M.C.* 301 (*base*) 45

45b As **45,** but star in l. field. *B.M.C.* 81-82; *R.I.C.* 272 45

45c As last, but without star. (*G. R. Arnold coll.*) 45

45d (A). As last. *B.M.C.* 300 45

45c 46

46 Quinarius. As before, large star in field l. *B.M.C.* 83; *R.I.C.* 273 .. 325

51 Denarius. (A). R. TEMPORVM FEL., Felicitas seated l. between two children, holding flower and sceptre. *B.M.C.* p. 578, *; *R.I.C.* 274 .. 70

52 R. VENVS VICTRIX, Venus stg. l., holding helmet, transverse spear and shield. *R.I.C.* 275 60

52a R. — Venus stg. l., holding helmet and spear; spear at l. side. *B.M.C.* p. 621 (*irregular; Oldroyd*) 60

52b (A). R. — Venus stg. l., holding statuette or child in outstretched arms and transverse spear; at side, shield on base. *B.M.C.* p. 578, †; *R.I.C.* 275 note (*Stirling hoard*) 60

53 R. VESTA, Vesta, veiled, stg., holding palladium and sceptre (Hy.; *rev. of Julia Domna. B.M.C.* p. 542, (c) (*ancient forgery ?*); *R.I.C.* 276 .. ..

53a R. VIRTVS AVG., Virtus seated l., holding branch and spear reversed (Hy., *plated; rev. of Severus Alexander*). *B.M.C.* p. 542, (d) (*ancient forgery ?*); *R.I.C.* 279 (*Lawrence*) .. ..

SEVERUS ALEXANDER
222-235 A.D.

Bassianus Alexianus was born at Arce in Phoenicia in 208 A.D., *the son of Gessius Marcianus and Julia Mamaea. Through the sagacious policy and persuasion of Julia Maesa, his grandmother, he was adopted by Elagabalus in* 221 *and given the title of Caesar: he then took the names Marcus Aurelius Alexander. He was a most popular youth possessed of talents, courage and every personal accomplishment. On the death of Elagabalus he was at once acknowledged emperor by the praetorian guards and confirmed by the enraptured Senate the following day. He at once added Severus to his name. For nine years Alexander ruled the empire wisely and well, and its condition was much improved; but in* 231 *troubles on its eastern frontiers compelled him to take the field against the Parthians, whom he defeated in* 232. *Almost at once, however, similar troubles on the German frontier necessitated a western campaign. A band of factious soldiers, instigated by the Thracian savage, Maximinus, at that time one of Alexander's guards, slew Alexander and his mother at their camp near Mainz on* 22nd *March,* 235 A.D.

Obverse legends.

As Caesar

A.   M . AVR . ALEXANDER CAES. After July 10th, 221 A.D.

As Emperor

B.   IMP . ALEXANDER PIVS AVG. A.D. 231-5

C.   IMP . C . M . AVR . SEV . ALEXAND . AVG. A.D. 222-8

D.   IMP . SEV . ALEXAND . AVG. A.D. 228-31

Obverse types.

All portraits are to the right unless otherwise indicated, and the busts are seen from the back unless indicated by f.

bd.   Bare-headed bust right, draped

l.   Laureate head right

lsd.   „   bust right, slight drapery

ld.   „   „   „   draped

ldc.   „   „   „   draped and cuirassed

f.   Added to the foregoing, if seen from the front

For the first years of his reign, the portrait is quite young, as he was only thirteen at succession. Three years later he has side-whiskers and from then on he is shown progressively more bearded.

Mints.

All coins are attributed to Rome by *B.M.C.* and *R.I.C.* unless (A) for Antioch is given after the bust.

B.M.C. numbers followed by * indicate that the coin was not in the British Museum at the time the catalogue was written.

The antoninianus (double denarius) was not struck under this reign, and was not re-introduced until the joint reign of Balbinus and Pupienus, 238 A.D.

1 Denarius. Dl. ℞. ABVNDANTIA AVG., Abundantia stg. half-right, empty-ing cornucopiae held in both hands. *B.M.C.* 591 note; *R.I.C.* 184 (*R. D. hoard*) £30

1a   23

1a Dlsd. ℞. — As last. *B.M.C.* 591-4; *R.I.C.* 184..   25
1b Dld. ℞. — As last. *R.I.C.* 184 (*Ciani*)   30
1c Dl. ℞. — As before, but Abundantia stg. l. *R.I.C.* 184A (*R. D. hoard*)   35
1d Dlsd. ℞. — As last. *B.M.C.* 591 note; *R.I.C.* 184A (*R. D. hoard*)   35
2 As **1** or **1a** (*base, plated or Æ*). *B.M.C.* 591 note ..   ..
9 Cld. ℞. AEQVITAS AVG., Aequitas stg. half-left, holding scales and cornu-copiae. *B.M.C.* 329-31; *R.I.C.* 127   25
9a Cldc. ℞. — As last. *R.I.C.* 127 (*Lawrence*)   25
10 Quinarius. Cld. ℞. — As last. *B.M.C.* 332*; *R.I.C.* 128   ..   150
11 Denarius. Cld(A). ℞. — As before, but with star in field l. *B.M.C.* 1033-5; *R.I.C.* 274   25
11a Cld(A). ℞. — As last, but without star. *B.M.C.* 1049 (*reads* AVENITAS). *R.I.C.* 274   35
11b Cldc(A). ℞. — As last. *B.M.C.* 1048   35
11c As last (*base*). *B.M.C.* 1048 note (*in B.M.*)   ..   ..   ..
12 As **11** (*base, plated or Æ*). *B.M.C.* 1033 note   ..   ..   ..
13 Dld (*Cohen says, young bust, but that does not go with this legend*). ℞. — As **9**. *R.I.C.* 185 ..   ..
13a Dl. ℞. — As last (*Tinchant cat.*)   40
13b Dldc(A). ℞. — As **11**. *B.M.C.* 1011* (*Voetter*)   40
15 Medallion. Bldc. ℞. AEQVITAS AVGVSTI, the Three Monetae stg. front, hd. l., each holds scales and cornucopiae; at the feet of each, a pile of metal or coins. *B.M.C.* p. 79 note; *R.I.C.* 228; *Gnecchi*, p. 46, 1   *Very rare*
16 C, but CAES., ld. ℞. — As before. *B.M.C.* 206A* note; *R.I.C.* 128A   *Very rare*
17 C, but CAES., ldc. ℞. — As last. *B.M.C.* 206A*; *R.I.C.* 128A; *Gn.* 4   *Very rare*
18 C, but ALEXANDER, ldcf. (*Cohen has* 'son buste lauré'). ℞. — As last. *B.M.C.* 552*; *R.I.C.* 186 (ld.); *Gn.* 3   ..   ..   ..   *Very rare*
19 IMP . CAES . M . AVREL . ALEXANDER PIVS FELIX (or FEL.) AVG., ldc. (*Cohen has* 'même buste'). ℞. — As before, but the centre Moneta has hd. facing. *B.M.C.* 551; *R.I.C.* 229 (ld.); *Gn.* 2   ..   ..   *Very rare*
21 Denarius. C (*or perhaps* CAES. *for* C.), l. ℞. AETERNITATIBVS, woman stg., leaning on column and holding globe and javelin. *B.M.C.* 472 note (*must be a misreading of* **192**); *R.I.C.* 129-30   ..   ..   ..
23 Cld. ℞. ANNONA AVG., Annona (*Cohen*, Abundantia) stg. front, hd. l., holding corn-ears and cornucopiae; at her feet l., modius filled with corn-ears. *B.M.C.* 341-4; *R.I.C.* 133   25
23a C, but ALEXANDER, ld. ℞. — As last (*plated or Æ*). *B.M.C.* 341 note; *R.I.C.* 133A   ..   ..
23b Dl(A). ℞. — As last. *B.M.C.* 1069 (*irregular*)   35
24 Quinarius. Cld. ℞. — As last. *B.M.C.* 345; *R.I.C.* 134   ..   150
26 Denarius. Bl. ℞. — As last (Hy.). *B.M.C.* 968*; *R.I.C.* 230   ..

27 Denarius. Dl. ℞. ANNONA AVG., Annona stg. front, hd. l., holding corn-ears and cornucopiae, her r. foot on prow. *B.M.C.* 496-7; *R.I.C.* 187 .. ₤30

27a Dl. ℞. — As last, but double cornucopiae (*Mazzini cat.*) 35

28 Cld. ℞. — As **27.** *B.M.C.* 469; *R.I.C.* 135 30

29 Dl. ℞. — As **23**, but anchor instead of cornucopiae. *B.M.C.* 673; *R.I.C.* 188 25

29a Dlsd. ℞. — As last. *B.M.C.* 674-6; *R.I.C.* 188 25

30 Quinarius. Dl. ℞. — As last. *B.M.C.* 677 note; *R.I.C.* 189.. .. 150

31 Dld. ℞. — As last. *R.I.C.* 189 (*possibly a wrong description of next*) .. 150

31a Dlsd. ℞. — As last. *B.M.C.* 677 150

32 Denarius. Dl. ℞. — Annona stg. r., holding rudder on globe, and modius filled with corn-ears; her l. foot on prow. *B.M.C.* 595-6; *R.I.C.* 190 25

32a Dlsd. ℞. — As last. *B.M.C.* 597; *R.I.C.* 190 25

33 Quinarius. Dlsd (and l?). ℞. — As last. *B.M.C.* 598; *R.I.C.* 191 .. 150

34 Denarius. Cldc. ℞. — As last (Hy.). *B.M.C.* 969*; *R.I.C.* 136 ..

33   38

38 Cldc(A). ℞. CONCORDIA, Concordia seated l., holding patera and cornu-copiae (*Cohen says*, sometimes double). *B.M.C.* 1050; *R.I.C.* 275 (*who also gives Cld, as in B.M., but it is not in catalogue*) 25

39 As last (*base, plated or Æ*). *B.M.C.* 1050 note (*who possess three examples*)

39a Dldc. ℞. — As last (*base*). *B.M.C.* 1050 note (*in B.M.*) ..

39b Dld. ℞. — As last (Hy.). *B.M.C.* 1067; *R.I.C.* 276 ..

41a Dl. ℞. DEANA LVCAFERA, Diana stg. l., holding torch (Hy.). *R.I.C.* 303 (*reading corrected when the coin was in our possession*) .. ..

42 Cl. ℞. DIANA LVCIFERA, Diana walking l., holding torch (Hy.; *rev. of Julia Domna*). *B.M.C.* 970*; *R.I.C.* 304 .. ..

43 Cl(?). ℞. FECVND . AVGVSTAE, Fecunditas stg. (Hy.). *B.M.C.* 971*; *R.I.C.* 305 .. ..

44 Cld. ℞. FELICITAS AVG., Felicitas stg. half-left, sacrificing out of patera over lighted altar and holding caduceus. *B.M.C.* 470-1; *R.I.C.* 137 .. 25

45 Dl. ℞. — As last. *B.M.C.* 498*; *R.I.C.* 192 30

46 As last (*base, plated or Æ*). *B.M.C.* 498* note .. ..

46a Dldc. ℞. — As last. (*Tinchant cat.*) 30

47 C (*Cohen gives* CAES. *for* C.) l(A?). ℞. FELICITAS TEMPORVM, as before (*irregular, some barbarous*). *B.M.C.* 1070*; *R.I.C.* 277 .. .. ..

48a Cldc(A?). ℞. FIDES EXERCIT. (or EXERCIV.), Fides seated l., holding standard in each hand (or holding standard, another standard behind her). *B.M.C.* 1071 (*irregular*); *R.I.C.* 278 .. ..

49 C (*Cohen and R.I.C. give* CAES. *for* C.) l. ℞. FIDES EXERCITVS, Fides seated l., holding two standards. *B.M.C.* 220 note; *R.I.C.* 138 .. ˙. ..

49b Clsd(A). ℞. — Fides seated l., holding standard and cornucopiae. *R.I.C.* 279 (*B.M., but it is not in catalogue*).. .. ..

50 Cld. ℞. — As **49** (*some, if not all, base or Æ*). *R.I.C.* 220 note; *R.I.C.* 138 (*obv.* Clsd) (*R. D. hoard*) .. ..

51 Dl. ℞. FIDES MILITVM, as last. *B.M.C.* 684-7; *R.I.C.* 193 25

51a Dlsd. ℞. — As last (*Brussels*) 30

51b Dld. ℞. — As last. *R.I.C.* 193 (*Baldwin*) 30

52   52b

52 Cld. ℞. — Fides stg. front (or slightly l.), hd. l., holding standard in
each hand. *B.M.C.* 220-6; *R.I.C.* 139 .. .. £25
52a Cl. ℞. — As last. *B.M.C.* 219; *R.I.C.* 139 30
52b Cld(A). ℞. — As last, but hd. r. (*G. R. Arnold*).. 30
53 As **52** (*base, plated or Æ*). *B.M.C.* 220 note .. .. ..
57 Dlsd. ℞. — Fides stg. r. (or front, hd. r.), holding vexillum and transverse standard. *B.M.C.* 737*; *R.I.C.* 194 30
57a Dlsd. ℞. — As last, but Fides seated l. *B.M.C.* 1072 (*irregular*) .. 35
57b Cl. ℞. — As **57**. *B.M.C.* 972*; *R.I.C.* 139 note (Cld) (*R. D. hoard*) .. 35
57c C, AV. for AVG., lsd. ℞. — As last. *R.I.C.* 139A note (*R. D. hoard*)
(139A — Cld. — *is not in Ashmolean*) 30

58   65

58 Blsd. ℞. — As last. *B.M.C.* 762-3; *R.I.C.* 231 25
59 Dlsd. ℞. — Jupiter, nude, stg. half-left, holding thunderbolt and
sceptre, eagle at feet; facing him, the emperor stg. r., sacrificing over tripod
and being crowned by Mars who stands behind him; behind Jupiter, a
standard. *B.M.C.* 681; *R.I.C.* 195 (*Cohen's description and illustration are
from B.M. coin, so probably only one obv. exists and not Dl. as given by
Cohen and R.I.C.*) 350
62a Cl. ℞. FORTVNAE FELICI, Fortuna seated l., holding cornucopiae and
resting elbow on chair. *R.I.C.* 139B .. ..
63 Dl (and possibly lsd). ℞. FORTVNAE REDVCI, Fortuna stg. front, hd. l.,
holding rudder on globe and cornucopiae. *B.M.C.* 738; *R.I.C.* 196 .. 25
64 Bl. ℞. — As last. *B.M.C.* 765; *R.I.C.* 232 25
64a Blsd. ℞. — As last. *B.M.C.* 765 note; *R.I.C.* 232 25
64b Blsd. ℞. — Fortuna seated l. *R.I.C.* 233 (*Tinchant, but not in his mss.
catalogue*) .. ..
65 Abd. ℞. INDVLGENTIA AVG., Spes walking l., holding up flower and
raising her skirt. *B.M.C.* Elagabalus 264-5; *R.I.C.* 2 200
70 Cld. ℞. IOVI CONSERVATORI, Jupiter stg. front, hd. l., nude except for
cloak hanging behind, holding thunderbolt and sceptre. *B.M.C.* 56-60;
R.I.C. 141 (*also gives* Clsd *in error*) 25
70a As last (*base*). *B.M.C.* 56 note (*in B.M.*) .. ..
70b Cldc. ℞. — As before. *R.I.C.* 141 (*Lawrence*) 30
71 Dlsd. ℞. — As last. *B.M.C.* 55 note; *R.I.C.* 198 .. .. ..
73 Dlsd. ℞. — Jupiter stg. half-left, nude except for mantle over arms,
holding sceptre and thunderbolt over small figure of Sev. Alexander.
B.M.C. 690-1; *R.I.C.* 200 30
73a Dl. ℞. — As last. *R.I.C.* 200 30

76 Denarius. Bldcf. R. IOVI PROPVGNATORI, Jupiter, nude but for cloak, stg. front in fighting attitude, inclined to l., hd. r., holding thunderbolt raised. *B.M.C.* 790-3; *R.I.C.* 235 .. .. £25
77 Bld. R. — As last. *B.M.C.* 790* note; *R.I.C.* 236 .. .. ..
78 Dl. R. — As last (Hy.). *B.M.C.* 973*; *R.I.C.* 201 .. .. ..

84   108a

83 Bldcf. R. — As before, but also holds eagle. *B.M.C.* 824; *R.I.C.* 238   25
84 Bldf. R. — As last. *B.M.C.* 825; *R.I.C.* 239   25
89 Bldf. R. IOVIS PROPVGNATOR, as **76.** *B.M.C.* 799 note; *R.I.C.* 240 ..   30
90 Bldcf. R. — As last. *B.M.C.* 799; *R.I.C.* 241   30
92 Dl. R. IOVI STATORI, Jupiter, naked, stg. front, hd. r., holding sceptre and thunderbolt. *B.M.C.* 697-8; *R.I.C.* 202   25
93 As last (*plated, base or Æ*). *B.M.C.* 697 note .. .. ..
95 Cld. R. IOVI VLTORI, Jupiter, half-naked, seated l. on throne, holding Victory and sceptre or reversed spear. *B.M.C.* 233-7; *R.I.C.* 144 ..   25
96 Quinarius. As last. *B.M.C.* 238; *R.I.C.* 145   150
97 Denarius. Cl. R. — As last. *B.M.C.* 232; *R.I.C.* 143   30
97a ·Dl. R. — As last (Hy., *plated*). *B.M.C.* 974*; *R.I.C.* 203 (*Ashmolean*)
101 Cl. R. — Jupiter seated facing within hexastyle temple; also showing a courtyard surrounded by a covered arcade with arches. *B.M.C.* 207* and pl. 8 (*Modena*); *R.I.C.* 146   400
105 Dl(A). R. IVCVNDITATI AVG., Jucunditas (Gaiety) seated r., holding globe and sceptre. *B.M.C.* 1073* (*irregular*); *R.I.C.* 280   100
106a Cldc(A). R. LIBEALITAS AVG., as next. *B.M.C.* 1047; *R.I.C.* 283 ..   35
108 Cld. R. LIBERALITAS AVG., Liberalitas stg. front (or half-left), hd. l., holding abacus and cornucopiae. *B.M.C.* 6; *R.I.C.* 148   25
108a Cldc. R. — As last. *B.M.C.* 3-5; *R.I.C.* 148   25
108b Cldc(A). R. — As last. *B.M.C.* 1043-7; *R.I.C.* 281   30
109 As **108** or **108a** (*base, plated or Æ*). *B.M.C.* 6 note .. .. ..
115 Cl. R. LIBERTAS AVG., as last. *B.M.C.* 3 note; *R.I.C.* 151   40
115a Cldc. R. — As last. *B.M.C.* 3 note; *R.I.C.* 151   40
118 Cld. R. LIBERALITAS AVG . II, as last. *B.M.C.* 212-3; *R.I.C.* 153 ..   35
128 Cldc. R. LIBERALITAS AVG . III, as last. *B.M.C.* 309 note; *R.I.C.* 154..   30
128a Cld. R. — As last. *B.M.C.* 309-11; *R.I.C.* 154   30

133 Dl. R. LIBERALITAS AVG . IIII, as last. *B.M.C.* 558; *R.I.C.* 205.. ..   30

134 Quinarius. As last. *B.M.C.* 559; *R.I.C.* 506   ..   ..   ..   £175
135 Denarius. As last (*base, plated or Æ*). *B.M.C.* 558 note   ..   ..
142 Bldcf. ℞. LIBERALITAS AVG . V, as last. *B.M.C.* 946*; *R.I.C.* 243   ..   40
143 Dl(A ?). ℞. LIBERALITAS AVGG . V, as last (*barbarous*). *B.M.C.* 946*
note (*misdescribed*); *R.I.C.* 282 (*misdescribed*)   ..   ..   ..
145a Cl(A). ℞. LIBERITAS AVG., as last. *R.I.C.* 284 note (*R. D. hoard*)   ..
146 Cl(A). ℞. — Libertas stg. half-left, holding pileus and long sceptre;
in field, star. *B.M.C.* 1036 note; *R.I.C.* 284   ..   ..
147 Cld(A). ℞. LIBERTAS AVG., as last. *B.M.C.* 1036; *R.I.C.* 286   30
147a Cl(A). ℞. — As last. *R.I.C.* 286 (*possibly in error*)   ..   ..   ..
148 As 147 (*base, plated or Æ*). *B.M.C.* 1036 note   ..   ..
149 Dld(A). ℞. — As before. *B.M.C.* 1012-3; *R.I.C.* 285   30
150 Cld. ℞. — Libertas stg. half-left, holding pileus and transverse spear.
B.M.C. 64 note; *R.I.C.* 155   30
151 Cld(A). ℞. — As before. *B.M.C.* 1036 note; *R.I.C.* 287   30
152 Cld. ℞. — Libertas stg. half-left, holding pileus and cornucopiae.
B.M.C. 64 and 315* (plate 11, older hd.); *R.I.C.* 156   25
152a Cld(A). ℞. — As last, but Libertas stg. front, hd. l. *B.M.C.* 1053;
R.I.C. 288   30
152b Cldc(A). ℞. — As last. *B.M.C.* 1054; *R.I.C.* 288   30
152c Cldc. ℞. — As **152**. *B.M.C.* 62-3   25
156 Cld (*Cohen has* EV. *for* SEV.). ℞. MAISAI (or MAISI) AVG., Julia Maesa stg.
front, hd. l., leaning against column and sacrificing at altar, holding
sceptre. *B.M.C.* 1074* (*irregular*); *R.I.C.* 310 (*who also gives obv.* Cl)   250
156a Bl. ℞. MARS PROPVG., Mars, in military dress, walking r., holding
transverse spear and shield. *B.M.C.* 833 note; *R.I.C.* 244 (*and obv.*
Blsd) ..   ..
156b Antoninianus. C. Rad. bust dr. and cuir. r. ℞. MARS VICTOR, Mars
hastening r., holding trophy and spear. *B.M.C.* p. 32, 4 (*modern forgery*);
R.I.C. 157   ..   ..
156c As last, but SEVE. for SEV. on *obv.* *R.I.C.* 157 note (*Lawrence: plated*) ..
158 Denarius. Dl. ℞. MARS VLTOR, as **156a** (Hy.). *B.M.C.* 976*; *R.I.C.* 207
159 As last (*base, plated or Æ*). *B.M.C.* 976* note   ..   ..   ..
161 Bld(f?). ℞. — As last. *B.M.C.* 833 note; *R.I.C.* 246   25

152b   161a

161a Bldcf. ℞. — As last. *B.M.C.* 831-3; *R.I.C.* 246   25
161b Bldcf. ℞. — As last, but Mars running. *B.M.C.* 834-6   25
161c Bldf. ℞. — As last. *B.M.C.* 837   25
161d Cld. ℞. — As before, but Mars walking (Hy.). *B.M.C.* 975*   ..
162 Quinarius. Bl. ℞. — As **156a**. *B.M.C.* 839; *R.I.C.* 247   150
162a Blcdf. ℞. — As **161b**. *B.M.C.* 838; *R.I.C.* 247   150
166 Denarius. Bld (*Cohen says*, same bust *in error*). ℞. — Mars, in military
dress, stg. front, hd. l., holding spear and shield resting on ground, against
which standard. *B.M.C.* 802 note; *R.I.C.* 248 (*probably the next*)   ..
166a Blsd. ℞. — As last. *B.M.C.* 802; *R..IC.* 248   30
166b Blcdf. ℞. — As last. *B.M.C.* 803-3A   30

173 Denarius. Cld. ℞. MARTI PACIFERO, Mars, in military dress, stg. front, hd. l., holding branch and reversed spear. *B.M.C.* 72; *R.I.C.* 160 .. £25

173a Cldc. ℞. — As last. *B.M.C.* 68-71; *R.I.C.* 160 25

173b Cld(A). ℞. — As last. *R.I.C.* 289 (*not in B.M. as stated*) .. ..

174 Quinarius. Cld. ℞. — As last. *B.M.C.* 73*; *R.I.C.* 161 175

175 Denarius. As last (*base, plated or Æ*). *B.M.C.* 72 note .. ..

177 Cld. ℞. MARTI VICTORI, Mars, nude, walking, holding spear and trophy. *R.I.C.* 162 .. ..

178 Cld. ℞. MONETA AVG., Moneta stg. front (or half-left), hd. l., holding scales and cornucopiae. *B.M.C.* 204 note; *R.I.C.* 163 50

181 Cld and/or Cldc (A). ℞. NOBILITAS, Nobilitas stg. r., holding spear or long sceptre and palladium (?; *Cohen says* javelin). *B.M.C.* 1055-6; *R.I.C.* 290 75

181a As last, but Victory for spear. *R.I.C.* 290 note (*R. D. hoard*) .. ..

183   187a

183 Cld. ℞. PAX AETERNA AVG., Pax stg. front, hd. l., holding olive-branch and long sceptre. *B.M.C.* 131-5; *R.I.C.* 165 25

183a Cldc. ℞. — As last. *B.M.C.* 129-30; *R.I.C.* 165 25

183b Cld(A). ℞. — As last. *R.I.C.* 291 (*not in B.M.C. as stated*) .. ..

184 Quinarius. As 183. *B.M.C.* 136; *R.I.C.* 166 175

187 Denarius. Cld. ℞. PAX AVG., as before, but Pax running l. *B.M.C.* 363-7; *R.I.C.* 168 25

187a Cldc. ℞. — As last (*G. R. Arnold*) 25

188 As 187 (*base, plated or N*). *B.M.C.* 363 note .. ..

191 Dl. ℞. PERPETVITATI AVG., Perpetuitas or Securitas standing almost front, leaning against column, hd. l., holding globe and transverse sceptre. *B.M.C.* 499-502; *R.I.C.* 208 35

192 Cld. ℞. — As last. *B.M.C.* 472; *R.I.C.* 169 40

193 As last (*base, plated or Æ*). *B.M.C.* 472 note .. ..

194a Cld. ℞. PIETAS AVG., Pietas stg. half. l., dropping incense on to lighted altar with r. hand and holding incense-box in l. *R.I.C.* 170 (*Tinchant cat.*) 35

194b Dld. ℞. — As last. *R.I.C.* 209 (*B.M., but not in cat.*) .. .. ..

195 Cl(A). ℞. — As last. *B.M.C.* 1057 note; *R.I.C.* 292 35

195a As last, but NVC for AVG. on *rev.* *R.I.C.* 292 note .. .. ..

195b Cld(A). ℞. — As 195. *B.M.C.* 1057 35

195c As last (*base*). *B.M.C.* 1057 note (*two in B.M.*) .. ..

196 Cldc(A). ℞. — As last. *B.M.C.* 1058-60; *R.I.C.* 293 25

196a As last (*plated*). *B.M.C.* 1058 note (*in B.M.*) .. ..

196b Cldc. ℞. PIETAS AVG., Piety stg. half-left, as last few, but dropping incense from l. hand and holding box in r. (*irregular*). *B.M.C.* 1075 ..

197 As **196** but *obv.* ends AV. *B.M.C.* 1058 note; *R.I.C.* 293 note £30

198 Abd. ℞. PIETAS AVG., priestly emblems—lituus, knife, sacrificial jug, simpulum and sprinkler. *B.M.C.* Elagabalus 266-7; *R.I.C.* 3 200

200 C (*Cohen gives* ALEXAN.) ld (*possibly of Eastern mintage, if it exists*). ℞. PIETAS MILITVM, Fides or Pietas stg., placing r. hand on standard, behind another standard (? type of **52**). *B.M.C.* 220 note; *R.I.C.* 171 .. .. For PIETAS NVC., *see* **195a**.

201 Dld(A). ℞. P . M . TR . P . COS, Mars stg. half-left, holding branch and reversed spear, star in field. *B.M.C.* 1009-10; *R.I.C.* 262 30

201a Dldc(A). ℞. — As last. *B.M.C.* 1007-8; *R.I.C.* 262 30
This reverse legend and type may exist with obv. legend C.

201 bis Dld and/or ldc (A). ℞. — Fortuna stg. front, hd. l., holding rudder (on globe *in B.M.*) and cornucopiae; usually with star in field. *B.M.C.* 1006; *R.I.C.* 263 35

202 Cld(A). ℞. — As last, but without star. *B.M.C.* 1026 note; *R.I.C.* 265 35
R.I.C. 264 *gives the same piece, but with star, as in the B.M. and pl. 4, 18, but the piece illustrated is R.I.C.* 267 (*see our* **223a**), *so R.I.C.* 264 *may not exist.*

202a As last, but reading ALEXD or ALEXAN. *R.I.C.* 265 note for latter .. 35

198   204

204 Cld. ℞. P . M . TR . P . COS . P . P., Jupiter, naked, but for cloak behind over arms, stg. front, hd. l., holding thunderbolt and long sceptre (*B.M.C.* says spear, *but illustration looks more like* sceptre). *B.M.C.* 16-8; *R.I.C.* 5 25

204a Cldc. ℞. — As last. *B.M.C.* 13-15; *R.I.C.* 5 (*Baldwin*) 25

204b As last (*base*). *B.M.C.* 13 note (*in B.M., ex. Lawrence*) .. .. ..

204c Cld. ℞. — As before, but with eagle at feet (*Dr. Busso Peus*) 40

206a Cld. ℞. — Mars stg. front, hd. l., holding olive-branch and spear. *B.M.C.* 28 note (*R. D. hoard*) 25

207   207a

207 As last, but spear reversed. *B.M.C.* 28-9; *R.I.C.* 7 25

207a As last, with star in field (A). *B.M.C.* 1032*; *R.I.C.* 266 30

208 As **207** (*base, plated or Æ*). *B.M.C.* 28 note .. ..

208a Cldc. ℞. — As **207**. *B.M.C.* 27; *R.I.C.* 7 25

208b Cldc(A). ℞. — As last. *R.I.C.* 266 30

212 Cldc(A?). ℞. — Sol. rad., stg. l. (head r.?), raising r. hand and holding whip (Hy.?). *B.M.C.* 1088 note; *R.I.C.* 8 35

212a Denarius. Cld. ℞. P . M . TR . P . COS . P . P., Liberalitas stg. front, hd. l., holding abacus and cornucopiae. *B.M.C.* 6 note (*R. D. hoard*) ..   £40

215 Cld and/or lsd. ℞. — Libertas stg. front, hd. l., holding pileus and cornucopiae. *B.M.C.* 21 note; *R.I.C.* 11   30

216 Cldcf. ℞. — As last. *B.M.C.* 21-3   25

R.I.C. 12 *gives a quinarius* (*obv.* Cl) *of this type, but B.M.C. says the reference given describes quite a different coin.*

216a Quinarius. Cl. cuir., but not draped. ℞. — As last; *R.I.C.* 12 note

218 Denarius. Cld. ℞. — Salus seated l., resting l. arm on throne and feeding out of patera a snake coiling up from altar. *B.M.C.* 34-8; *R.I.C.* 14   25

218a Cldc. ℞. — As last. *B.M.C.* 33; *R.I.C.* 14 (*Lawrence*)   25

223 Cld. ℞. — Fortuna stg. half-left, holding rudder on globe and cornucopiae. *R.I.C.* 9   35

223a Cld(A). ℞. — As last, but with star in field. *B.M.C.* 1026-31; *R.I.C.* 267   25

224 As one or both of the last two (*plated or* Æ). *B.M.C.* 1026 note (*Ashmolean, plated*) .. ..

224a Dld. ℞. — As **223** (Hy.). *R.I.C.* quote (*R. D. hoard*) .. ..

226 Dldc. ℞. — Emperor stg. in slow quadriga l., holding branch and eagle-topped sceptre. *B.M.C.* 11 note; *R.I.C.* 17 .. ..

226a Cld. ℞. — Emperor stg. front, hd. l., holding branch and leaning on reversed spear. *B.M.C.* 28 note; *R.I.C.* 17A (*Evans*) (*probably the same as* **207**) .. ..

227 *Obv.?* ℞. P . M . TR . P . COS . P . P . P., lion holding thunderbolt in its jaws (Hy.; *rev. of Caracalla*). *B.M.C.* 977*; *R.I.C.* p. 72, † .. ..

227a Cldc(A). ℞. P . M . TR . P . COS . II . P . P., Liberalitas stg. l., holding abacus and cornucopiae (*irregular*). *B.M.C.* 1076*; *R.I.C.* 310A (*R. D. hoard*)   40

227b Cld. ℞. — The Nymphaeum (or Thermae Alexandri; *see* **297**). *B.M.C.* p. 32 (*modern forgery*) .. ..

227c Cld. ℞. P . M . TR . P . I . COS . P . P., Pax stg. front, hd. l., holding olive-branch and sceptre. *B.M.C.* 101 note; *R.I.C.* 27 note (*R. D. hoard*)   40

229 Cld. ℞. P . M . TR . P . II . COS . P . P., Jupiter stg., as **204**. *B.M.C.* 87-9; *R.I.C.* 19   25

229a Cldc. ℞. — As last (*New York*) .. ..

229b Quinarius. As **229**. *B.M.C.* 90; *R.I.C.* 20   175

231   236

231 Denarius. Cld. ℞. — Mars stg., as **207**. *B.M.C.* 92-8; *R.I.C.* 23 ..   25

231a Cld(A). ℞. — Mars stg., as **201**. *B.M.C.* 1041*   30

232 Quinarius. As **231**. *B.M.C.* 99*; *R.I.C.* 24   175

233 Denarius. As **231** (*base, plated or* Æ). *B.M.C.* 92 note .. ..

233a As **231**, but spear not reversed. *B.M.C.* 92 note   25

234 Cld. ℞. — Mars walking r., carrying spear and trophy (Hy.?). *B.M.C.* p. 28; *R.I.C.* 25   35

236 Cld. ℞. — Pax stg., as **227c** *B.M.C.* 101-5; *R.I.C.* 27   25

236a As last (*base*). *B.M.C.* 101 note (*Ashmolean*) .. ..

237 Cld(A). ℞. P . M . TR . P . II . COS . P . P., Fortuna stg. l., as **223a.** *B.M.C.* 1042; *R.I.C.* 268 .. .. £25

237a Cld. ℞. — As last. *R.I.C.* 29 (*this could be a mistake for last*) 25

237b **Quinarius.** As before. *B.M.C.* 1042 note; *R.I.C.* 30 (sceptre for cornucopiae) 175

238a Cld. ℞. — Providentia stg. facing, hd. l., holding wand over globe at feet and long sceptre. *B.M.C.* 110* (*Vienna*) 175

239 **Denarius.** Cld. ℞. — Salus seated l., feeding serpent entwined around altar. *B.M.C.* 117-22; *R.I.C.* 32 25

239a Cldc. ℞. — As last (*Brussels*) 25

239b Cld(A). ℞. — As last. *R.I.C.* 269 (*in B.M., possibly a mistake for next*)

239c Cldc(A). ℞. — As last, a second snake coiled around waist. *B.M.C.* 1077 (Æ).

247 Cld ? ℞. — The Coliseum with three figures. *B.M.C.* p. 129; *R.I.C.* 33

247a Cld. ℞. P . M . TR . P . II . COS . II . P . P., Providentia stg. l., leaning against column, holding wand over globe at her feet and cornucopiae. *R.I.C.* 310B (*irregular; R. D. hoard*).. 35

249   255

249 Cld. ℞. P . M . TR . P . III . COS . P . P., Jupiter stg., as **204.** *B.M.C.* 160-2; *R.I.C.* 35 25

251 Cld. ℞. — Mars stg., as **207.** *B.M.C.* 163-4; *R.I.C.* 37 25

254 Cld. ℞. — Pax stg., as **227c.** *B.M.C.* 167-9; *R.I.C.* 40 25

255 Cld. ℞. — Salus seated, as **218.** *B.M.C.* 176; *R.I.C.* 42 25

256 Cld. ℞. — The emperor, in military dress, stg. front, hd. l., holding globe and reversed spear. *B.M.C.* 178-82; *R.I.C.* 44 25

257 As last (*base, plated or Æ*). *B.M.C.* 178 note .. ..

258 Cl. ℞. — As before. *B.M.C.* 183; *R.I.C.* 44 25

260 Cl. ℞. P . M . TR . P . IIII . COS . P . P., Mars, naked except for cloak floating out, walking r., holding spear transversely and trophy over shoulder. *B.M.C.* 246-9; *R.I.C.* 45 25

261 As last (*base, plated or Æ*). *B.M.C.* 246 note .. ..

263a Cld (and/or ldc ?). ℞. — Aequitas stg. l., holding scales and cornucopiae (Hy. ?). *R.I.C.* 51 .. ..

270 Cld. ℞. — The emperor stg., as **256.** *B.M.C.* 253-4; *R.I.C.* 48 .. 25

276 Cld. ℞. — The emperor stg. half-left, sacrificing out of patera over tripod and holding scroll. *B.M.C.* 259-62; *R.I.C.* 50 25

277 As last (*base, plated or Æ*). *B.M.C.* 259 note .. ..

279a Cld. ℞. P . M . TR . P . IIII . COS . III . P . P., Sol stg. front, hd. l. (Hy., *base; rev. of Elagabalus*). *B.M.C.* 278 .. ..

281 Cld. ℞. P . M . TR . P . V . COS . II . P . P., Mars walking r., as **260.** *B.M.C.* 353-6; *R.I.C.* 53 25

289 Cld. ℞. P . M . TR . P . V . COS . II . P . P., the emperor sacrificing, as **276.** *B.M.C.* 373-6; *R.I.C.* 55 25

294a Cldcf. ℞. — emperor in slow quadriga l., holding eagle-tipped sceptre and branch. *B.M.C.* 318; *R.I.C.* 56A 200

296 D!. ℞. — The emperor walking. *B.M.C.* p. 151 (*is* **351** *altered by tooling*); *R.I.C.* 57 (*wrongly described*) .. ..

297   **Denarius.** Cld. ℞. P . M . TR . P . V . COS . II . P . P., the Nymphaeum (or Thermae) of Severus Alexander. *B.M.C.* 323; *R.I.C.* 59   ..   .. £1,250

305   Cld. ℞. P . M . TR . P . VI . COS . II . P . P., Mars walking r., as **260**. *B.M.C.* 409-13; *R.I.C.* 61   25

306   **Quinarius.** As last. *B.M.C.* 414*; *R.I.C.* 62   150

307   **Denarius.** As last (*base, plated or Æ*). *B.M.C.* 409 note   ..   ..

312   Cld. ℞. — Aequitas stg. front, hd. l., holding scales and cornucopiae. *B.M.C.* 294-8; *R.I.C.* 64   25

312a   C, but C . II . RVR . for C . M . AVR, l. ℞. — As last. (*Æ, irregular*). *B.M.C.* 1079   ..   ..

315   Cld. ℞. — Annona (*Cohen*, Abundantia) stg. half-left, holding two ears of corn over modius and cornucopiae. *B.M.C.* 403-4; *R.I.C.* 65 ..   25

318   Cld. ℞. — (*Cohen omits* II *after* COS), Pax stg., as **227c**. *B.M.C.* 420 note; *R.I.C.* 66   30

319   Cld. ℞. — Pax running l., holding olive-branch and transverse sceptre. *B.M.C.* 420-4; *R.I.C.* 67   25

325   Cld. ℞. — The emperor sacrificing, as **276,** but sometimes stg. facing, hd. l.   *B.M.C.* 430-5; *R.I.C.* 70   25

332   Cld. ℞. P . M . TR . P . VII . COS . II . P . P., Mars walking r., as **260**. *B.M.C.* 453-5; *R.I.C.* 73   25

333   As last (*base, plated or Æ*). *B.M.C.* 453 note

333a   Dld. ℞. — As last (Hy.). *R.I.C.* 73 note (*R. D. hoard*)   ..   35

333b   Dl. ℞. — As last. *R.I.C.* 82 (*Brussels*)   35

336   Cld. ℞. — Mars, in military dress, stg. half-right, holding reversed spear and resting hand on shield. *B.M.C.* 473*; *R.I.C.* 74   30

337   Dl. ℞. — As last. *B.M.C.* 503-5; *R.I.C.* 83   25

337a   Dlsd. ℞. — As last. *R.I.C.* 83

337b   **Quinarius.** As **337**. *B.M.C.* 506*; *R.I.C.* 84 (*Rome*)   ..   175

338   Cl. ℞. — As **336**. but Mars l.   *B.M.C.* 473* note (*not in Copenhagen as Cohen says*); *R.I.C.* 75   ..   ..

341   Dl. ℞. — Sol stg. l., raising r. hand and holding globe. *B.M.C.* p. 341 (TR . P. *number presumably misread*); *R.I.C.* 76   ..   ..   ..

346   Cld. ℞. — Aequitas stg., as **312**. *B.M.C.* 449-50; *R.I.C.* 78   25

347   Cld. ℞. — Pax stg. l., as **227c**. *B.M.C.* 458 note; *R.I.C.* 79 ..   35

348   Cld. ℞. — Pax running l., as **319**. *B.M.C.* 458-9; *R.I.C.* 80   25

351   Dl. ℞. — Severus Alexander as Romulus, bare-headed in military dress, hurrying r., holding transverse spear and trophy over shoulder. *B.M.C.* 507-10; *R.I.C.* 85   30

351a   **Quinarius.** As last. *B.M.C.* 511; *R.I.C.* 86 (*Trau*)   175

355   Dl. ℞. — Severus Alexander, laur., walking r., holding spear and club ? on shoulder. *B.M.C.* 511 note; *R.I.C.* 87 (*probably the same as last*)   ..   175

356   As last, but without club and with shield at his feet. *B.M.C.* 511 note; *R.I.C.* 88   175

357   **Denarius.** Cld. ℞. — Sev. Alexander sacrificing half-left, as **276**. *B.M.C.* 463-4; *R.I.C.* 81   30

362   Dl. ℞. P . M . TR . P . VII . COS . III (sic) . P . P., Virtus walking, holding branch and spear (Hy. ?). *B.M.C.* p. 163 (*not in Vienna*); *R.I.C.* 89   ..

363 Dl. R. — Virtus or soldier stg. r., holding spear and shield. *B.M.C.* 601 note; *R.I.C.* 90 (*probably a misreading for next*) .. .. ..

364 Dl. R. P . M . TR . P . VIII . COS . III . P . P., Mars, in military dress, stg. half-right, holding reversed spear and resting l. hand on shield. *B.M.C.* 601-2; *R.I.C.* 91 .. .. £25

364a Dlsd. R. — As last (*Brussels*) 25

364   365

365 Dl. R. — Mars, in military dress, hurrying l., holding branch, spear and shield. *B.M.C.* 603-5; *R.I.C.* 92 25

365a Dlsd. R. — As last. *B.M.C.* 606 (*Plevna hoard*) 25

366 Dl. R. — Mars walking r., as **260.** *B.M.C.* 609 note (*this could be a misdescription*); *R.I.C.* 93 .. ..

370 Dl. R. — (*Cohen omits* III *in error*), Annona stg. half-left, r. foot on prow, holding two corn-ears and cornucopiae. *B.M.C.* 599-600; *R.I.C.* 94 25

370a Dlsd. R. — As last. *R.I.C.* 94 25

370b Cl. R. — As last (*base*). *R.I.C* 94 (*in B.M., but not in cat.*) .. ..

371 Dl. R. — Libertas stg. front, hd. l., holding pileus and sceptre. *B.M.C.* 568-9; *R.I.C.* 95 25

371a Dlsd. R. — As last. *R.I.C.* 95 (*Tinchant cat.*) 25

375 Dl. R. — Sev. Alexander as Romulus hurrying r., as **351.** *B.M.C.* 608; *R.I.C.* 97 30

376 Dlsd. R. — Emperor in slow quadriga r., holding eagle-tipped sceptre. *B.M.C.* 575 note (*says the coin Cohen quoted from is a cast; possibly from the aureus that has turned up since*); *R.I.C.* 99 .. ..

388 Dl. R. P . M . TR . P . VIIII . COS . III . P . P., Sol. cloak over shoulder, stg. half-left, raising r. hand and holding whip. *B.M.C.* 623; *R.I.C.* 101 .. 25
There is a modern forgery of this piece, B.M.C. p. 32, 3.

388a Dlsd. R. — As last. *B.M.C.* 624; *R.I.C.* 101 25

389 Bl or lsd. R. — As before (Hy.; *plated*). *B.M.C.* 979*; *R.I.C.* 106

391 Dl. R. — As **388,** but Sol stg. half-right, looking l., holding globe. *B.M.C.* 630; *R.I.C.* 102 25

391a Dlsd. R. — As last. *B.M..C* 631-3; *R.I.C.* 102 25

392 As one of the last two (*base, plated or Æ*). *B.M.C.* 630 note .. ..

395 Dl or lsd. R. — Sev. Alexander, as Romulus, hurrying r., as **351.** *B.M.C.* 621*; *R.I.C.* 104 35

399a Cld. R. P . M . TR . P . IIIIII . OS . II . P . P., Pietas stg. l., sacrificing over altar (*irregular, barbarous style*). *R.I.C.* 312 (*as in B.M., but not in cat.; possibly misdescription of next*) .. ..

400 Cld(A ?). R. P . M . TR . P . VIII . OS . II . P . P., emperor stg. l., sacrificing over tripod (*irregular and Æ*). *B.M.C.* 1080; *R.I.C.* 273 .. ..

401 Denarius. Dl. R. P . M . TR . P . VIIII . COS . III . P . P., Sev. Alexander, in military dress, stg. r., holding transverse spear and globe. *B.M.C.* 616; *R.I.C.* 105 .. .. £30
401a Dlsd. R. — As last (*Brussels*) 30
402 As last (*base, plated or* Æ). *B.M.C.* 616 note .. ..
409 Blsd. R. P . M . TR . P . X . COS . III . P . P., Mars or Virtus stg. front, hd. l., resting r. hand on shield and holding reversed spear. *B.M.C.* 774; *R.I.C.* 108 30
409a Bl. R. — As last. *B.M.C.* 774 note; *R.I.C.* 108 (*R. D. hoard*) .. 30
410 Dl. R. — As last. *B.M.C.* 746 note; *R.I.C.* 107 30
410a Dlsd. R. — As last. *B.M.C.* 746 30
410b Dldc. R. — As last. *B.M.C.* 746 note, *R.I.C.* 107 30
411 Bldf. R. — Sol naked except for cloak over shoulders, stg. facing, hd. l., raising r. hand and holding globe. *B.M.C.* 807 note; *R.I.C.* 109 .. 25
411a Bldcf. R. — As last. *B.M.C.* 807; *R.I.C.* 109 25
416a Blsd. R. — As before, but whip for globe. *B.M.C.* 770-1; *R.I.C.* 109 note 25
417 Bld. R. — As last, but Sol walking. *B.M.C.* 770 note; *R.I.C.* 110 .. 30
417a Blsd. R. — As last. *R.I.C.* 110 30

427 Bldcf (and ldf?). R. P . M . TR . P . XI . COS . III . P . P., Sol stg., as **411**. *B.M.C.* 855; *R.I.C.* 112 25
428 (*R.I.C.* 113) is wrongly described from B.M., it is our **434c** .. ..
434 Bl and/or lsd. R. — As last, but Sol walks l. holding whip, as **417**. *B.M.C.* 862 note 25
434a Bld. R. — As last. *R.I.C.* 114 (*Brussels*) 25
434b Bldcf. R. — As last. *B.M.C.* 862-3; *R.I.C.* 114 25
434c Quinarius. Dl. R. — As last. *B.M.C.* 864; *R.I.C.* 115 175
434d Bld. R. — As last. *B.M.C.* 864 note; *R.I.C.* 115 175
434e Bldc. R. — As last. *B.M.C.* 864 note (*Hunterian*) 175
434f Denarius. Alcdf. R. — As before, but Sol holds rock instead of globe. *B.M.C.* 862 note; *R.I.C.* 117 (*possibly wrongly described*) .. .. ..
440 Bldf. R. P . M . TR . P . XII . COS . III . P . P., Sol walking l., as **417**. *B.M.C.* 930-1; *R.I.C.* 120 25
448 Bldf and/or ldcf. R. P . M . TR . P . XIII . COS . III . P . P., as last. *B.M.C.* 950-2; *R.I.C.* 123 25
452 (*R.I.C.* 124) has been misread, it is **365**. *B.M.C.* p. 208 .. ..
453 Bldf. R. P . M . TR . P . XIIII . COS . III . P . P., as **417**. *B.M.C.* 963; *R.I.C.* 125 30
453a Bldcf. R. — As last. *B.M.C.* 962 30
460 Cldc. R. PONTIF . MAX . TR . P . II . COS . P . P., Roma seated l. holding Victory and spear, shield beside throne (*base or* Æ). *B.M.C.* 1063 note
460a Dld. R. As last or next. *B.M.C.* 1063 note; *R.I.C.* 270 (*also specimen in B.M., plated*) .. ..
470 Cldc. R. PONTIF . MAX . TR . P . II . COS . II . P . P., as **460**. *B.M.C.* 1063 note; *R.I.C.* 271
470a Cld. R. — As last. *B.M.C.* 1063-5; *R.I.C.* 271 and 306 30
470b As last, but PONTE. *B.M.C.* 1066; *R.I.C.* 271 note .. .. ..
470c As **470** (*base*). *B.M.C.* 1063 note (*Spink*) .. ..

470d As **470,** but COS . III. *B.M.C.* 1063 note; *R.I.C.* 271 note (*R. D. hoard*)
It is possible that all the last seven are hybrids with rev. of Elagabalus

483 Cld. ℞. PONTIF . MAX . TR . P . VII . COS . II . P . P., as before (*base, plated* or Æ). *B.M.C.* 1081* (*irregular*); *R.I.C.* 272 .. ..

483a Cld or l. ℞. PONT . M . II . COS . P . P., emperor stg. l., holding globe and spear (*irregular*). *B.M.C.* 1082*; *R.I.C.* 313 .. ..

488 Dldcf. ℞. PROFECTIO AVG., Alexander, in military dress, on horseback r., holding transverse spear. *B.M.C.* 747*; *R.I.C.* 210 .. .. ..   £200

495 Cld(A). ℞. PROVID . DEORVM, Providentia stg. half-left (or front, hd. l.) holding wand over globe and long sceptre. *B.M.C.* 1062; *R.I.C.* 294 ..   25

495a Cldc(A). ℞. — As last. *B.M.C.* 1061   25
495b As **495,** but obv. reads ALIXAD. *R.I.C.* 294 note (*R. D. hoard*) .. ..
496 As **495** (*base, plated or* Æ). *B.M.C.* 1062 note (*two in B.M.*) .. ..
497 As **495,** but PROVAD (*base, plated or* Æ). *B.M.C.* 1062 note; *R.I.C.* 295
497a Cldc. ℞. PROVID . DEORVM, Providentia stg. l, leaning against column. *R.I.C.* 172 (*Ciani*)   40
497b Cld(A). ℞. — As **495,** but cornucopiæ for sceptre. *R.I.C.* 294 note (*R. D. hoard*)   30
498 Cld. ℞. PROVIDENTIA AVG., as **495.** *B.M.C.* 138-40; *R.I.C.* 173 ..   25
498a Cld(A). ℞. — As last. *R.I.C.* 296 (*B.M., but not in cat.*) . ..

501 Bld. ℞. — Providentia (*Cohen,* Prudence; *R.I.C.,* or Annona) stg. front, hd. l., holding corn-ears over modius filled with corn-ears and holding cornucopiae. *B.M.C.* 875 note; *R.I.C.* 250   25
501a Bl. ℞. — As last. *B.M.C.* 875 note; *R.I.C.* 250 (*Ashmolean*)   25
501b Blsd. ℞. — As last. *B.M.C.* 875-9; *R.I.C.* 250   25
501c Bldc. ℞. — As last. *B.M.C.* 875 note; *R.I.C.* 250 (*but not in B.M.*) ..
502 As **501** (*base, plated or* Æ). *B.M.C.* 875 note .. ..
502a **Quinarius.** Bldcf. ℞. — As before. *B.M.C.* 880* (*Vienna*) ..   200
508 **Denarius.** Bl. ℞. — As before, but Providentia holds anchor in place of cornucopiae. *B.M.C.* 814 note; *R.I.C.* 252   25
508a Blsd. ℞. — As last. *B.M.C.* 813-4; *R.I.C.* 252   25
508b Bldcf. ℞. — As last. *R.I.C.* 252 (*Brussels*)   25
512 Cld. ℞. — As **495,** but spear for sceptre. *B.M.C.* 138 note; *R.I.C.* 174   25
515a Cl and/or lsd and/or ld. ℞. PVDICITIA. Pudicitia seated l. on throne, about to draw veil and holding transverse sceptre (Hy., *base; rev of Julia Maesa*). *B.M.C.* 980; *R.I.C.* 307
527 IMP . MARCO AVR . SEV . AL . AV, ldc. ℞. SACERDOS VRBIS, emperor, in military dress, stg. l beside altar, holding branch and sceptre (Æ, *irregular*). *B.M.C.* 1083*; *R.I.C.* 297 .. ..

528 Denarius. Cld. ℞. SALVS AVGVSTI, Salus stg. half-left, feeding out of
bowl snake she holds in her arms. *B.M.C.* 479-80; *R.I.C.* 176 ..   ..   £25
528a Antoninianus. B, rad. bust dr. and cuir. r. ℞. — Salus stg. l., holding
branch. *B.M.C.* p. 32, modern forgery 5 ..   ..
528b Dld(A ?). ℞. SALVS PSVLAS, as next. *B.M.C.* 1084* (*irregular*); *R.I.C.*
298 note (*R. D. hoard*)   ..   ..

530   543

530 and **532** Cldc. ℞. SALVS PVBLICA, Salus seated l., feeding from patera
snake coiling up from altar, elbow resting on side of throne. *B.M.C.*
77-80; *R I.C.* 178   25
531 As last or next (*base, plated or Æ*). *B.M.C.* 77 note   ..   ..   ..
532a Cld. ℞. — As last. *B.M.C.* 81-2; *R.I.C.* 178   25
535 Dld(A). ℞. — As last, but star in field l. *B.M.C.* 1014-15; *R.I.C.* 298   25
535a Dldc(A). ℞. — As last. *B.M.C.* 1016   25
535b As last, but star in field r. *B.M.C.* 1017   25
535c Cld(A). ℞. — As **535**. *B.M.C.* 1037 * (*Vatican*)   30
536a Cldc(A ?). ℞. SECVLI FELICITAS, Felicitas stg. l., holding patera and long
caduceus; on l., modius filled with corn-ears. (Hy.; *rev. of Julia Maesa*).
B.M.C. 1068*; *R.I.C.* 299   ..   ..
543 Bldf. ℞. SPES PVBLICA, Spes walking l., holding flower and raising skirt.
B.M.C. 896; *R.I.C.* 254   25
544 Quinarius. Bldcf (*wrongly described by Cohen*, ld). ℞. — As last.
B.M.C. 901; *R.I.C.* 255   175
544a Bl. ℞. — As last. *B.M.C.* 901 note; *R.I.C.* 255 (*Vienna, ex Vierordt*)   175
544b Denarius. Blsd. ℞. — As last. *B.M.C.* 895   25
545 As **543** (*base, plated or Æ*). *B.M.C.* 896 note   ..   ..
546 Bldcf. ℞. — As before. *B.M.C.* 897-900; *R.I.C.* 254   25
546a Dl. ℞. — As last (Hy.). *B.M.C.* 981   ..   ..
554 Cld(A ?). ℞. TEMPORVM FELICITAS, Felicitas stg. l., holding caduceus
and cornucopiae; star ? in field. *B.M.C.* 1070* note (*irregular*); *R.I.C.*
179   ..   ..
554a IMP . CAE . MAR . AV . SEV . ALX, ldc. ℞. VENVS CAELISTIS, Venus stg. l.,
holding sceptre (Hy., *base or Æ*; *rev. of Julia Soaemias*). *B.M.C.* 1085
(*irregular*); *R.I.C.* 308..   ..   ..
554b Cld. ℞. VENVS VICTRIX, Venus stg. l., holding helmet and leaning on spear,
shield at feet (Hy., *plated; rev. of Julia Mamaea*). *B.M.C.* 982*; *R.I.C.*
309   ..   ..
554c Obv. not given. ℞. VESTA, Vesta stg. l., holding palladium and sceptre
(Hy., *plated?; rev. of Julia Mamaea*). *Seaby's Bull.*, Feb. 63, B1500   ..

556   566b

556 Dl. R. VICTORIA AVG., Victory stg. half-left, holding wreath and palm. B.M.C. 700-1; R.I.C. 212. *Illustrated at bottom of last page* £25

556a Dlsd. R. — As last. B.M.C. 702; R.I.C. 212 25

558 Bl and/or lsd. R. — Victory stg. half-left, resting r. hand on shield at side and holding palm in l.; at her feet, captive kneeling with hands tied behind back. B.M.C. 778 note; R.I.C. 257 35

558a As before, but captive seated l. B.M.C. 778; R.I.C. 257 35

558b Dl. R. — As last, but resting l. hand on shield and palm in r. B.M.C. 753*; R.I.C. 216 (*Ball cat.*) 35

558c Dl (and lsd ?). R. — As **556**, with captive kneeling at feet. B.M.C. 700 note; R.I.C. 213 35

558d Dl. R. — Victory stg. l., holding palm in l. hand and placing r. on trophy, below which sits captive. B.M.C. 700 note; R.I.C. 214 35

559 Cld(A). R. — Victory running r., holding wreath and palm; star in field r. B.M.C. 1038-40; R.I.C. 301 25

559a Cldc(A). R. — As last (*base*). B.M.C. 1038 note; R.I.C. 300 .. ..

560 Dldc (and Dld). R. — As before, but without star. R.I.C. 215 .. 25

561 Dldc(A). R. — As last. B.M.C. 1020-4; R.I.C. 302 25

561a Dld(A). R. — As last. B.M.C. 1018-9; R.I.C. 302 25

561b As last (*base*). B.M.C. 1018 note (*two in B.M.*) .. ..

562 Bl or lsd(A). R. — As before. B.M.C. 1020 note (*who says the coin that Cohen catalogued is a cast forgery*); R.I.C. 258 .. .. ..

563 Cl. R. — Victory running l., holding wreath and palm. B.M.C. 268; R.I.C. 180 25

564 Cld. R. — As last. B.M.C. 269-73; R.I.C. 180 25

566 Dl and/or lsd. R. VICTORIA AVGVSTI, Victory stg. r., l. foot on helmet, inscribing VOT / X on shield attached to palm-tree. B.M.C. 638 note; R.I.C. 218 35

566a Dl. R. — As before, but Victory hold shield above knee, no palm-tree. B.M.C. 638-41; R.I.C. 219 30

566b Dlsd. R. — As last. (*G. R. Arnold*). *Illustrated at bottom of last page* 30

576   580a

576 Cld. R. VIRTVS AVG., Virtus, in military dress, stg. r., holding reversed spear and resting l. hand on shield. B.M.C. 278-82; R.I.C. 182 .. 25

577 **Quinarius.** As last. B.M.C. 283*; R.I.C. 183 175

578 **Denarius.** Cl and/or lsd. R. — As last. B.M.C. 278 note; R.I.C 182 30

579 Dl. R. — Virtus, in military dress, stg. half-right, holding Victory and resting l. hand on shield, upright spear rests against l. arm. B.M.C. 709-11; R.I.C. 220 25

579a Dlsd. R. — As last. R.I.C. 220 (*in B.M., but not in cat.*) 30

579b Bl. R. — As last. B.M.C. 983*; R.I.C. 259A (*R. D. hoard*) 35

579c Dl. R. — Virtus, in military dress, stg. r., holding spear and resting l. on shield. B.M.C. 1089 (*irregular*) 35

580 Denarius. Dl. R. VIRTVS AVG., Virtus seated l. on cuirass, holding branch and spear or sceptre, sometimes shield behind. *B.M.C.* 653-5; *R.I.C.* 221 .. .. £25

580a Dlsd. R. — As last. *B.M.C.* 656-7; *R.I.C.* 221 25

581 Bl. R. — Virtus, in military dress, stg. r., foot on helmet, holding sceptre and parazonium. *B.M.C.* 780 note; *R.I.C.* 259 30

581a Blsd. R. — As last. *B.M.C.* 779-80; *R.I.C.* 259 30

582 Dl. R. — As last. *B.M.C.* 754 note; *R.I.C.* 222 30

582a Dlsd. R. — As last. *B.M.C.* 754 30

582b As one of the last two (*plated or Æ*) (*Paris*) .. .. ..

584 Dl. R. — Emperor as Romulus, bare-headed, in military dress, walking r., carrying transverse spear and trophy over shoulder. *B.M.C.* 522-3; *R.I.C.* 224 30

585 As last, but emperor laureate. *B.M.C.* 522 note; *R.I.C.* 225 30

586 Dl. R. — Emperor, in military dress, stg. l., r. foot on helmet, holding globe and reversed spear. *B.M C.* 647; *R.I.C.* 226 25

586a Dlsd. R. — As last. *B.M.C.* 648; *R.I.C.* 226 25

586b As **586**, but rather unusual style. *B.M.C.* 647 note (*probable contemporary forgery, in B.M.*) .. ..

587 Quinarius. As **586a**. *B.M.C.* 649*; *R.I.C.* 227 175

584   596

596 Denarius. Bldcf. R. VOTIS / VICEN / NALI / BVS within laurel-wreath. *B.M.C.* 819; *R.I.C.* 261 150

596a Bldf R. As last (*Mazzini cat.*) 150

597 *Restitution of Trajan Decius.* **Antoninianus.** DIVO ALEXANDRO, hd. or bust rad. r. R. CONSECRATIO, lighted altar with two palmettes 75

598 — Bust rad. r. R. — Without palmette 75

599 — — R. — Eagle stg., looking l. 75

SEVERUS ALEXANDER and JULIA MAMAEA

2 Medallion. IMP ALEXANDER PIVS AVG . IVLIA MAMAEA AVG . MATER AVG , busts of Alex Sev ldc. r. and J. Mam. ds. l. R. AEQVITAS AVGVSTI., the Three Monetae. *R.I.C.* 316 .. .. *Extremely rare*

13 Denarius. Dl. R. IVLIA MAMAEA AVG, her dr. bust r. without diadem. *B.M.C.* p. 193 (*perhaps a later fabrication*); *R.I.C.* 315 .. .. ..

ORBIANA

Sallustia Barbia Orbiana was a wife of Severus Alexander who he married about 225-6 A.D. Almost nothing is known about her, but some have presumed that she was his third wife, and that Mamaea was jealous of her and compelled Alexander to banish her to Africa.

Obverse legend and type
Unless otherwise stated
SALL . BARBIA ORBIANA AVG., her diademed bust draped, right.

References.
All are to Severus Alexander numbers.

1   2

1 **Denarius.** R. CONCORDIA AVGG., Concordia seated l. on throne, holding
   patera and double cornucopiae. *B.M.C.* 287-90; *R.I.C.* 319 ..   ..   £200
2 **Quinarius.** As last. *B.M.C.* 291; *R.I.C.* 320   650
9 **Denarius.** R. MINERVA VICTRIX, Minerva stg. l., holding Victory and
   spear, shield at feet (Hy.; *rev. of Caracalla*). *B.M.C.* 984*; *R.I.C.* 322
10 R. PROPAGI IMPERI, emperor and empress stg. clasping hands (Hy.; *rev.
   of Plautilla*). *B.M.C.* 985*; *R.I.C.* 323 ..   ..
11 R. PVDICITIA, Pudicitia seated l., r. hand up to face, and holding sceptre.
   (Hy.; *rev. of Julia Maesa*). *B.M.C.* 986*; *R.I.C.* 324 ..   ..   ..
11a R. SAECVLI FELICITAS, Felicitas stg. front, hd. l., sacrificing out of patera
   over lighted altar, and holding long caduceus; star in field (Hy.; *rev. of
   Julia Maesa*). *B.M.C.* 987; *R.I.C.* 325 ..   ..
12 R. VENVS GENETRIX, Venus seated l., holding patera and sceptre (Hy.;
   rev of Julia Mamaea). *B.M.C.* 989*; *R.I.C.* 326 ..   ..
13 R. — Venus stg., holding apple and spear (Hy.; *rev. of Julia Mamaea*).
   B.M.C. 988*; *R.I.C.* 327. ..   ..

JULIA MAMAEA

*Julia Mamaea was the daughter of Julius Avitus and Julia Maesa, sister of Julia Domna.
She was the mother of Severus Alexander, and the real power behind the throne, and was
assassinated with her son in 235 A.D.*

Obverse legends.
A. IVLIA MAMAEA AVG.
B. IVLIA MAMAEA AVGVSTA.

Obverse types.
d. Bust draped right
ds. „   „   „ wearing diadem (stephane)
dsc. „   „   „   „   „ all on crescent

References.
All are to Severus Alexander numbers
(A) indicates that it is attributed to mint of Antioch.

1 bis (*Cohen*, p. 498) **Denarius.** Ad. R. ABVNDANTIA AVG., Abundantia
   (Hy.). *B.M.C.* 990*; *R.I.C.* 369 ..   ..
1a Ad. R. AEQVITAS AVG., Aequitas stg. l., holding scales and cornucopiae
   (Hy.). *B.M.C.* 991* (*Sussex Arch. coll.*); *R.I.C.* 369A ..   ..   ..
2 **Medallion.** Bdsc, but to l. R. AEQVITAS PVBLICA, the Three Monetae stg.
   front, each holds scales and cornucopiae; at feet of each, pile of metal or
   coins. *B.M.C.* 554*; *R.I.C.* 328 ..   ..   *Extremely rare*
3 **Denarius.** A, but MAMMAEA, ds. R. ANNONA AVG., Annona stg. l.,
   holding cornucopiae and corn-ears (Hy. ?). *B.M.C.* 992* note; *R.I.C.* 366
3a (*Cohen*, p. 498) Ads. R. — Annona stg. holding corn-ears over modius
   and cornucopiae (Hy.). *B.M.C.* 992*; *R.I.C.* 370 ..   ..   ..

4 Denarius. Ad(A). ℝ. CONCOBDIA, Concordia stg. l., sacrificing at altar, holding double cornucopiae; star in field. *B.M.C.* 1090* (*irregular*) ..

4a Ad. ℝ. CONCORDIA, Concordia stg. l., holding double cornucopiae (?Hy.). *R.I.C.* 329 (*Budapest*) .. ..

4b Ads. ℝ. CONCORDIA AVGG., Concordia seated l., holding double cornu-copia (Hy.; *plated* ?). *R.I.C.* 330 .. ..

5 Ads. ℝ. FECVND . AVGVSTAE. Fecunditas stg. l., stretching out r. hand to little boy stg. r. and stretching up arms towards her, she holds cornu-copiae. *B.M.C.* 917-9; *R.I.C.* 331 .. .. £35

6 Ads. ℝ. — Fecunditas seated l., stretching out hand to child before her, l. elbow rests on back of chair. *B.M.C.* 913-15; *R.I.C.* 332 40

7 Quinarius. As last. *B.M.C.* 916*; *R.I.C.* 333 300

14a Denarius. Ad(A). ℝ. FELICITAS EXERCI, Felicitas seated l., holding caduceus and cornucopiae, between legionary eagle and standard. *R.I.C.* 367A (*Gantz*) 75

17   24

17 Ads. ℝ. FELICITAS PVBLICA, Felicity stg. facing, hd. l., legs crossed and leaning l. elbow on column, holding caduceus transversely. *B.M.C.* 483-5; *R.I.C.* 335 30

17a Another, very similar. *B.M.C.* 1091 (*irregular; ex Lawrence*) .. ..

19 Quinarius. As **17.** *B.M.C.* 486; *R.I.C.* 336 300

20 Denarius. As **17** (*base, plated or Æ*). *B.M.C.* 483 note .. ..

24 Ads. ℝ. — Felicitas seated l. on chair, holding caduceus and cornu-copiae. *B.M.C.* 658-9; *R.I.C.* 338 35

24a Quinarius. As last. *B.M.C.* 660; *R.I.C.* 339 (*Lawrence*) 350

29a (*Cohen*, p. 498) **Denarius.** Ads ? ℝ. FIDES MILITVM, Fides stg. (Hy.). *B.M.C.* 993*; *R.I.C.* 371 (*Vienna*) . .. .

29b Ads ? ℝ. — Fides seated l., holding two standards (Hy.; *rev. of Sev. Alex.*) *Seaby's Bull.*, Feb. 63, B1470 .. ..

30 Ad(A). ℝ. FORTVNA REDVX, Aequitas stg. l., holding scales and cornu-copiae. *B.M.C.* 1092* (*irregular*); *R.I.C.* 368 .. .. ..

31 Ads. ℝ. IVNO, Juno stg. l., holding patera and sceptre. *B.M.C.* 43 note; *R.I.C.* 340 60

31a As last with peacock at Juno's feet. *B.M.C.* 43 note; *R.I.C.* 340 note .. 60

32 Ads. ℝ. IVNO AVGVSTAE, Juno seated l., holding flower (?) and swathed infant (?). *B.M.C.* 755-8; *R.I.C.* 341 35

35 Ad. ℞. IVNO CONSERVATRIX, Juno, diad. and veiled, stg. half-left, holding patera and sceptre; at feet, peacock stg. **half-left,** turning head back to catch drops out of patera. *B.M.C.* 43-8; *R.I.C.* 343 .. .. .. £30

37

37 Quinarius. As last. *B.M.C.* 49; *R.I.C.* 344 300

38 Denarius. As **35** (*base, plated or* Æ). *B.M.C.* 43 note (*two in B.M.*) ..

41a As **35**, but MAMIAS for MAMAEA. (Hy.; *base or plated*). *B.M.C.* 43 note and 43A (*Addendum,* p. 260); *R.I.C.* 343 note 45

42a Ads. ℞. LIBERALITAS AVG . IIII, Liberalitas stg. l. holding abacus and cornucopiae (Hy.; *rev. of Alexander*). *B.M.C.* 994; *R.I.C.* 372 .. ..

42b (*Cohen,* p. 498) Ads. ℞. LIBERTAS AVG. Libertas stg (Hy.). *B.M.C.* 995*; *R.I.C.* 373 .. ..

42c Ads(A). ℞. LIBERTAS AVGVSTI, Libertas seated l. holding pileus and sceptre. *B.M.C.* 1092 (*irregular*); *R.I.C.* 374 (*hybrid*) .. .. ..

47 Quinarius. Ad. ℞. PAX AETERNA AVG., Pax stg. front or half-left, hd. l., holding olive-branch and long sceptre (Hy.; *rev. of Alexander*). *B.M.C.* 997*; *R.I.C.* 345 .. ..

47a Denarius. As last. *B.M.C.* 996* (*Kress sale*) .. ..

48 Ads. ℞. PIETAS AVGVSTAE, Pietas stg. front, hd. l., dropping grains of incense into lighted altar and holding box of perfume. *B.M.C.* 821-2; *R.I.C.* 346 45

49 As last (*base, plated or* Æ). *B.M.C.* 821 note .. ..

49a Ads. ℞. P . M . TR . P VI . COS . II . P . P., Aequitas stg. front, hd. l., holding scales and cornucopiae (Hy.; *rev. of Alexander*). *B.M.C.* 998*; *R.I.C.* 374A (*R. D. hoard*) .. ..

50 Ads. ℞. P . M . TR . P . VIII . . . Sol stg. (Hy., *plated*). *B.M.C.* 999*; *R.I.C.* 375 .. ..

50a Ads. ℞. P . M . TR . P . VIIII . COS . II . [P . P.], Alexander, as Romulus, bare-headed, in military dress, hurrying r., holding transverse spear and trophy over shoulder (Hy.; *rev. of Alexander*). *B.M.C.* 1000 (*Elveden find*)

50b Ads. ℞. PONTIF TR . P . III, Alexander stg. l. (Hy.) *B.M.C.* 1001*; *R.I.C.* 375A (*Trau*) .. ..

50c Ads. ℞. PROVIDENTIA AVG., Providentia stg. front, hd. l., holding two corn-ears over modius, and anchor (Hy.; *rev. of Alexander*). *B.M.C.* 1002* (*Kress sale*) .. ..

52 Ads. ℞. PVDICITIA, Pudicitia seated l., raising veil and holding sceptre (Hy.; *rev. of Maesa*). *B.M.C.* 1003*; *R.I.C.* 347 .. .. ..

53 As last (*base, plated or* Æ). *B.M.C.* 1003* note .. .. ..

53a Ads? ℞. — Pudicitia stg. l., holding patera and sceptre, altar at feet (*irregular ?*). *Seaby's Bull.*, *Feb.* 63, B1496 .. ..

55 Ads. ℞. SAECVLI FELICITAS, Felicitas stg. front, hd. l., sacrificing out of patera over lighted altar and holding long caduceus (Hy.; *rev. of Maesa*). *B.M.C.* 1005*; *R.I.C.* 348 .. ..

56 Ads? ℞. SALVS AVGVSTI, Salus stg. half-left, feeding out of bowl, snake she holds in her arms? (Hy.; *rev. of Alexander*). *B.M.C.* 1004*; *R.I.C.* 349 .. ..

58a Ads? ℞. TEMPORVM FELICITAS, Felicitas stg. l., holding caduceus and cornucopiae (Hy., *ancient forgery: rev. of Elagabalus*). *Seaby's Bull.*, *May* 1964, B355 .. ..

60 Denarius. Ads. ℞. VENERI FELICI, Venus stg. half-right, holding sceptre and Cupid. *B.M.C.* 189; *R.I.C.* 351   .. ..   £35
61 Quinarius. As last. *B.M.C.* 189 note; *R.I.C.* 352   350
68 Denarius. Ads. ℞. VENVS FELIX, Venus stg. r., holding sceptre and Cupid. *B.M.C.* 189 note; *R.I.C.* 353   .. ..

72 Ads. ℞. VENVS GENETRIX, Venus stg. front, hd. l., holding apple and sceptre; before her, Cupid stg. r. with hands raised. *B.M.C.* 152-3; *R.I.C.* 355   35
73 Ad. ℞. — As last. *B.M.C.* 152 note; *R.I.C.* 356   .. .. ..

76   81

76 Ads. ℞. VENVS VICTRIX, Venus stg. half-left or front, hd. l., holding helmet and sceptre; at feet l., shield. *B.M.C.* 713-7; *R.I.C.* 358   ..   35
77 As last (*base, plated or Æ*). *B.M.C.* 714 note; *R.I.C.* 358   .. ..
81 Ads. ℞. VESTA, Vesta, veiled, stg. half-left, holding palladium and sceptre. *B.M.C.* 381-7; *R.I.C.* 360   30
82 Quinarius. As last. *B.M.C.* 388*; *R.I.C.* 361   350
85 Denarius. Ads. ℞. — Vesta, veiled, stg. half-left, holding patera and transverse sceptre. *B.M.C.* 440-3; *R.I.C.* 362   35
86 Quinarius. As last. *B.M.C.* 444; *R.I.C.* 363   300
87 Denarius. As before (*base, plated or Æ*). *B.M.C.* 440 note   .. ..
90 Ad. ℞. — Vesta seated l., holding palladium and transverse sceptre. *B.M.C.* 380 note; *R.I.C.* 364..   .. ..
90a Ads. ℞. VICTOR. AVG (or AVGG)., Victory stg. l., holding wreath and palm (Hy.). *B.M.C.* 1005A* (*Ball*); *R.I.C.* 376 ..   ..
90b Ads. ℞. VICTORIA AVG., Victory walking r., holding wreath and palm (*plated*). *R.I.C.* 365 (*in B.M., but not in cat.*)   .. ..

MAMAEA, SEVERUS ALEXANDER and ORBIANA

1 Small medallion (or double denarius). IVLIA MAMAEA AVG . MAT . AVGVSTI, diad. bust of Mamaea dr. l. ℞. IMP . SEV . ALEXANDER AVG . SALL . BARBIA ORBIANA AVG., laur. dr. and cuir. bust of Alexander r. facing diad. and dr. bust of Orbiana l. *B.M.C.* 308*   .. ..   *Extremely rare*
1a As before, but bust of Mamaea to r. *R.I.C.* 318 ..   ..
1b As 1, but *rev.* legend starts IMP . SEVERVS. *R.I.C.* 318 note   .. ..

MAXIMINUS I
235-8 A.D.

Caius Julius Verus Maximinus was born in Thrace in 173 A.D. of peasant stock; his father was Micea, a Goth, and his mother, Abada, an Alanian. He was originally a herdsman, before entering the Roman cavalry. His extraordinary size and strength attracted the attention of Septimius Severus and he gained rapid promotion. During the reign of Alexander he commanded a legion and later became governor of Mesopotamia. In the war against Persia he showed his courage and capability. He accompanied Alexander into Germany and in 235 was in charge of levies of recruits on the Rhine. On Alexander's assassination, which he might have been associated with, the army proclaimed him emperor. He made his son, Maximus, Caesar.

His reign was characterised by his hatred of the Senate and ruthless cruelty towards anyone suspected of conspiracy against him. The abortive rebellion of the Gordiani in Africa in March 238, was soon followed by a similar defection in Rome, when Balbinus and Pupienus were elected joint emperors by the Senate. Maximinus, therefore, advanced upon Italy and besieged Aquileia, but his efforts were unsuccessful and his troops finally mutinied and murdered him and his son, Maximus on 24 June, 238.

Obverse legends.
A. IMP . MAXIMINVS PIVS AVG.
B. MAXIMINVS PIVS AVG . GERM

Obverse types.
ld. laureate bust right, draped

ldc. „ „ „ draped and cuirassed

f. Bust seen from front; all the rest are seen from side or behind

e. Early portrait rather like Sev. Alexander before the Rome engravers knew what Maximinus was really like.

All his coinage is attributed to Rome.

2 **Denarius.** Bldc. ℞. AEQVITAS AVG., Aequitas stg. half-left, holding scales and cornucopiae (Hy.; *rev. of Sev. Alexander*). *B.M.C.* 233*; *R.I.C.* 95 .. ..

3 **Medallion.** Bldcf. ℞. AEQVITAS AVGVSTI, the Three Monetae stg. facing, hds. l., each holding scales and cornucopiae; at their feet, piles of metal or coins, or a die. *B.M.C.* 226*; *R.I.C.* 18 .. *Extremely rare*

5 Aldcf ℞. — As last. *B.M.C.* 136A; *R.I.C.* 7 .. .. *Extremely rare*

5a **Quinarius.** Aldc. ℞. CONCORDIA AVG., Concordia stg. l., holding patera and cornucopiae (*modern forgery*). *B.M.C.* p. 33, 2 .. .. ..

6 **Denarius.** Aldc. ℞. FELICITAS PVBLICA, Felicitas stg. l., holding caduceus and cornucopiae (Hy.; *rev. of Julia Mamaea?*). *B.M.C.* 234* (*this is probably a misdescription of the next*).. .. ..

6a Aldc. ℞. — Felicitas stg. facing, hd. l., legs crossed and leaning l. elbow on column, holding caduceus (Hy.; *rev. of Julia Mamaea*). *R.I.C.* 96 (*Berlin*) .. ..

7 **Denarius.** Aldce. ℞. FIDES MILITVM, Fides stg. facing, hd. l., holding standard in each hand. *B.M.C.* 1; *R.I.C.* 7A £40

7a   37

7a Aldc. ℞. — As last. *B.M.C.* 58-61; *R.I.C.* 7A   35

8 **Quinarius.** As last. *B.M.C.* 62*; *R.I.C.* 7A   500

8a **Denarius.** As **7a** (*plated or base*). *B.M.C.* 58 note; *R.I.C.* 7A note   ..

8b As last (*semi-barbarous*). *R.I.C.* 7A note (*in B.M., but not in cat.*)   ..

9 Bldc. ℞. — As before. *B.M.C.* 137-8; *R.I.C.* 18A   35

16 Ald. ℞. INDVLGENTIA AVG., Indulgentia seated l., extending r. hand and holding transverse sceptre. *B.M.C.* 31* (pl. 34, *Paris*); *R.I.C.* 8 (*curious style*)   85

18a Aldc. ℞. LIBER . AVGGGG., emperor stg. l., between standards (*modern forgery*). *B.M.C.* p. 32, 1   ..   ..

19 Aldc. ℞. LIBERALITAS AVG., Liberalitas stg. front, hd. l., holding abacus and cornucopiae. *B.M.C.* 45; *R.I.C.* 10   45

29a **Quinarius.** Aldc. ℞. MARTI PACIFERO, Mars, in military dress, stg. l., foot on helmet, holding branch and spear. *B.M.C.* 34* (*Vienna*); *R.I.C.* 11 (*Trau*)   500

31 **Denarius.** Aldce. ℞. PAX AVGVSTI, Pax stg. half-left (or facing, hd. l.), holding branch and transverse sceptre. *B.M.C.* 5-6; *R.I.C.* 12   40

31a Aldc. ℞. — As last. *B.M.C.* 68-71; *R.I.C.* 12   35

31b Ald. ℞. — As last (*Mazzini cat.*)   35

32 **Quinarius.** As **31a.** *B.M.C.* 68 note; *R.I.C.* 12   500

33 **Denarius.** As **31** or **31a** (*base, plated or Æ*). *B.M.C.* 68 note; *R.I.C.* 12 note   ..   ..

33a As before, but reading MAXIMIVS. *R.I.C.* 12 note (*Berlin*)   ..   ..

37 Bldc. ℞. — As **31.** *B.M.C.* 144-6; *R.I.C.* 19   35

37a **Quinarius.** As last. *B.M.C.* 147*; *R.I.C.* 19 (*de Quelen*)   550

41 **Denarius.** As last (*base, plated or Æ*). *B.M.C.* 44 note; *R.I.C.* 19 note
N.B. *Cohen 44-49 accidently gives obv. B for obv. A.*

45 **Quinarius.** Alde or ldce. ℞. P . M . TR . P . P . P., emperor stg. almost front, hd. l., between two standards, raising r. hand and holding long sceptre (*Cohen and R.I.C.* spear) in l. *B.M.C.* 13*; *R.I.C.* 1   500

46 **Denarius.** Aldce. ℞. — As last. *B.M.C.* 11-12; *R.I.C.* 1   35

46a Alde. ℞. — As last. *B.M.C.* 9-10   35

46b MAXIMINVS PIVS AVG., lde(?). ℞. — As last. *R.I.C.* 1 (*P. Whiteway*) ..   65

47 Aldce. ℞. — As before, but three standards. *B.M.C.* 9 note; *R.I.C.* 1 note   55

51 Aldc?. ℞. P . M . TR . P . II . COS . P . P., emperor seated in triumphal quadriga, holding ivory baton (*unknown today*). *B.M.C.* 55 note; *R.I.C.* 2

55   64

55 Aldc. R . — As **45,** but sometimes spear for sceptre. *B.M.C.* 77-9;
R.I.C. 3   ..   ..   £35
56 Bldc. R . — As last. *B.M.C.* 157-8; *R.I.C.* 4   40
64 Bldc. R . P . M . TR . P . III . COS . P . P., as last. *B.M.C.* 161-3; *R.I.C.* 5   40
65 **Quinarius.** As last. *B.M.C.* 164; *R.I.C.* 5   500
66 **Denarius.** As last (*base, plated or Æ*). *B.M.C.* 161 note; *R.I.C.* 5 note
66a Aldc. R . — As last (Hy.). *B.M.C.* 235*; *R.I.C.* 98   ..   ..   ..
70 Bldc. R . P . M . TR . P . IIII . COS . P . P., as before. *B.M.C.* 219-20; *R.I.C.* 6   45
73a Aldc. R . P . M . TR . P . VI . COS . II . P . P., Aequitas stg. as 2 (Hy., *plated;
rev. of Sev. Alexander*). *B.M.C.* 237*; *R.I.C.* 99   ..   ..   ..
73b Aldc. R . P . M . TR . P . VIII . COS . III . P . P., Libertas stg. l., holding pileus
and transverse sceptre (Hy.; *rev. of Sev. Alexander*). *B.M.C.* 238*;
R.I.C. 100 (*R. D. hoard, semi-barbarous*)   ..   ..
73c Aldc. R . P . M . TR . P . VIIII . COS . III . P . P. (Hy.; *rev. of Sev.
Alexander*). *B.M.C.* 239; *R.I.C.* 101   ..   ..
73d Aldc. R . PODTVNAE REDVCI, Fortuna stg. l., holding rudder on globe and
cornucopiae. *B.M.C.* 244* (*irregular*); *R.I.C.* 104 (*barbarous*) (*R. D.
hoard*) ..   ..

77a

75 Bldc. R . PROVIDENTIA AVG., Providentia stg. facing, hd. l., holding
wand over globe and cornucopiae. *B.M.C.* 170-1; *R.I.C.* 20   35
77 Aldce. R . — As last. *B.M.C.* 15-16; *R.I.C.* 13   35
77a Aldc. R . — As last. *B.M.C.* 86-8; *R.I.C.* 13   35

78 **Quinarius.** As last. *B.M.C.* 89; *R.I.C.* 13   500
79 **Denarius.** As last (*base, plated or Æ*). *B.M.C.* 86 note; *R.I.C.* 13 note
79a As **75,** but without globe. *R.I.C.* 13 note (*Lawrence*)   40
79b As **75.** *B.M.C.* 245 (*irregular*); *R.I.C.* 105 (*barbarous*) (*Lawrence*)   ..

85 Denarius. Aldce. ℞. SALVS AVGVSTI, Salus seated l., feeding out of patera a snake rising from altar, resting l. arm on chair. *B.M.C.* 21-2; *R.I.C.* 14 .. .. £35

85a Aldc. ℞. — As last. *B.M.C.* 99; *R.I.C.* 14 35

86 Quinarius. As 85 or 85a. *B.M.C.* 99 note; *R.I.C.* 14 ..

87 Denarius. As before (*base, plated or Æ*). *B.M.C.* 99 note; *R.I.C.* 14 note

91 Bldc. ℞. — As last. *B.M.C.* 173*; *R.I.C.* 21 45

91a Quinarius. As last. *B.M.C.* 174*; *R.I.C.* 21 500

85a   99a

95a Denarius. Aldc. ℞. VICT . AETERN., Victory flying l., holding wreath in both hands; before her, shield (Hy.; *plated?*). *B.M.C.* 246 * (*irregular*); *R.I.C.* 15 .. ..

99 Aldce. ℞. VICTORIA AVG., Victory running r., holding out wreath and palm over l. shoulder. *B.M.C.* 25-6; *R.I.C.* 16 35

99a Aldc. ℞. — As last. *B.M.C.* 105-7; *R.I.C.* 16 35

99b As last (*base*). *B.M.C.* 106 note (*Lawrence*) .. ..

103a Bldc. ℞. — As last. *B.M.C.* 181*; *R.I.C.* 22 (*R. D. hoard*) ..

107   117a

107 Bldc. ℞. VICTORIA GERM., Victory stg. half-left, holding wreath and palm; at her feet, German captive seated l., hd. r., probably hands tied behind back. *B.M.C.* 186-9; *R.I.C.* 23 40

108 Quinarius. As last. *B.M.C.* 190; *R.I.C.* 23 550

112 Denarius. Aldc. ℞. VICTORIA GERMANICA, Maximinus in military dress, std. l. with captive at feet; he raises r. hand and holds short sceptre in l., and is being crowned by Victory, who holds palm. *B.M.C.* 112*
        if it exists 500

116a Aldc? ℞. VIRTVS AVG., Virtus stg. l., holding globe and leaning on spear. *B.M.C.* 248* (*irregular*); *R.I.C.* 106 (*barbarous; Budapest*) .. ..

117 Aldce. ℞. VOTIS / DECENNA / LIBVS in laurel wreath. *B.M.C.* 38-9; *R.I.C.* 17 150

117a Aldc. ℞. — As last (*G. R. Arnold coll.*) 150

1   2

PAULINA

Paulina is presumed to have been the wife of Maximinus, but history knows nothing of her.

1 **Denarius.** DIVA PAVLINA, her veiled and dr. bust r. R. CONSECRATIO,
peacock facing, with tail in splendour, hd. l. *B.M.C.* 135; *R.I.C.* 1.
Illustrated at bottom of page before £350

2 — — R. — Paulina, holding sceptre and raising hand, seated l. on
peacock, flying r., to heaven. *B.M.C.* 127-8; *R.I.C.* 2. *Illustrated at bottom
of last page* 300

2a As last (*base*). *B.M.C.* 127 note (*Ashmolean*) .. ..

MAXIMUS

*Caius Julius Verus Maximus was the son of Maximinus and was probably made Caesar
at the same time as his father was created Augustus. He was murdered at the same time as
his father.*

Obverse legends and type.

A. IVL . VERVS MAXIMVS CAES., A.D. 235-6

B. MAXIMVS CAES . GERM., A.D. 236-8

C. MAXIMVS CAESAR GERM., A.D. 236-8

All pieces have his bare-headed bust draped right.

1   10

1 **Denarius.** A. R. PIETAS AVG., lituus, knife, jug, simpulum and sprinkler.
B.M.C. 118; *R.I.C.* 1 140

1a As last (*base or plated*). *B.M.C.* 118 note; *R.I.C.* 1 note (*Lawrence*) ..
Becker made dies based on Cohen 1.

3 B. R. — As last (*Cohen omits* simpulum). *B.M.C.* 201-3; *R.I.C.* 2 .. 150

9a B. R. P . M . TR . P . III . COS . P . P., Maximinus stg. l., between two
standards, raising r. hand and holding sceptre (Hy.; *rev. of Maximinus*).
B.M.C. 241*; *R.I.C.* 15 (*Vierordt*) .. ..

10 B. R. PRINC . IVVENTVTIS, the young prince, in military dress, stg. half-
left, holding baton and transverse spear with point downwards; to r.,
two standards. *B.M.C.* 211-2; *R.I.C.* 3 125

10a **Quinarius.** As last. *R.I.C.* 3 (*Vienna*) .. .. .. *Extremely rare*

11 **Denarius.** As last (*base, plated or Æ*). *B.M.C.* 211 note; *R.I.C.* 3 note ..

11a C. R. PRINCIPI IVVENT, Maximus stg. half-left, holding globe and leaning
on reversed spear. *R.I.C.* 4 (*Hunterian*) .. ..

15a B. R. SALVS AVGVSTI, Salus seated l., feeding from patera snake rising
from altar, elbow on back of chair (Hy.; *rev. of Maximinus*). *B.M.C.* 249
(*irregular*); *R.I.C.* 16 .. ..

15b As last (*barbarous*). *R.I.C.* 18 (*De Quelen*) .. ..

15c A. R. — As last (*barbarous*). *R.I.C.* 17 .. ..

GORDIAN I, AFRICANUS

238 A.D.

Marcus Antonius Gordianus was the son of Metius Marulus and Ulpia Gordiana and born about 157 A.D. *He was distinguished for his moral and intellectual excellence, and he soon obtained public offices. His aedileship was a splendid one, for his family's riches enabled him to serve that magistrature with great brilliance. He was consul for the first time in* 213 *and his second consulate was with Alexander Severus in* 229. *The emperor sent him into Africa as pro-consul, and appointed his son to be his lieutenant; in that province he won great popularity. When in* 238 *a rebellion against the tyranny of Maximinus broke out in the province, Gordian was petitioned to accept the purple, and although then* 80 *years of age he agreed. He associated his son with him as joint-ruler and a deputation was sent to Rome to ask for the confirmation of the Senate. This was readily granted and Maximinus declared a public enemy; but before the deputies could return to Africa both the Gordiani had perished. The governor of Mauretania, Capellianus, enraged against Gordian, marched upon Carthage with a numerous army. The younger Gordian with what troops he could muster, went out to meet him and was killed in the ensuing battle. When the news reached Gordian I he ended his own life after a reign of only* 36 *days.*

Obverse legend and type:

IMP . M . ANT . GORDIANVS AFR . AVG., his laureate bust, draped and cuirassed right.

1 **Denarius.** (IMP . C . M . ANT . GORDIANVS AFR AVG., laur. hd. ?). ℞. CONCORDIA AVG., Concordia seated, holding patera and double cornucopiae (Hy.; *rev. of Pupienus*). *B.M.C.* 33* note; *R.I.C.* p. 176 note (*this may be an inaccurate description of Gordian II, no.*1) .. .. ..

2   8

2 ℞. P . M . TR . P . COS . P . P., emperor, laur. and togate, stg. facing, hd. l., holding branch and short sceptre (*R.I.C.* wearing parazonium). *B.M.C.* 1-3; *R.I.C.* 1 (*R.I.C.* 2—female figure instead of emperor—*is according to B.M.C. only a poorly preserved example of this*) £700

4 ℞. PROVIDENTIA AVGG., Providence l. *This is probably Gordian II* ..

8 ℞. ROMAE AETERNAE, Roma seated l. on throne, holding Victory and long sceptre. *B.M.C.* 8-9; *R.I.C.* 4 700

10 ℞. SECVRITAS AVGG., Securitas seated l. on throne, holding short transverse sceptre. *B.M.C.* 11; *R.I.C.* 5 700

13 ℞. VICTORIA AVGG., Victory walking l. *This is probably Gordian II* ..

15a ℞. VIRTVS AVGG., Virtus stg. l. *R.I.C.* 6 (*probably Gordian II*) ..

157

GORDIAN II, AFRICANUS

238 A.D.

Marcus Antoninus Gordianus was born 191 A.D., the son of Gordian I and Fabia Orestilla. He was a great student with a large library. He was quaestor under Elagabalus, praetor and consul under Severus Alexander, who later appointed him legatus to his father in Africa. He was acknowledged as joint emperor with his father and was killed a few weeks later, fighting valiantly at the head of his troops.

Obverse legend and type:
As Gordian I, but he is bald in front of the laurel-wreath.

1 Denarius. ℞. CONCORDIA AVGG., Concordia seated l., holding patera and double cornucopiae (Hy.; *rev. of Pupienus*). *B.M.C.* 33; *R.I.C.* p. 176 ..

2a ℞. FIDES EXERCIT., clasped hands holding winged caduceus. *R.I.C.* p. 164 (*Lawrence; curious forgery*) .. ..

2b ℞. LIBERALITAS AVGG. I (and II), two emperors seated l. on curule chairs (*forgery; rev. of Philip I and II*). *B.M.C.* p. 249, c .. .. ..

3 CAES. M . ANT . GORDIANVS AFR . AVG., laur. bust dr. r. ℞. PIETAS AVG., sacrificial implements (*plated; forgery of Gordian III*). *B.M.C.* p. 248, (b); *R.I.C.* 16 .. ..

3a — Bare-headed bust dr. r. ℞. As last (*forgery*). *B.M.C.* p. 248, (b); *R.I.C.* 15 .. ..

5 ℞. PROVIDENTIA AVGG., Providentia stg. facing, hd. l., leaning against column with legs crossed, holding wand over globe at her feet and cornucopiae. *B.M.C.* 19-20; *R.I.C.* 1 .. .. £700

7 As last (*base, plated or Æ*). *B.M.C.* 19 note; *R.I.C.* 1 note .. ..

8 ℞. ROMAE AETERNAE, Roma seated. (*probably Gordian I*) .. ..

9a ℞. SALVS AVG., Salus stg. facing, hd. l., feeding serpent held in her arms (*plated; forgery*). *B.M.C.* p. 249,(d); *R.I.C.* p.164 (*Lawrence, now in B.M.*)

10 ℞. SECVRITAS AVGG., Securitas seated (*probably only Gordian I*) ..

12 ℞. VICTORIA AVGG., Victory walking l., holding wreath and palm. *B.M.C.* 28; *R.I.C.* 2 700

14 ℞. VIRTVS AVGG., Virtus stg. half-left, holding spear (sometimes reversed) and leaning on shield. *B.M.C.* 30; *R.I.C.* 3 700

14a *Obv.* reads IMP . CAES . M . ANT. etc. ℞. VIRTVS AVG., Virtus stg. l., holding globe and spear. *R.I.C.* 3 note (*Hunterian, curious style and fabric*) ..

15a *Obv.* as last. ℞. No legend, legionary eagle between two standards. *B.M.C.* p. 249, (e) (*forgery*) .. ..

158

BALBINUS
238 A.D.

Decimus Caelius Balbinus was born in 178 A.D. *of a very noble family. He governed several provinces with justice and mildness, he had also been consul twice. The Senate having heard of the death of the Gordiani, and realising that they had now incurred the active enmity of Maximinus, elected two of their number as joint rulers, one was Balbinus, the other Pupienus. The latter gathered troops to oppose the advance on Rome of Maximinus, whilst Balbinus was given the task of directing the civil administration. Although Maximinus was checked and ultimately murdered by his own men, neither the ordinary citizens nor the army had any love for their two new rulers. After a short period of civil strife and disorder, a number of the praetorian guards invaded the palace, dragged out the two emperors and murdered them, after a reign of ninety-nine days.*

Obverse legends.
A. IMP . C . D . CAEL . BALBINVS AVG.
B. IMP . CAES . D . CAEL . BALBINVS AVG.

Obverse types.
ldc.   Laureate bust draped and cuirassed right, seen from the front
rdc.   Radiate bust draped and cuirassed right, seen from the front

1 **Antoninianus.** Ardc. ℞. AMOR MVTVVS AVG., two clasped hands (Hy.; *rev. of Pupienus*). *B.M.C.* 99*; *R.I.C.* p. 172   ..   ..

2 Brdc? ℞. CARITAS MVTVA AVC., as last (Hy.; *rev. of Pupienus*). *B.M.C.* 100*; *R.I.C.* p. 172   ..   ..

3 Brdc. ℞. CONCORDIA AVGG., as last. *B.M.C.* 67-70; *R.I.C.* 10 ..   .. £200

5a **Denarius.** Aldc. ℞. — Concordia seated l. on throne, holding patera and double cornucopiae (Hy.; *rev. of Pupienus*). *B.M.C.* 101*; *R.I.C.* 1 (*Nisch hoard*)   ..   ..

6 **Antoninianus.** Brdc. ℞. FIDES MVTVA AVGG., two clasped hands. *B.M.C.* 71-3; *R.I.C.* 11   200

8 **Denarius.** Aldc. ℞. IOVI CONSERVATORI, Jupiter, naked, cloak over arms, stg. facing, hd. l., holding thunderbolt and long sceptre. *B.M.C.* 22; *R.I.C.* 2   250

10   17

10 Aldc. ℞. LIBERALITAS AVGVSTORVM, Liberalitas stg. facing, hd. l., holding abacus and cornucopiae. *B.M.C.* 1; *R.I.C.* 3   250

14 **Antoninianus.** Brdc? ℞. PATRES SENATVS, two clasped hands (Hy.; *rev. of Pupienus*). *B.M.C.* 102*; *R.I.C.* p. 172   ..   ..

15 **Denarius.** Aldc. ℞. PAX PVBLICA, Peace seated l. on throne, holding branch and sceptre (Hy.; *rev. of Pupienus*). *B.M.C.* 103*; *R.I.C.* 4   ..

17 **Antoninianus.** Brdc. ℞. PIETAS MVTVA AVGG., as **14.** *B.M.C.* 74-6; *R.I.C.* 12   225

18 **Denarius.** Aldc (*Cohen gives* rdc *in error*). ℞. P . M . TR . P . COS . II . P . P., Felicitas stg. front, hd. l., holding caduceus and long sceptre (*R.I.C. says* short sceptre *in error*). *B.M.C.* 32; *R.I.C.* 6   250

20 Aldc. R. — Emperor, togate, stg. front, hd. l., holding branch and short
     sceptre (*R.I.C.* parazonium). *B.M.C.* 26-7; *R.I.C.* 5 ..   ..   .. £175
23 Aldc. R. PROVIDENTIA DEORVM, Providentia stg. front, hd. l., holding
     wand over globe and cornucopiae. *B.M.C.* 33; *R.I.C.* 7   175
     Becker forged dies from this type.

27   32

27 Aldc. R. VICTORIA AVGG., Victory stg. half-left or front, hd. l., holding
     wreath and palm over shoulder. *B.M.C.* 37-8; *R.I.C.* 8   175

28 **Quinarius.** As last, but wreath held downward. *B.M.C.* 39; *R.I.C.* 8   *Unique*
32 **Denarius.** Aldc. R. VOTIS / DECENNA / LIBVS in wreath. *B.M.C.* 6 (*ex.*
     Lawrence); *R.I.C.* p. 172; also *G. R. Arnold, ex Ferguson*   350

PUPIENUS

238 A.D.

Marcus Clodius Pupienus Maximus was born about 164 A.D. *of humble parents. He
entered the military service and for his exploits in the field the Senate elected him into their
body. He was consul twice and governed the provinces of Bithynia and Gaul with great credit.
Victorious over the Samatians and the Germans he was rewarded with the Prefecture of
Rome. He was elected joint-emperor with Balbinus and saw to the military side of the
partnership. It was mainly through his endeavours that the empire was delivered from the
tyranny of Maximinus. He was murdered with Balbinus after having reigned three months
and three days*

Obverse legends.

A. IMP . C . M . CLOD . PVPIENVS AVG.
B. IMP . CAES . M . CLOD . PVPIENVS AVG.
C. IMP . CAES . PVPIEN . MAXIMVS AVG.

Obverse types.

ldc. Laureate bust draped and cuirassed right, seen from behind
rdc. Radiate bust draped and cuirassed right, seen from behind

1 **Antoninianus.** Brdc. R. AMOR MVTVVS AVGG., two clasped hands.
     B.M.C. 77-9; *R.I.C.* 9 (a)   200

2 Crdc. R. — As last. *B.M.C.* 82-6; *R.I.C.* 9 (b)   200

3 Antoninianus. Crdc. ℞. CARITAS MVTVA AVGG., as last. *B.M.C.* 87-91;
R.I.C. 10 (b) £200
4 Brdc. ℞. — As last. *B.M.C.* 80; *R.I.C.* 10 (a)   225
5 Brdc. ℞. CONCORDIA AVGG., as last (Hy.; *rev. of Balbinus*). *B.M.C.* 106*;
R.I.C. p. 176 ..   ..

6   12

6 Denarius. Aldc. ℞. CONCORDIA AVGG., Concordia seated l. on throne,
holding patera and double cornucopiae. *B.M.C.* 42; *R.I.C.* 1 ..   175
10 Aldc? ℞. FELICITAS AVGG., Felicitas stg., holding caduceus and spear.
B.M.C. p. 200; *R.I.C.* p. 176 (*unknown today; doubtful or false ?*) ..
11 Antoninianus. B or Crdc? ℞. FIDES MVTVA AVGG. (AVGG. *omitted by
Cohen—in error ?*), two clasped hands (Hy.; *rev. of Balbinus*). *B.M.C.*
107*; *R.I.C.* p. 176 ..   ..
12 Denarius. Aldc. ℞. IOVI CONSERVATORI, Jupiter, naked, cloak over arms,
stg. facing, hd. l., holding thunderbolt and long sceptre. *B.M.C.* 44 *;
R.I.C. 2   250
14 Aldc. ℞. LIBERALITAS AVGVSTORVM, Liberalitas stg. facing, hd. l., holding
abacus and cornucopiae. *B.M.C.* 9 *; *R.I.C.* 3   250
19 Antoninianus. Brdc. ℞. PATRES SENATVS, two clasped hands. *B.M.C.*
81; *R.I.C.* 11 (a)   225
21 Crdc. ℞. — As last. *B.M.C.* 92-4; *R.I.C.* 11 (b)   200

22 Denarius. Aldc. ℞. PAX PVBLICA, Pax seated l. on throne, holding, branch
and short transverse sceptre. *B.M.C.* 46-7; *R.I.C.* 4   175
25 Antoninianus. ? ℞. PIETAS MVTVA AVGG., clasped hands (Hy.; *rev. of
Balbinus*). *B.M.C.* 109 *; *R.I.C.* p. 176 ..   ..

26   29

26 Denarius. Aldc. ℞. P . M . TR . P . COS . II . P . P., Felicitas stg. facing,
hd. l., holding caduceus and long sceptre. *B.M.C.* 52-4; *R.I.C.* 6   ..   175
29 Aldc. ℞. — Emperor, togate, stg. half-left, holding branch and short
sceptre (*R.I.C.* parazonium). *B.M.C.* 50*; *R.I.C.* 5   250
33 Aldc. ℞. PROVIDENTIA DEORVM, Providentia stg. front, hd. l., holding
wand over globe and cornucopiae (Hy.; *rev. of Balbinus*). *B.M.C.* 110*;
R.I.C. 7 (*unknown today*)   ..   ..
43 Aldc. ℞. VOTIS / DECENNA / LIBVS within wreath. *B.M.C.* 15* and pl. 44
(*Hunterian*); *R.I.C.* p. 176   350

INDEX.

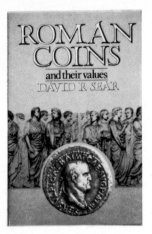

ROMAN COINS
and Their Values

by D. R. Sear
3rd Revised Edition 1981
£10·00 $25·00

A general catalogue of Roman coins, with values, containing biographical and historical details, and descriptions of over 4300 coins

376 pages, with chronological tables, twelve plates and many half tone illustrations in text.

ROMAN SILVER COINS

by H. A. Seaby
New editions revised by
D. R. Sear and Robert Loosley

Vol. I.   Republic to Augustus
£7·50 $16·00
Vol. II. Tiberius to Commodus
£12·00 $30·00
Vol. III. Pertinax to Balbinus and Pupienus
£10·00 $22·50
Vol. IV. Gordian III to Postumus
£10·00 $22·50

The text of the above volumes has been revised to include the latest valuations, new coins and the latest research, and contains new photographic illustrations.

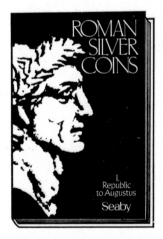

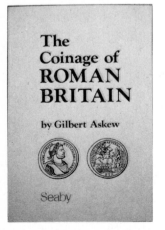

THE COINAGE OF ROMAN BRITAIN

by Gilbert Askew
£4·75 $12·00

Second edition with new introduction. The most compact listing of the Roman coins relating to the Province of Britannia.

A DICTIONARY OF ROMAN COINS

by S. W. Stevenson
£16·00 $35·00

First published in 1889, this is a reprint of the most comprehensive dictionary of Roman coin types, legends, emperors, etc., ever published in a single volume and contains much information for students of Roman coinage not assembled elsewhere.

929 pages, several hundred illustrations.

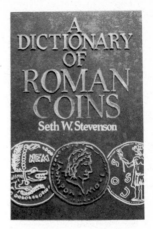

GREEK IMPERIAL COINS and Their Values

The Local Coinages of the Roman Empire
by David R. Sear
£27·50 $55·00

Arranged chronologically by emperors, this catalogue is unique in providing the collector with the only comprehensive and authoritative guide devoted specifically to the local coinages of the Roman Empire. Includes the "quasi-autonomous" series and completes the listing of contemporary coinages begun in "Greek Coins and their Values".

Over 6000 coins described and valued with 1750 photographs and 10 maps.

THE EMPERORS OF ROME AND BYZANTIUM

Chronological and Genealogical Tables for History Students and Coin Collectors
by David R. Sear
£5·00 $12·50

An introduction, plus 75 tabulated sheets giving dates, relationships, cause of death, and many other life details of all the Roman and Byzantine emperors.

GREEK COINS
and Their Values
by D. R. Sear

Vol I. **Europe**
£12·50 $27·50

Vol. II. **Asia & Africa,**
including the Hellenistic
Monarchies.
£14·00 $35·00

The most comprehensive priced guide to
Greek coins ever published. The average
collector should be able to locate all the
types he is likely to encounter in one
denomination or another. Useful
historical notes and illustrated preface.
Altogether 7956 coins listed with 3356
photographs of coins in the British
Museum.

GREEK COIN TYPES AND THEIR IDENTIFICATION

by Richard Plant
£10·00 $24·00

Nearly 3000 Greek coins are listed and
illustrated, concentrating on types not
immediately identifiable from their
inscriptions or subjects represented. Place
of issue, date, denomination, metal and
size are given. An invaluable aid to the
identification of Greek and 'Greek
Imperial' coins.

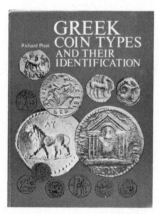

Please send for a complete list of our numismatic publications and
current book and accessory catalogue.

Seaby Coin and Medal Bulletin. A monthly magazine for all interested
in numismatics. Specimen copy upon request.